TRAVELERS' TALES BOOKS

Country and Regional Guides

30 Days in Italy, 30 Days in the South Pacific, America, Antarctica, Australia, Brazil, Central America, China, Cuba, France, Greece, India, Ireland, Italy, Japan, Mexico, Nepal, Spain, Thailand, Tibet, Turkey, Alaska, American Southwest, Grand Canyon, Hawai'i, Hong Kong, Middle East, Paris, Prague, Provence, San Francisco, South Pacific, Tuscany

Women's Travel

100 Places Every Woman Should Go, 100 Places in France Every Woman Should Go, 100 Places in Greece Every Woman Should Go, 100 Places in Italy Every Woman Should Go, 100 Places in the USA Every Woman Should Go, 50 Places in Rome, Florence, & Venice Every Woman Should Go, Best Women's Travel Writing, Family Travel, Gutsy Mamas, Gutsy Women, Mother's World, Safety and Security for Women Who Travel, Wild with Child, Woman's Asia, Woman's Europe, Woman's Passion for Travel, Woman's Path, Woman's World, Woman's World Again, Women in the Wild

Body & Soul

Adventure of Food, Food, How to Eat Around the World, Love & Romance, Mile in Her Boots, Pilgrimage, Road Within, Spiritual Gifts of Travel, Stories to Live By, Ultimate Journey

Special Interest

365 Travel, Adventures in Wine, Danger!, Fearless Shopper, Gift of Birds, Gift of Rivers, Gift of Travel, Guidebook Experiment, How to Shit Around the World, Hyenas Laughed at Me, It's a Dog's World, Leave the Lipstick, Take the Iguana, Make Your Travel Dollars Worth a Fortune, More Sand in My Bra, Mousejunkies!, Not So Funny When It Happened, Penny Pincher's Passport to Luxury Travel, Sand in My Bra, Soul of Place, Testosterone Planet, There's No Toilet Paper on the Road Less Traveled, Thong Also Rises, What Color is your Jockstrap?, Whose Panties Are These?, World is a Kitchen, Writing Away

Travel Literature

The Best Travel Writing, Deer Hunting in Paris, Ghost Dance in Berlin, Shopping for Buddhas, Kin to the Wind, [Coast] Fire Never Dies, Kite Strings of the Southern Cross, La[s], Rivers Ran East, Royal Road to Romance, Heaven, Take Me With You, Trader Ho, Tracks in Japan, The Guidebook Expe[r]

TRAVELERS' TALES

THE GUIDEBOOK EXPERIMENT

Discovering Exploration in a Hyper-Connected World

DAVID BOCKINO

Travelers' Tales
An imprint of Solas House, Inc.
Palo Alto

Travelers' Tales is a trademark of Travelers' Tales/Solas House, Inc.
2320 Bowdoin Street, Palo Alto, California 94306. www.travelerstales.com

Art Direction: Kimberly Nelson Coombs
Cover Illustration: Man Writing on Leaves, India, 1774-1781. Copyright ©
    National Library of France.
Page Layout: Scribe Inc., using the fonts Granjon, Nicolas Cochin, and
    Ex Ponto
Production Director: Susan Brady

Library of Congress Cataloging-in-Publication Data
Available upon request

Library of Congress Cataloging-in-Publication Data

Bockino, David
  The guidebook experiment : discovering exploration in a hyper-connected world / David Bockino.
          pages cm
  Summary: "The Guidebook Experiment shows readers how to
mitigate the effects of an information-saturated world and discover the
wonders associated with true exploration"--
Provided by publisher.
  ISBN 978-1-60952-092-2 (paperback)
1. Voyages and travels. 2. Explorers 3. Discoveries in geography. I. Title.
  G465.B63 2015
  910--dc23
                                             2015021632

First Edition
Printed in the United States
10 9 8 7 6 5 4 3 2 1

To Emily, of course

Contents

Prologue: The Guidebook Experiment

Day 6–Georgetown, Guyana: It's karaoke night
at the Sleep-In International, an irritating (and
unavoidable) epilogue to the events of the past few
hours. After my visit to the police station, I had used
one of the hotel's calling cards to call my wife. I said
I had been defeated—I had no money, no credit cards,
no idea where to go for help—and was ready to abandon
the experiment. But she convinced me to stay, to march
on through this methodological hiccup, and so here I
am, in my hotel room, penniless, listening to the grating
melodies of 1980s American pop ballads.

The purpose of my trip to the Guianas, a journey I had ceremoniously designated the "guidebook experiment," had been to determine how the recent proliferation of guidebook-related material—how the explosion of travel blogs and restaurant reviews and backpacking message boards and digital mapping applications on top of the already vast library of print-related guides to nearly every city, region, and country on the planet—had changed the way we see the world. That was how I ended up trapped one night in a hotel in Georgetown, the capital of Guyana, with a black eye and barely a dollar to my name, listening to middle-aged men serenade their female companions with the unmistakable passion of forlorn American rock 'n' roll musicians. My presence in that hotel at that very moment seemed to embody, in all its pathetic glory, the results of my experiment.

But I must back up; no proper experiment begins with its findings. Most, instead, begin with an introduction—an explanation of the experiment's purpose, a justification of its design, and a description of its participants. And so before I explain how I endured and eventually escaped my karaoke purgatory, I must first explain how I ended up there in the first place. That particular story begins not in Guyana but in Montana, on the trail of two of the most famous guidebook-less travelers of all time. It was there that the guidebook experiment was launched.

CHAPTER I

ℐ℘ ℐ℘ ℐ℘

Guidebook (In)Dependence

I had always imagined the confluence of the Madison, Jefferson, and Gallatin rivers, a historic landmark located a few miles north of Three Forks, Montana, to more closely resemble a flattened tripod, with each river neatly draining into a pool out of which would flow the beginning of the mighty Missouri River. But nature is rarely so tidy and although I had two maps, several interpretive signs, and an audio recording as guides when I arrived at the designated Three Forks viewpoint, it still took me a while to figure out which waterway was which. The trick was that all three rivers were not in fact visible from this exact spot. To my left was the Madison while straight ahead of me was the Jefferson. Both of these rivers joined to form the Missouri which then continued downstream to my right. The Gallatin, however, the third of the "three forks," diverged from the Missouri a short distance after this convergence. It was therefore hidden from view, thus rendering my visible expectation of the confluence—a symmetrical three prongs converging into one river—inaccurate.

Regardless of my expectations, the location remains, as Meriwether Lewis had said, "an essential point in the geography of this western point of the continent." The transcontinental Lewis and Clark expedition had arrived at the Three Forks in late July 1805, a little over a year into their journey, after following the Missouri River from its mouth

over a thousand miles to the east. Their objective had been
to follow the river to its source and to continue west to the
Pacific Ocean. But after seeing that two of the three rivers at
the Three Forks "appeared as if they had been cast in the same
mold,"[1] the explorers decided that to call either of the two the
Missouri "would be giving it a preference which its size does
not warrant," and therefore it is at the Three Forks that the
explorers decided the Missouri River officially began.

Now the decision—which fork to follow? With little
information to guide them, Lewis and Clark surveyed the
area. They climbed hills, they measured the rivers' widths,
and they advanced a few miles up each option to scout the
terrain. Both men agreed that the northernmost river, the
one they had named after the President of the United States
Thomas Jefferson, was the logical choice. Clark mentioned in
his journal that it "appears to have the most water and must
be considered as the one best calculated for us to ascend" while
Lewis wrote that "its direction is much more promising than
any other." But the assessment of the Three Forks is best seen
as a prologue rather than as a conclusion—it signifies the start
of the most difficult part of the expedition, the beginning of a
strenuous march over unknown land, and the first of a series
of choices that would ultimately determine the fate and success of the entire Lewis and Clark expedition.

I sat down at the site's picnic table and looked out over the
water. The State Park brochure touts the area of the Missouri
Headwaters as "one of the few places appearing almost exactly
as viewed by Lewis and Clark." This is not bravado; the park
is simply pristine. And I was fortunate to have visited on a
perfect Montana evening. The temperature was ideal, aided

---

[1] As this narrative (rightfully) exists separate from the library of books com-
prehensively detailing the history of the Lewis and Clark expedition, I have
occasionally changed the spelling or use of a word within these quotations
to represent its modern day equivalent and to make the text more accessible.

by a slight breeze, and the foreboding clouds that had earlier commanded the sky and threatened rain had made way for several pockets of bright blue sky through which rays of sunshine filtered down. Even the mosquitoes that had so bothered the expedition in the heat of summer remained dormant, not yet ready to emerge from their winter hiatus.

Lewis and Clark had been quick to anoint the Jefferson as the proper route to follow toward the Pacific Ocean. But I wondered which way I would have gone. Past the Madison River, the fork to my left, were distant snow-capped mountains. Past the Jefferson River, the fork straight in front of me, were much smaller and more accessible hills. From this information, one could surmise that the route to the Pacific was in fact up the Madison, as geographical theories suggested the existence of an additional chain of high altitude mountains before the distant ocean. So it was only when I took out my compass (well, the compass on my phone) and saw that the upstream flow of the Jefferson was almost perfectly due west, and therefore more directly in line with the route the expedition hoped to maintain, that I changed my mind and proudly concluded that, yes, I would have made the same decision as the two captains.

I had come to Montana, as so many before me had done, to follow in the footsteps of Meriwether Lewis and William Clark, the two men sent by United States President Thomas Jefferson to find "the most direct and practicable water communication" across the continent. During their journey, which lasted from May 1804 to September 1806, Lewis, Clark and their team learned more about what would become the United States than any man or woman had before or has since. Armed with an extensive knowledge of history, botany, biology, and geography, the men systematically and thoroughly catalogued their route up the Missouri River, over the mountains of the west, and down the Columbia River, detailing where they traveled, how they arrived at each destination, what those destinations looked like, and why future travelers should or should not follow them. I was neither a historian nor botanist, neither a biologist nor geographer. But I was indeed a traveler and my interest in Lewis and Clark stemmed mostly from the expedition as a journey over previously undocumented land rather than as an important economic or political turning point. As historian John Logan Allen has written, "Perhaps the single most striking feature of American geographical knowledge of the Northwest before Lewis and Clark was the almost total lack of good information on the western interior."

The next morning I hiked around the park's grounds and climbed a small limestone outcropping designated as "Lewis Rock" by the park's brochure: "Way up at the top, 200 years ago, Captain Meriwether Lewis stood looking out over the Headwaters of the mighty Missouri River." The view from the rock was remarkable, vast green plains stretching out in all directions and save for the road that dissected the park and a few houses, almost entirely untouched by modern society. Rabbits and chipmunks scurried over the rocks; to my left I could hear the rush of the Gallatin River. From this height, Lewis could have gazed out over the open land plotting the expedition's path west, where distant mountain ranges interrupted the landscape's level uniformity. If Lewis had bought into the geographical assumptions of his time—and all indications are that he did—then these mountains, what the explorers hoped constituted the Continental Divide, represented an essential landmark for their journey west. It is easiest to think of the Divide as a triangle; rivers that begin on the right side of the triangle flow east toward the Atlantic Ocean and the Gulf of Mexico, rivers that begin on the left side of the triangle flow west to the Pacific Ocean. The Lewis and Clark expedition was predicated on a theory that the headwaters of the Missouri River (or whichever rivers fed into the Missouri) existed at a point high up the right side of the triangle. When the expedition, traveling upstream on the Missouri, reached this point, it would pack up the canoes, walk over the triangle's crest, and find the headwaters of a western flowing river on the other side where it could then put the canoes back in the water and travel downstream straight into the Pacific Ocean. But this was all conjecture; Lewis and Clark, in fact, had no idea what lay beyond those mountains. And their route to that point had been determined not through confirmed intelligence but through educated intuition, an aggregation of local Indian knowledge, and good old-fashioned luck. The rest of their journey would involve the same.

I packed up my tent and drove southwest toward Lemhi Pass, the spot where Lewis and Clark first crossed the Continental Divide. The area approaching the pass is sparsely populated and the one town I passed, Grant, looked virtually abandoned. At the designated turn-off, a sign noted that the gravel road which led up the mountain remained closed due to snow but it was moved off to the side and having seen another car come through a few moments earlier, I ignored the warning and drove on. Halfway up, an interpretive sign indicates the general location where one of the expedition's men had triumphantly bestrode the river they had been following for over a year: "Two miles below [the pass], McNeal had exultingly stood with a foot on each side of this little river and thanked his God that he had lived to bestride the mighty and heretofore deemed endless Missouri." The road ends with a final steep switchback and a sign announcing one's arrival at the Continental Divide.

It's difficult to imagine a more perfect historical landmark than Lemhi Pass; apart from any changes Mother Nature may have caused and a few wooden fence posts, it remains exactly as Lewis and Clark had seen it. The Forest Service deserves much of the credit—they smartly positioned the parking and signage for the site behind a small ridge, meaning that the view from the crest is unblocked by even the transportation one arrives in. To that end, it's best to let Meriwether Lewis describe the scene: "After refreshing ourselves we proceeded on to the top of the dividing ridge from which I discovered immense ranges of high mountains still to the west of us with their tops partially covered with snow. I now descended the mountain about ¾ of a mile which I found much steeper than on the opposite side, to a handsome bold running creek of cold clear water." Those ranges were still there, still covered in snow, and obviously still immense. There's even a sign-posted trail down the western side of the divide following the small creeks and puddles that eventually form the Lemhi River, although the exact spot where Lewis tasted the water is unknown.

I was again the only visitor at this landmark, meaning my Lemhi Pass experience was actually *less* crowded than Lewis's (he had arrived with three other expedition members). And although there was little to do but read the signs and wander from ridge to ridge, I still lingered for almost two hours, enjoying the personal panorama. When it was time to leave, I again ignored the warnings of the Forest Service and attempted to descend what my guidebook said was the more scenic path into Idaho. But my decision proved costly three miles later when I discovered persistent snowdrifts still blocking the road and I was forced to make a precipitous three-point turn on the narrow mountain ledge. I circled back to Lemhi Pass and instead proceeded down the alternate road, a more direct, steeper, albeit less interesting route.

I camped that evening on a freshly cut plot of grass on the banks of the Salmon River. The campground's hosts, a pleasant couple who lived out of their RV, charged me $5 and told me to take my pick of sites—I was the only resident for the night. I prepared my tent, washed up, and took a short walk around the area. The evening was tranquil and I was unhurried. As the sun slowly set behind the mountains, I used my propane stove to prepare a small meal of chicken and rice. Over a hot cup of tea, I read about Lewis and Clark's rather different experience in this region over two hundred years before. Although they had made it over Lemhi Pass unscathed, their difficulties were just beginning:

> *We proceeded on through thickets in which we were obliged to cut a road, over rocky hill sides where our horses were in perpetual danger of slipping to their certain destruction and up and down steep hills, where several horses fell, some turned over, and others slipped down steep hill sides, one horse crippled and two gave out. With the greatest difficulty and risk, we made five miles and encamped.*

The next morning I followed the expedition's route up the two-lane U.S. Route 93, listed conveniently on my map as *Lewis and Clark Trail.* Lewis didn't write regularly in his journal as the expedition passed through the area; Clark did, but he was mostly preoccupied with the safety of his horses and men. It's a shame—one wonders what the explorers would have said about seeing those lush valleys and fertile hillsides for the first time, had they been unconcerned with simple survival.

Soon, the road began to rise, meandering between narrow gorges covered in loose rock. An interpretive sign highlighted a jagged chasm in the mountains explored by Clark in the hopes of resuming travel via river. But it would not be—"The passage of either with canoes is entirely impossible"—and so the expedition continued on foot. Today, the route is still slow going, especially when caught behind a lumbering semi. But the near inaccessible conditions have been mitigated by modern technology; the road is in fact trodden enough to support a ski resort at the pass over which the expedition crossed.

On the way down the mountain, the expedition encountered a group of Salish (Flathead) Indians. Clark wrote, "Those people received us friendly, threw white robes over our shoulders and smoked in the pipes of peace. We encamped with them and found them friendly." I stopped here as well, at a site designated as Ross's Hole, and bought a coffee from a kind woman at the Sula Country Store and Resort where "Coffee is always on and it's always fresh!" Shortly thereafter, the severity of the terrain to the west, the land over which the expedition would have to cross, became apparent. These were the Bitterroot Mountains, described by one expedition member as "the most terrible mountains I ever beheld," and on this late May afternoon, both the mountains' summits and the cavernous valleys surrounding them were covered in snow. Seventy miles later I reached Lolo, Montana and made a left toward the final stop on my Lewis and Clark excursion, Travelers' Rest State Park.

Compared to the other landmarks where I had been the only visitor, Travelers' Rest was a veritable carnival. According to its brochure, among the park's 25,000 annual visitors were 2,500 school children sent on field trips for historical immersion. At least a hundred of these children, two school buses full, were there when I visited. Some frolicked around the park's grassy lawns playing ring toss and football. Others scampered around the interactive exhibits in the museum or patiently sat through the park's lectures. Their presence reflected the site's importance as the "only scientifically verified Lewis and Clark campsite in the nation," a designation confirmed through a trail of archaeological evidence that culminated in the discovery of mercury vapor in the camp's suspected latrine. That residue was subsequently said to have originated in Dr. Benjamin Rush's Bilious Pills, the notorious catchall medicine that had been prescribed for the expedition in Philadelphia.

But I was interested in the site for another reason, its importance to the actual journey. The expedition had stopped at Travelers' Rest (named by Lewis in his journal) after a difficult few weeks—they had labored up the rocky Jefferson River, trudged over Lemhi Pass, slogged up and over another high-altitude pass, and descended on through the Bitterroot Valley. The captains had so far kept the expedition safe and on course, but the going had been rough and the men were tired. To the west lay the Bitterroot Mountains, the inevitable and daunting obstacle separating the expedition from the Pacific Ocean. Travelers' Rest, then, was the calm before the storm. What existed beyond those mountains was mostly unknown; the meager information the men did have of the route up Lolo Pass and toward navigable waters had been gleaned from their Indian guide. But the Corps of Discovery certainly didn't know what we do now—that the next ten days would be the most difficult of the entire journey.

I walked past the playing schoolchildren and over a small bridge to reach the actual location of the campsite, an open field tucked back from the museum and visitor center. A dirt trail rings the site while numbered signposts, corresponding to the park's free brochure, designate sections of note. Just past the park's barbed wire boundaries were the trailers and small houses of the residents of Lolo, Montana; it was clear the landmark had been carved out of otherwise occupied land. Looking past those houses, one begins to see the foothills of the Bitterroots, hilly summits now capped by large single-family homes. Beyond those, more mountains.

And so we have come to the point of the narrative where I'm supposed to tell the readers that I closed my eyes and imagined what it would have been like to be Meriwether Lewis and William Clark. That I stood at the Travelers' Rest campsite and gazed west, imagining how it would have felt to have already endured so much and yet to still know so little about what lay beyond Lolo Pass, over the mountains, on the path to the Pacific Ocean. The interpretive signs at various monuments, in fact, had instructed me to do just that—"Imagine what it would have been like to go forth into unknown territory . . ."

But none of that happened. The fact was, although I had never been there, I knew exactly what lay beyond Travelers' Rest; I had studiously researched it for the past two months. I knew about the roads that funneled down into the middle of Idaho and the campgrounds within the Clearwater National Forest. I knew that Lewiston was approximately two hundred miles west and Seattle another three hundred miles past that. I had even watched videos of *other* travelers visiting various sites along my route—Clark's Lookout, Three Forks, Lemhi Pass. My very presence at Travelers' Rest, meanwhile, could be attributed not to a union of fortuitous encounters and shrewd instinct but rather to the execution of a list of diligently pre-planned maneuvers. In my world, even spontaneity is arranged. While standing upon the pass, for example, I had used my phone to locate the nearest campgrounds, having decided on the spot not to backtrack through Montana but to instead continue down the western side of the Divide into Idaho. I was supposed to pretend what it was like to not have a map or a guidebook, to pretend as if the land in front of me was *terra incognita*. But the fact was the guidebook (and all its extensions) was the very reason I was there; pretending not to have one, then, was not only difficult, it was near impossible.

There had been, however, one small guidebook-less moment during my Lewis and Clark excursion. It had originated at a rest stop off Interstate 15 where one of the many signs along the route had encouraged me to "Use Montana for your own discoveries!" My original plan was to continue south on the highway to the town of Dillon where I could then reverse course, heading back up north on a different road to hit a few additional expedition landmarks. But I had grown tired of highway driving and had decided at the rest stop to instead cut across the mountains using a "gravel road" that would ostensibly eliminate the need for backtracking.

It was a terrible idea. The road, which according to the map went in an almost perfectly eastern direction, was in fact a shifty one-way path through steep isolated terrain. Gravel turned to rocks and I was soon regretting my decision, bouncing over jagged boulders and inching through small streams. I began to pass turn-offs toward towns that weren't even listed on my map: Rochester—6 miles, Moose Town— 2 miles. After a short while, I wasn't even going east anymore; my car's compass was rapidly rotating between north and northwest as I navigated the tight mountain curves. With an inadequate map and no service for my phone, I blindly drove on, choosing the straighter option whenever I had a choice. As I continued, the path got steeper and I soon began to see bits of snow on the side of the road. While I never felt like I was in mortal danger (I did, after all, have food, water, and camping equipment with me), it was an anxious drive, and my entire body tensed as I thought about the possibilities of a flat tire or, worse, my $30,000 rented SUV stuck in a shallow ditch. After about an hour and a half, a sliver of hope—a road sign littered with bullet holes (probably from nearby hunters) pointing toward the interstate I had initially turned off from. When I finally reached the highway, two hours had passed, I had wasted a quarter tank of gas, my car was covered in dirt, and I was twenty miles *behind* from where I had originally started. Lewis and Clark I am not.

꧁ ꧁ ꧁

I had become intrigued with the Lewis and Clark journey precisely because it was the antithesis of every trip I have ever taken. In *Undaunted Courage: Meriwether Lewis, Thomas Jefferson, and the Opening of the American West*, a historical narrative of the Lewis and Clark expedition, Stephen Ambrose writes, "Only a tiny number of people have ever had the experience of not knowing what they would see when they got to the top of the mountain or turned into the river or sailed around the tip of a continent." He is referring, of course, to the privileged few who have had these types of virgin encounters—men like Meriwether Lewis and William Clark as well as history's other great explorers, Christopher Columbus and Captain James Cook and Ernest Shackleton—who were propelled into action not by a well-defined route, but by ambitious theories, salacious rumors, a burning curiosity, an addiction to adventure, and a desire for fame and glory.

The trips were rarely smooth; unknown destinations bring unknown difficulties and many of these explorers fell victim to the obstacles encountered on their expeditions. Their stories, some of the most compelling tales in history, are filled with accounts of scurvy and revolts, malaria and war. Ferdinand Magellan, after successfully establishing his namesake strait and effectively creating a westward link between Europe and Asia, was stabbed and bludgeoned to death after picking a fight in the Philippines. Henry Hudson, during his search for the elusive Northwest Passage, was either killed or cast adrift by an apparently homesick crew. Robert Scott, after enduring the disappointment of seeing another flag already planted at the South Pole, couldn't survive a harsh blizzard that engulfed his team on the way back, and eventually died in his tent. And yet despite their misfortune, they remain the envy of modern day explorers everywhere for a simple yet powerful reason: they had no idea what they were going to see. And with that experience comes the invaluable opportunity to form the first opinion, to create the first description—in essence, to develop the first "guidebook."

Some travelers liken themselves to these explorers. Not I. Ever since I can remember, I have traveled with the help of a guidebook, often obsessively so. It's an overdependence that can partly be explained by two personal characteristics. One, I'm a natural introvert and would much rather consult a book (or a website, for that matter) on where to eat and what to see than an actual human being. And two, I have always had a fierce desire to control my surroundings, to mitigate the unforeseen—I strongly believe that what can't be expected can at least be prepared for. These traits have resulted in my becoming an extremely efficient (and, admittedly, somewhat socially withdrawn) traveler, someone who has always found it prudent to arrive, be it across the street or across the world, dutifully prepared, with sufficient information to both maximize enjoyment and to minimize the possibility of setbacks and complications. I have never been one to "let myself get lost"; on the contrary, I've always found the notion quite disturbing. My reliance on guidebooks is so absolute, in fact, that I've always believed that if my professional career ever necessitated one of those comma-delineated biographies, the kind that can be found on the book jackets of nearly every travel book published over the past thirty years, it would have to be properly annotated, to explain not only what I did, but how I got there in the first place: "David Bockino has climbed mountains in Bolivia (Summitpost.org), eaten raw goat heart in Mongolia (Lonely Planet), and traveled by train through the southern hinterlands of Africa (Seat61.com)." Although my experiences were indeed extraordinary, they were hardly exceptional—each of my trips was the result of meticulous planning, the utilization of information culled from travelers who had already completed the journey. Those guidebook extensions had played such an integral part in the experiences that I always felt they should be properly credited, the same way a musician might recognize each sample used in his or her record.

My earliest travel memories, coincidentally, correspond with my earliest guidebook memories. One year, after the announcement of a family vacation to Walt Disney World, my affinity for collecting information about potential destinations revealed itself through a dependence on Birnbaum's famous Walt Disney World guidebook, considered by many to be the definitive source on the destination. Its thorough descriptions were a window to the World, the only window I had, and I used its recommendations ("Space Mountain is a very popular attraction—plan on visiting as soon as the park opens") to map out itineraries, tweaking the schedules to align with my prioritized attractions. To the chagrin of my family, the guidebook would accompany me to most meals, and while I wolfed down my oatmeal or picked at my pizza, my finger would trace appropriate routes from attraction to attraction.

By the time the trip arrived, I had my whole family equipped for the journey. I had detailed plans, and if those were interrupted, I had detailed backup plans. I knew the stories behind all the rides, the quickest paths between stops, the coolest restaurants, the quirkiest shops, the places to avoid, the prices, the secrets, the lingo—I knew everything. Or, more precisely, I knew everything Birnbaum wanted me to know. Because for better or for worse, I had put my trust in that book, my faith in its recommendations. Even before we left, the guide was dog-eared and wrinkled, well-worn from its journey around my house, and when we were finally ready to depart, it was the first thing I packed—the most important item in my suitcase. I wouldn't have dreamt of leaving without it.

Twenty years later, I set off traveling once again, this time on a much more ambitious excursion. My plan was to travel for seven months, visiting more than twenty countries on four continents. It was an intricate journey, designed to let me see as much of the world as possible in a short timeframe and on a limited budget, and I knew that preparation was the key to its success. Fortunately, the guidebook had evolved significantly since my foray into Disney World and there was ample information available for nearly every destination, no matter how remote, on my itinerary.

The backbone of my preparation was, of course, the standard print guidebook, and I purchased the most updated edition I could find for each region. The online extensions of these guidebooks helped me distill the copious information even further, allowing me to flip through photo galleries and to consult interactive maps. The most valuable guidebook advancement, however, was the abundance of online consumer-generated content, now available instantaneously and effortlessly—blogs, message boards, videos—all of which I combed through extensively in the months leading up to my trip. I found images of possible hotels, read reviews of prospective restaurants, and watched videos of potential hiking trails. When I discovered a noticeable gap in my knowledge (such as the cost for a particular bus route), I would post a question to an online message board, and the answer would almost always materialize within twenty-four hours.

While my preparation for Disney World had involved rough notes scribbled on the edges of my guidebook, my preparation for the larger trip involved elaborate spreadsheets, complete with proposed itineraries, estimated costs, and detailed visa information. And once on the road, my level of adherence remained high. I would check my guidebook for sightseeing recommendations, consult the message boards to manage logistical difficulties, and rely on online reviews for hotel approvals. My reliance was admittedly a tad extreme, but I was certainly not alone. Everywhere I went, travelers would be accessing the same information and consulting the same sources; in essence, using the same guidebooks. And although I was unbothered by the modern day traveler's near-ubiquitous reliance on guidebook information (after all, I was a practicing advocate) I couldn't help but wonder how that kind of dependence, something akin to addiction, has changed the way we see and experience the world around us. I vowed to find out.

Apart from the critical developments and advances in transportation—such as the steamboat, the locomotive, and the airplane—no tool has influenced the world of travel more than the guidebook. In fact, one can argue that the genre, almost two thousand years old, has evolved congruently with the act of travel itself. For hundreds of years, guidebooks complemented and facilitated specific traveling motivations. Going on a pilgrimage? Here's a guidebook. Going to Italy to study antiquity? Here's a guidebook. The books, often cumbersome and wordy, were written for audiences with well-defined, unambiguous traveling goals. Only after the industrial revolution, when travel reached the masses and people began to venture out solely for enjoyment, did the guide-book begin to resemble the form we see today. Trusted brands emerged—Baedeker and Frommer's and Lonely Planet—and the opinions and experiences of a few soon determined the actions of many. It was, of course, an inherently capitalistic relationship; the traveler, with neither the time, resources, nor desire (or some combination of the three) to wander aimlessly, would instead enlist the help of the "professional," paying a fee for efficient and timely information.

But thanks to two fundamental media-related shifts over the past decade or so, the guidebook has evolved once again. First, there's been a change in how content is being distrib-uted. Once relegated to traditional print-based delivery, travel information can now be disseminated through a multitude of digital extensions such as websites, e-books, and mobile applications. But second, and perhaps more importantly, there's been a change in *who* is doing the distributing. Much has been made of the Internet's ability to connect disparate groups of people—to mobilize revolutions, to inspire philanthropy, to uncover injustice. But far too little has been said about the web's ability—the "amateurs," as we will call them—to consistently and continuously update the map of the world. Global in nature and vastly accessible, the Internet is uniquely positioned to provide comprehensive information about any corner of the planet. A modern day traveler interested in visiting Peru, for example, can read a trip report about the Cordillera Blanco, watch a user-created video about the trek into Machu Picchu, and check reviews of Lima hotels, all while procuring suggestions from a message board about his or her proposed two-week itinerary. Where the traditional guidebook might lack clarity, these amateur guidebook creators are ready to fill in the gaps. Reliability and accountability, once the lynchpins of the traditional guidebook, have been replaced by accessibility and breadth.

Because of this evolution, travel advice, once restricted to niche avenues of distribution, now emerges from a seemingly infinite number of outlets. And yet each piece of information contained within this universe—every price, every picture, every opinion—can ultimately be classified under one of the three pillars of the overall guidebook structure. It is this unifying categorization that bridges the gap between the professionals and amateurs, and allows us to discuss them as a singular, albeit amorphous, entity.

The first pillar involves logistical information: content designed to tell the traveler where to go and how to get there. The earliest guidebooks, operating in a technologically limited environment, were often forced to use tangible objects to delineate notable attractions (i.e., from Pausanias's *Description of Greece*—"As you turn from Daulis on to the high road for Delphi and go forward, you will come to a building on the left of the road called Phocicum"). Today's guidebooks, on the other hand, are able to be not only more comprehensive, since information (e.g., taxi fares, bus schedules) has become increasingly attainable, but also more precise, thanks to technical advances like mobile phones and digital mapping software.

The second pillar of the guidebook structure is description: objective content designed to show the traveler what he or she will encounter. Simple descriptive language—"The Eiffel Tower is 320 meters high"—is now supplemented with high-resolution photography and panoramic video. No longer does the prospective traveler lie awake before the trip wondering what the destination will look like. Instead, his or her enthusiasm is piqued by becoming immersed in the destination during preparation—by watching documentaries, by reading blog posts, and by perusing pictures of friends, family, and strangers.

The third pillar is perhaps the most interesting of the three: subjective content designed to tell travelers why they should be going there in the first place. As we will see, early guidebooks were often promoted to a distinct group of travelers (say, religious pilgrims), thereby making the "why" fairly straightforward. It's only when "travel for the sake of travel" became prominent sometime in the nineteenth century that the guidebook industry faced a dilemma—which destinations should they recommend and why? The decisions often fell to the authors themselves, and guidebook brands became synonymous with certain types of travel. With the emergence of the Internet—and the birth of the amateur guidebook creator—the third pillar became even more muddled. And while many sites have attempted to normalize individuality by creating systems of aggregate opinion, inside those aggregators remains a vast amount of influential guidebook-related content easily accessible and, more importantly, easily misconstrued.

That we're allowing random people around the world—without knowing if they're a misanthrope, a vegan, or an anarchist—to justify or belittle our choice of hotel, restaurant, or museum, speaks volumes for the universality of the guidebook structure. No matter what side you advocate, guidebook-heavy or guidebook-less, there's no denying the influence the ever-expanding structure has had on the world of travel. There are few places on our planet for which information is not instantaneously available. This is important. Not because it is a crisis, as many cynics would argue, but because it has dramatically changed the way we interact with and experience these destinations.

As a serial guidebook adherent, I wanted to understand what the proliferation of guidebook material means to our society, in essence, to understand the guidebook effect.

The manifestation of this contradiction, a curiosity regarding guidebook-less travel combined with a complete reliance on guidebook-related material, meant that in order to determine the true effects of the guidebook evolution, I would need to conduct my own guidebook experiment: a systematic study in which I traveled guidebook-less to a destination I knew virtually nothing about. Because I harbored no ill feelings toward the guidebook genre (quite the contrary in fact), I had no intention of setting out on an idealistic anti-guidebook traveling endeavor. My guidebook experiment, therefore, was not some sort of delusional attempt to avoid all facets of the tourism industry and I was under no illusion that my itinerary would totally skirt the guidebook-recommended route. In fact, I was interested to see how often it would intersect. If a restaurant looked appetizing, I would eat there. If a guesthouse looked comfortable, I would stay there. Whether the destination was the top ranked attraction or left out of the guidebook spectrum entirely was immaterial. The point was to mitigate the abundant information of the current guidebook structure, to eliminate the incessant handholding in an effort to explore and discover the destination at my own pace, and to ultimately uncover the effects the guidebook has on the overall act of travel.

And what better way to understand the effects of the guidebook evolution than to link my journey with the greatest guidebook-less journey in American history? Meriwether Lewis and William Clark not only traveled guidebook-less, they did so successfully, returning to Washington having catalogued a vast swath of the continent. By searching for commonalities between their journey and my own, I hoped to uncover a series of shared themes—aspects of both trips that had been significantly affected by the absence of guidebook-related material.

My goal was simple: I wanted to see what would happen when the guidebook was taken away. But before I began my experiment, I felt it was necessary to understand the origins of the guidebook and how it had evolved over the past two thousand years. That investigation began not in some far-flung locale but rather much closer to home, in my own library.

INTERLUDE — LEWIS AND CLARK: INSPIRATION

While the inspiration for my proposed journey stemmed from an interest in the proliferation of guidebook material, the inspiration for the Lewis and Clark expedition began long before either man was even born, when a young Thomas Jefferson, the individual more responsible for the launch of the expedition than any other, was introduced to a concept that had originated hundreds of years earlier, from the discoveries of a different, equally famous, explorer.

In the late fifteenth century, Christopher Columbus set off from Spain with the purpose of finding a western trade route to the Orient. Columbus of course failed miserably, ending up in the Caribbean and stubbornly refusing to believe that the lands he encountered were not, indeed, Asia. But while the discovery of The New World was a surprise to many, and despite the added problem of an entirely new continent standing in the way, the desire to find a western route from the Atlantic Ocean to the Pacific Ocean, then regularly described as the Northwest Passage or the Passage to India, only increased.

As a small child, Thomas Jefferson was exposed to this obsession through both his father, a member of a company that had been awarded 800,000 acres west of the Appalachian Mountains, and through his teacher, the Reverend James Maury, who, as a member of the same company, had discussed sending a water-borne expedition across the continent. By the time of the American Revolution in the 1770s, Jefferson was obsessed with the concept of the Northwest Passage; he filled his library with books about North America and collected as much information as he could about its history and geography. For the United States to spread across the continent—Jefferson's ultimate vision—the soon-to-be President first needed to unlock the secrets of the interior. And the best way to do so was to unlock the secrets of the Northwest Passage, to find a passable route through the heart of North America.

His attempts began in 1783 when he wrote a letter to William Clark's brother, General George Rogers Clark, explaining that the English were attempting an expedition to California and asking if Clark would like to lead a similar mission for the United States. But Clark declined, citing a busy schedule. Three years later, Jefferson succumbed to the temptation yet again when John Ledyard, an old sailing mate of Captain James Cook, proposed a journey that would take him from Moscow through Siberia and across the Bering Strait to Alaska, from where he would ostensibly walk across the entire continent. Despite its obviously flawed design, Jefferson supported the plan. But it didn't work; Ledyard made it partly into Siberia before he was arrested and sent back to Poland. The most promising and professional attempt was made several years later when Jefferson enlisted a French botanist named Andre Michaux to "find the shortest and most convenient route of communication between the U.S. and the Pacific ocean, within the temperate latitudes." Michaux set off in June of 1793 and had barely begun before he was discovered to be a secret agent of the French and was sent back to Europe. Perhaps discouraged by the failures, or perhaps distracted by other, more important matters, such as running for the Presidency of the United States, Jefferson tabled his dreams for the immediate future.

They would not lie dormant for long. In 1793, a young Scotsman named Alexander Mackenzie set out from Fort Fork, about three hundred miles north of present day Edmonton in Alberta, Canada, with the intention of finding a route to the Pacific. Mackenzie was forced to abandon his all-water route but successfully made it to the Pacific Ocean only a few months after departing. In his book, which wasn't published until 1801 and didn't get to Thomas Jefferson until 1802, Mackenzie described a relatively straightforward path across the western part of the continent. This enthused both Jefferson and his young, ambitious secretary Meriwether Lewis, both of whom, according to historian Stephen Ambrose, "talked about little else than Mackenzie" in the summer of 1802. For Jefferson, Mackenzie's success was a cause for alarm, sparking a fear that the British would establish control of the

Northwest before the Americans. But for Lewis, the book was a challenge, and the knowledge that a trans-continental journey was indeed possible deepened his already intense thirst for adventure.

It was a thirst that had developed at an early age. Born in 1774 to William Lewis and Lucy Meriwether, Meriwether Lewis was a precocious young man. At eight or nine, he is said to have calmly shot dead a charging bull. At age ten, he is said to have played an integral role in keeping the family safe during an Indian attack. And at age nineteen, Lewis asked his father's friend, Thomas Jefferson, to appoint him head of the expedition that would attempt to cross the continent. Jefferson demurred, likely due to Lewis's youth and experience, and chose Michaux. A year later, a restless Lewis enlisted in the militia.

In 1799, Lewis was promoted to regimental paymaster, a post in which he was given free reign as a vagabond. During this time, as Ambrose explains, Lewis

> . . . *roamed the West, up and down the Ohio River—Cincinnati, Fort Wayne, Limestone, Maysville, Chillicothe, Wheeling—on a twenty-one-foot bateau, or keelboat, and a pirogue. He learned the craft of a waterman on western rivers. He traveled by horseback to forts south of the Ohio, riding through the wilderness carrying large sums in banknotes. . . . He kept extensive records—transfers, AWOLs, deserters, recruits. He established a reputation for thoroughness, accuracy, and honesty.*

In February 1801, shortly before his inauguration as President of the United States, Thomas Jefferson, involved in Lewis's life from an early age and impressed with his maturation as both a frontiersman and a soldier, wrote to the young captain and invited him to become his secretary: "Your knowledge of the Western country, of the army and all of its interests and relations has rendered it desirable for public as well as private purposes that you should be engaged in that office." Did Jefferson know he would eventually send Lewis to the Pacific Ocean? Historians remain divided over the issue. Nevertheless, in his letter to Lewis, the President stressed the secretary's capacity "not only to aid in the private concerns of the household, but also to contribute to the mass of information which it is interesting for the administration to acquire." Lewis, of course, agreed immediately: "I most cordially acquiesce, and with pleasure accept the office, nor were further motives necessary to induce my compliance." He set off for Washington in March of that year.

As the President's secretary, Lewis was given access to Jefferson's scholarly trove, described by historian John Logan Allen as "probably the finest collection of published materials on the American Northwest in any North America library." During his first few years on the job, Lewis used the material to further his wide-ranging education. He learned the intricacies of navigation, discussed the geography of the continent with renowned experts, researched the cultures of the North American Indians, and immersed himself within the sciences of botany, biology, and ornithology.

All of which led up to the publication of Mackenzie's narrative, reigniting Jefferson's prior obsession, and propelling the President into inevitable action. At some point in late 1802, Jefferson delivered to Lewis the news he had been waiting years to hear—he would be leading an American expedition to the Pacific Ocean. In a letter to the physician Benjamin Rush, Jefferson explained his choice:

> *Capt. Lewis is brave, prudent, habituated to the woods and familiar with Indian manners and character. He is not regularly educated, but he possesses a great mass of accurate observation on all the subjects of nature which present*

themselves here and will therefore readily select those only in his new route which shall be new.

And in a letter to another friend, Jefferson wrote the following well-known passage:

It was impossible to find a character who to a complete science in botany, natural history, mineralogy and astronomy, joined the firmness of constitution and character, prudence, habits adapted to the woods, and familiarity with the Indian manners and character, requisite for this undertaking. All the latter qualifications Capt. Lewis has.

A few months after accepting Jefferson's assignment, Lewis reached out to William Clark, a man he had known only briefly from their time in the army but had stayed friendly with in the decade since. Lewis knew that Clark's skills as a mapmaker and navigator, talents of which he was deficient, would be invaluable for the execution of an overland journey. In a letter dated June 19, 1803, Lewis asked Clark if he would serve as co-commander of the expedition. After outlining the general plan for the trip, Lewis wrote:

If therefore there is anything under those circumstances, in this enterprise, which would induce you to participate with me in its fatigues, its dangers and its honors, believe me there is no man on earth with whom I should feel equal pleasure in sharing them as with yourself.

Like Lewis, Clark enthusiastically agreed. But why? Why did these two men so readily surrender their time and risk their lives for such a difficult and lengthy ordeal? Part of it, of course, was loyalty to their country—raised as military men, assisting the young United States in all its endeavors was of the utmost important to both Lewis and Clark. And part of it must have been the anticipated glory—both men knew that if they returned, the expedition would certainly go down as one of the most famous in history. As Clark wrote in his reply to Lewis, "I anticipate the honors and rewards of the result of such an enterprise, should we be successful in accomplishing it."

And while those reasons undoubtedly played a significant role in their decisions, one can't help but assume that one of their motivations was in fact analogous to my own—that they simply wanted to explore a part of the world they knew little about.

CHAPTER 2

꧁ ꧁ ꧁

The Guidebook Evolution—
The Professionals

ust as one would expect from a proper guidebook aficionado, a small section of my office is reserved for retired volumes of guidebooks from previous trips. Logistically speaking, there's little reason to save these books—any return sojourn to their respective destinations would have to be arranged with more timely information. But my strict adherence to the guidebook means that these volumes represent my past journeys more thoroughly than any item ever could. Souvenirs are indicative of a single destination (say, a museum or a city); pictures indicative of a single point in time. The guidebooks in my library, on the other hand, embody entire trips, making it possible to fondly relive my journeys by simply flipping through their pages.

The largest member of this guidebook depository is a battered 1,200-page behemoth titled *Africa*. It bears the scars of liberal use—creased bindings, bent corners, and ketchup stains—and served as my constant companion through the Africa-specific portion of the previously mentioned around-the-world trip. My goal at that time was to travel overland from Johannesburg, South Africa to Kampala, Uganda, working my way slowly through the southern and eastern part of the continent. I had only one rule—I wanted to do it on my own. That meant no tours, no day trips, no bag lunches, no souvenir shops, and no South Africans holding microphones cracking jokes about rugby and elephants. To achieve this independence, I had enlisted the help of my monstrosity of a guidebook, hoping it could condense nearly twelve million square miles into digestible, bite-sized traveling chunks. But independence, of course, is a subjective construct. Although I was untethered to the incessant narration of a loquacious tour guide ("And over here we have *this*, and over there we have *that!*"), my unfamiliarity with the region and my tendency toward strict guidebook adherence meant I was instead heavily reliant on the advice within my guide's pages.

This reliance also meant I would regularly encounter other travelers, most of whom were as dependent on their own guidebook's instructions as I was. Historically speaking, these encounters are a relatively new phenomenon. When Henry Morton Stanley came to Africa in search of David Livingstone in 1871, he famously traveled 700 miles from the island of Zanzibar through dark jungle and scorching savannah before finding him on the shores of Lake Tanganyika in present-day Tanzania. But a 140 years later, the search for companionship on the continent has become remarkably easier. Within thirty minutes of arriving in most cities, I usually found myself at one of the guidebook's handful of recommended hostels or guesthouses, surrounded by dozens of travelers from all over the world. In this sense, the guidebook's role becomes akin to a magnet; finding fellow travelers to share a drink with is not a laborious and taxing ordeal but rather the expected culmination of a day's travel: "A mojito, I presume?"

Nowhere was this guidebook phenomenon more apparent than during my stay at Chachacha Backpackers, a sprawling centrally located hostel in Lusaka, Zambia. I had stopped in Lusaka for a few days not because of a particularly glowing recommendation—"There are few notable buildings, monuments or other sights"—but because it seemed like a good place to rest before I continued my trip north to Nairobi: "If you have to be in Lusaka for a few days you'll have no trouble passing the time pleasantly enough." During my first evening at the hostel, I made my way outside to the bar and sat in a lounge chair next to the pool. As the night progressed, the festivities around me increased. The music was turned up; toasts were made. As the merriment unfolded, I wondered how many people could possibly be traveling through Lusaka, Zambia at that very moment; I also wondered how many of those people were staying at the Chachacha. The percentage had to be quite high. In many ways, it was incredible that this moment was even possible, that travelers from the United States and Brazil and South Korea could arrive in Lusaka—a capital city relatively absent from the global conversation—and gravitate to a single patch of land no larger than a few acres. At the Chachacha, it seemed, the magnetic pull of the guidebook was particularly strong.

It was quickly apparent, however, that while our itineraries overlapped, they were also quite distinct; our motivations for being on the road varied considerably. There was the South African businessman who was heading west into Angola and onward to the country's capital Luanda. From there, he would continue north into the Democratic Republic of the Congo and to the city of Kinshasa. "Emerging markets," he told me. There was the American NGO worker who had arrived in Lusaka from the east, via Mozambique and Malawi, having spent most of her time hitchhiking and camping through both countries. Her goal was to continue up the eastern side of the continent until she reached Egypt. "Love being on the road," she said. As I met more of the Chachacha travelers, the diversity of traveling motivations increased. The fifty-year-old Englishman who had recently gotten divorced, quit his job, sold his house and left the country. The Australian high school graduates who were in the third month of their gap-year excursion. And on and on and on.

Why people choose to travel has for centuries influenced the ongoing evolution of the guidebook industry. And as Nicholas T. Parsons explains in *Worth the Detour: A History of the Guidebook*, the best and most complete chronicle of the guidebook available today: "One result of the huge increase in travel since the twentieth century, and hence the increased demand for travel literature of all kinds, is that guidebooks now extend from the impossibly macrocosmic to the obsessively microcosmic, dealing candidly with such hitherto unmentionable topics as *How to Shit in the Woods*." The formula is simple—more travelers mean more guidebooks. And my own library represents this diversity well. While some of my guidebooks aspire for breadth, such as the ones on specific countries (e.g., *Ireland* or *New Zealand*), or regions (e.g., *Southeast Asia On a Shoestring*), others aspire for depth (e.g., *Hiking in North Carolina* or *The Best Dive Bars in New York City*), indicating a potpourri of topical and geographical destination information.

It is on the third pillar of the guidebook structure, "the why," where these niche guidebooks—the "obsessively microcosmic"—excel. Specifically designed to cater to a certain audience, these guidebooks are able to issue their recommendations using a more authoritative tone, precisely because their users possess specific interests and motivations. The content inside *Hiking in North Carolina*, for instance, might be excruciatingly boring to a twenty-year-old aspiring musician in San Francisco, but incredibly appropriate fodder for a mountain-loving, New York transplant in Durham, North Carolina. And it's because of their emphasis on the "why" that these niche guidebooks, and not the mainstream Lonely

Planet or Fodor's, best help us understand the early beginnings of the guidebook industry.

꙾꙾   ꙾꙾   ꙾꙾

Travel as a leisurely diversion is a relatively recent development. Before the advent of modern conveniences such as the
eight-hour workday and the airplane, travel was mostly limited
to those with a specific reason or purpose. People traveled for
survival, for commerce, for their country, for religion, for education. The reasons for travel, in fact, were constantly evolving.

The same can also be said of the guidebook, a nebulously
defined genre of literature designed to help travelers get where
they needed to go. The world's earliest guidebooks were often
created reactively, as a response to an increase in a certain
type of travel. And because these pockets of travel were easily definable (a certain pilgrimage route, for instance), it was
easy for the guidebook creator to advise its reader, knowing
exactly what he or she was looking for, on precisely where
they should go and why.

As time passed, both the reasons for travel and the number
of travelers continued to increase. The guidebook industry
followed suit, issuing new editions and new content, tailoring
the pillars of their structure to each specific audience. Eventually, with the growth of the middle class, the appearance of
disposable income, and the development of free time, a new
traveler began to emerge, one who saw travel not as a means
to an end but as a recreation or hobby. "Travel for the sake
of travel," a drastic shift in traveler purpose and motivation,
forced the industry to respond yet again. Its answer was the
mass-market guidebook, a generic formula suitable to travelers of all shapes and sizes. The detailed maps and step-by-step
itineraries excelled at telling people where to go and how to
get there while the colorful pictures and lengthy descriptions
generated vivid scenes for the visitor before he or she arrived.

It was, like my *Africa* guidebook, the perfect companion for travelers of all purposes, or the traveler with no purpose at all.

And yet the mass-market guidebook had one major fault—because it was created to appeal to such a wide range of visitors, it was inherently inefficient. It was simply impossible for the publisher to include itineraries and suggestions for every type of traveler. So the guidebook's suggestions often came out as watered down blueprints designed more to avoid controversies than to break new ground. It's the reason we see exhausted Japanese clicking their way through their fifth hour at the Met or glassy-eyed Americans slogging their way through their thirty-seventh consecutive Italian cathedral. Stuck with a generic itinerary, and often unaware of or unconcerned with their trip's true purpose, the visitors follow the guidebook's advice blindly, tolerating the more banal experiences in the hopes of a better one around the corner.

To counter this inefficiency, and in an effort to respond to the continued increase in travel around the world, the guidebook evolved once again. The niche guides described above, *Hiking in North Carolina* and *The Best Dive Bars in New York City*, are the results of this response, as opportunistic publishers identify certain segments of the traveling population with a similar purpose. And with this innovation, the industry, ironically, has come full circle.

Because the term "guidebook" is so loosely defined, tracing its history is difficult. The genre simply did not develop linearly. From the tail end of Ancient Greece to the pilgrimages of the Middle Ages to the emergence of humanism and the enthusiastic search for knowledge, the guidebook adapted gradually, slowly emerging into the widespread genre we see today. The best way to understand the guidebook's evolution, then, is not through a continuous narrative of its development but through a review of the genre's most notable representatives during different moments in time—moments when the reasons and motives for travel were shifting and publishers attempted to cash in on the trends. Think of what follows, then, not as a true guidebook history but rather as a Guidebook Hall of Fame. While each of these "guidebooks"—from the nearly two thousand-year-old *Description of Greece* to Tony Wheeler's *Across Asia on the Cheap*—contains some combination of the three guidebook elements, the ratios and amounts vary wildly as writers and publishers of the individual titles built formats and styles appropriate for their particular audience. Regardless of their differences, however, it is these iconic books, albeit unintentionally, and for better or for worse, that eventually led to the publication of *How to Shit in the Woods.*

For an item that helped spawn the growth of an industry that contributes around $1 trillion annually to the global economy, the oldest-surviving complete guidebook ever uncovered may have very well been the worst selling guidebook of all time. It was so unsuccessful, some historians argue, that it wasn't read by anyone other than the author until the sixth century A.D., 350 years after its initial "publication." It was only then that Stephanus of Byzantium, a scholar interested in the manuscript for its geographical references, both rescued the document from a lifetime of neglect and immortalized its author (who remained anonymous on the manuscript) by giving him the name Pausanias.

Written sometime between 150 and 180 A.D., broken into ten sections, and translated into English as *Description of Greece* (or *Guide to Greece*), the first inductee in our Guidebook Hall of Fame was initially part of a larger genre of literature classified as periegetic, a category which scholar Christian Habicht explains, stems from the Greek word "periegeomai [meaning] 'to show around.'" Although very little of this work survives today, enough evidence has been amassed to reveal two distinguishing aspects of Pausanias's guide—aspects that have subsequently positioned the work as an important rung on the guidebook's evolutionary ladder.

First, the book was geographically ambitious. While many of these classic works focused on a single monument or region, Pausanias's tome was in fact a harbinger of my *Africa* guidebook—he aimed to cover all of Greece. Second, the author took his role as a guide very seriously. While the competition often resorted to "gossipy, colorful [and] frequently scabrous" language in an effort to attract an audience, Pausanias purposely avoided this kind of flamboyant verbiage. As Sir James Frazer, one of Pausanias's most respected translators, says, "If he lacked imagination he was the less likely to yield to that temptation of distorting and discoloring the facts to which men of bright fancy are peculiarly exposed." Guidebook historian Nicholas T. Parsons agrees:

> *The retrieval of those facts, the sifting of the grain from the chaff, the unemotional report of sanctuaries violated or cities pillaged, or of the wounds the Greeks inflicted on themselves through the internal strife that has brought them low, or finally the studied recall of an heroic past that is still present in the whispering ghosts he describes at Marathon—all this constitutes the author's homage to an idea and an ideal.*

This "ideal" was also reflected in the way Pausanias traveled. Habicht explains that the author canvassed the region using a remarkably disciplined method, one in which he "moves from the border by the shortest route to the capital, describes what is to be seen there, takes another road to the border, describing what seems worth recording, and then, returning to the capital and taking another road, continues until he finally crosses the border to another district, where again he goes straight to its center."

Still, while his methods were exhaustive, Pausanias remained dedicated to directing his readers toward what he felt were the most important destinations. The author, explains Habicht, "makes it clear that the oldest works, such as the wooden statues, unpolished as they are, are, to him, the most venerable, and those of the late archaic and classical periods, that is to say, of the fifth century BC, are the most perfect products of Greek art." The adherence to this particular task, however, often came at the expense of description. As Frazer suggests:

> *If he looks up at the mountains, it is not to mark the snowy peaks glistering in the sunlight against the blue, or the somber pine-forests that fringe their crests and are mirrored in the dark lake below; it is to tell you that Zeus or Apollo or the Sun-god is worshipped on their tops, that the Thyiad women rave on them above the clouds, or that Pan has been heard piping in their lonely coombs.*

Of the rivers that flow through Athens, for example, Pausanias describes them as "the Ilisus and its tributary the Eridanus" but says nothing about their orientation, their width, or their color. Instead, he chooses to relate an interesting, albeit mythological, story concerning their history: "This Ilisus is the river by which Oreithyia was playing when, according to the story, she was carried off by the North Wind. With Oreithyia he lived in wedlock, and because of the tie between him and the Athenians he helped them by destroying most of the foreigners' warships." There are hundreds of similar examples.

Unfortunately, the inclusion of all these mythological figures and legends made the text nearly indecipherable for the average reader. A baffling passage from the second volume of the guide, containing no less than ten Grecian characters, illustrates this difficulty all too well: "So even in his time poets lived at the courts of kings as earlier still Anacreon consorted with Polycrates, despot of Samos, and Aeschylus and Simonides journeyed to Hiero at Syracuse. Dionysius, afterwards despot in Sicily, had Philoxenus at his court, and Antigonus, ruler of Macedonia, had Antagoras of Rhodes and Aratus of Soli."

This kind of linguistic barbed wire also drastically increased the length of the book, which no doubt contributed to the lack of success noted previously—the guide was simply too cumbersome to take on a journey. Anyone who has traipsed through India or China or Africa with the accompanying Lonely Planet can attest to the difficulties caused by an unwieldy guidebook. So Pausanias's book was ignored, and the author, after dedicating so much of his life to the task, sank into anonymity for hundreds of years.

But let's return, for a moment, to the initial incentive behind Pausanias's guide—"to remind the Greeks of who they are and where they came from." This impulse, clearly ahead of its time, but now classified under the umbrella of patriotism or nationalism, would eventually be accepted as a legitimate reason to travel. It's why each year a million people visit Gettysburg, the site of the United States' most famous Civil War battle. Or why long lines of loyal Russians stream past Vladimir Lenin's preserved body in Moscow's Red Square nearly a century after his death. Or why more than ten million people, a vast majority of them Chinese, visit the Great Wall of China every year. Mankind's collective increase in knowledge has consequently allowed it to better understand the significance of certain places and events, and in turn, to embrace those places and events through travel. Guidebooks have followed, designed to hold the traveler's hand as he or she explores these battlegrounds, cemeteries, ruins, and tombs.

Pausanias, it seems, was born a few thousand years too early—it is easy to picture him alive today, a fake musket secured to his belt, leading an enthusiastic tour group through the grounds of Gettysburg, Pennsylvania.

ℐℬ   ℐℬ   ℐℬ

Although Pausanias's success as a guidebook writer was, at least initially, non-existent, his primary objective—to foster travel throughout Greece as an appreciation of the region's history—indirectly foreshadowed the next significant evolution of the guidebook genre, that of pilgrimage. Scholar Jas Elsner, in fact, argues that Pausanias's guide was promoting its own type of pilgrimage, its narrative "not only a journey through topography, but also a careful mytho-historical interpretation of the meaning of that topography."

And in terms of pilgrimages, there are few journeys better known than the Way of St. James to the Cathedral of Santiago de Compostela. Despite history being littered with examples of misguided pilgrims flocking to manufactured relics, Parsons argues "perhaps in no case has the will to believe triumphed so completely over the available historical and scientific facts as in that of the cult of St. James at Compostela in northwestern Spain." The basic story goes as follows: When Jesus Christ died, his disciples scattered throughout the world to spread the word of God. One of these men, Saint James, was sent to Spain where he succeeded in converting nine people. After returning to Jerusalem, he fell upon unfortunate luck and was promptly beheaded by an enemy in 44 A.D. Determined to get his body back to Spain, his followers took off for the coast where they auspiciously found a ship awaiting their arrival. Aided by angels, the boat returned to Spain, landing twenty or so kilometers from the current site of the Spanish town of Santiago de Compostela. The body of St. James was subsequently buried on a hillside and forgotten for nearly a millennium.

In the early ninth century, a hermit, guided by a large, bright star shining on an otherwise deserted hill, came across a tomb. Excited, the hermit quickly summoned the local

bishop who subsequently decreed that the body was in fact
that of Saint James. The fortuitous discovery was communi-
cated to King Alfonso II who, eager to encourage an influx of
tourism dollars to the area, rapidly pronounced Saint James
the patron saint of Spain and commissioned the building of
various monuments, including a church, at the site. With
Christian pilgrims anxious for a comparatively accessible pilgrimage route (Jerusalem, at this time, had been overrun by
the Turks) and despite the overwhelmingly flimsy evidence
on which its significance was established, Santiago de Compostela soon developed a reputation as one of the world's great
pilgrimage sites.

While there are dozens of examples, the most famous guidebook to Santiago de Compostela is undoubtedly Book Five of
the larger *Liber Sancti Jacobi* (or *Book of St. James*), probably
written around 1150 and attributed to a French writer named
Aymeric Picaud. While the designation of authorship is often
challenged, no such disagreement exists for the primary intent
of *Liber peregrinationis* (or *Pilgrim's Guide*)—to guide and
instruct travelers on the Way to St. James. As one historian
suggests: "[The author] seems to ask: 'If I were going on this
trip again, what would I need to know?'"

Compared to Pausanias's weighty tome, the *Pilgrim's
Guide* was light—eleven chapters and a relatively meager
14,000 words. The book, however, is packed with an abundance of practical advice including budgeting recommendations ("I have described these towns and stages so that
pilgrims setting out for Santiago, hearing this, can work out
the expenses necessary for their journey") and culinary suggestions ("Estella, full of good bread and the best wine and
meat and fish, and plenty of all good things"). Once safely
arrived at Santiago, the author delves into a painstakingly
accurate description of the church—"The Basilica of Santiago is the length of fifty-three men, from the west doorway

to the altar of St Salvador. It is thirty-nine men wide, from the French to the south doorway; in the inside, it is fourteen times a man's height"—dedicating separate, exhaustive sections to each architectural component of the Basilica (e.g., the windows, the South Doorway, the West Doorway).

But the reason the *Liber peregrinationis* endures in popular culture today, the reason a full English translation is available for free perusal online, and the reason Parsons calls it "one of the most entertaining European guidebooks ever written," is because of the French author's unabashedly jingoistic assaults on many of the Spanish inhabitants along the route. Of the village of Saint-Jean-de-Sorde, where the author was most likely accosted for unexpected fees, Picaud says "the boatmen are trouble—big trouble . . . they'll extort money for their services, whether you can afford it or not." And of the families in Gascony, the author says they are "fast-talking, obnoxious, and sex-crazed . . . overfed, poorly-dressed drunks" before softening the blow by adding: "They've two good characteristics: they are skilled warriors, and they give good hospitality to the poor."

Picaud's harshest venom, however, was reserved for the people of Navarre, today an autonomous community in northern Spain. The Navarrese, says the author, are "malicious, dark, hostile-looking types, crooked, perverse, treacherous, corrupt and untrustworthy, obsessed with sex and booze, steeped in violence, wild, savage, condemned and rejected, sour, horrible, and squabbling. They are badness and nastiness personified, utterly lacking in any good qualities." The angry ramblings, seemingly out of place in a work that has often been anointed Europe's "first guidebook," continue with severe and shocking accusations. The Navarrese, says Picaud, "also have sex with their farm animals. And it's said that they put a lock on the backsides of their mules and horses so that nobody except themselves can have at them."

But the author's warnings did little to diminish the popularity of the route—quite the contrary. The "Pilgrimage of Everyman," as one website calls it, continued to attract thousands of pilgrims, even through the more rational and increasingly skeptical years of the Renaissance and the Scientific Revolution. And the popularity continues today. In 2010, more than 270,000 pilgrims made the trek, nearly triple the amount of 1993, when the site received a designation as a UNESCO World Heritage Site, and over a hundred times more than in 1986, when the Cathedral at Santiago began to keep track. Not surprisingly, this popularity has resulted in more guidebooks for the route than ever before. And while the increase in guidebooks is inevitable, one can only hope that the local communities, when being described in contemporary guides, have been spared the presumably biased vitriol of previous authors.

Although it would endure in various shapes and forms, the act of pilgrimage would not survive unscathed. The advent of humanism, along with a new friction between secular and religious entities, brought with it a sense of efficiency and purpose to the world of travel. Suddenly, journeys to these once-revered destinations were viewed, according to scholar Justin Stagl, as frivolous endeavors, "treated with irony" by some and openly "attacked" by others. By the year 1550, "pilgrimage had ceased to be a plausible justification for travel."

The shift from religious pilgrimage toward a more structured traveling experience was indicative of the newfound emphasis placed on knowledge, and according to one author, the desire to "provide a comprehensive explanation of the world." And for scholarly men of the era, says Stagl, "the whole earth was for them a place where something could be learnt and where one could improve oneself."

What better way, then, to empirically collect earthly knowledge than to canvas the world systematically through the act of travel? But to simply travel would not do. Instead, these men "aimed at the standardization of the practice of travelling and the possible accumulation of its results."

What emerged was a genre of travel literature entitled ars apodemica, often translated as "the art of travel." Written by men with such grandiose names as Hieronymus Turler and Hilarius Pyrckmair and given such lumbering titles as *Methodus apodemica, in eorum gratia qui cum fructu in quocunque tandem vitae genere peregrinari cupiunt*, the manuscripts that make up the *ars apodemica* genre are not so much travel guides as they are guides toward a structured travel philosophy. Inside a modern day bookstore, for example, one can imagine the books sitting alongside *On the Road* or *Zen and the Art of Motorcycle Maintenance* rather than *Frommer's Italy*. But unlike those contemporary texts, the books produced under the *ars apodemica* umbrella were purposefully mundane. Parsons describes the genre as "eye-watering tedium." Stagl is less harsh, explaining the literary style as "deliberately plain, dry and realistic."

Although the genre was not widely adopted (one scholar aptly describes it as more "praised than read"), its emphasis on the educational aspect of travel had an indelible influence on one particular group—wealthy young men, the future of European aristocracy, who were sent off on lengthy journeys through Europe to learn about the world. The Grand Tour, as these trips would come to be known, was part experience, part education—an initiation, per se, designed to cultivate and refine at every stop of the journey. This "peripatetic liberal education" was accompanied by a private tutor, a man assigned to assist the young nobleman as he made his way through France, Italy, Germany, and beyond.

Sensing a new niche in the tourist marketplace, some of these tutors used their experience to produce Grand Tour-focused guidebooks. Probably the most famous of all, and the third entry to our Guidebook Hall of Fame, was one written by an English Roman Catholic priest and Grand Tour expert named Richard Lassels. Lassels's nearly seven hundred-page *The Voyage of Italy,* published posthumously in 1670, significantly advanced the Grand Tour literature, and according to at least one author, may very well claim the title of "the first true guidebook in the English language."

The most interesting part of the book is its beginning, a rambling introductory essay entitled "A Preface To The Reader Concerning Travelling." In it, Lassels first strains to justify his worth as a guidebook authority figure. This is attempted not only through the book's title page, where the short author bio ("By Richard Lassels, Gent, who Travelled through Italy Five times, as Tutor to several of the English Nobility and Gentry") is akin to a modern day travel writer boasting that he's "been to over sixty countries," but also through the first few pages, as he deflects anticipated criticism that his book is both too merry and too mocking.

Then, in a shrewd bit of guidebook promotion, Lassels happily expounds on the merits of the Grand Tour:

> *Travelling preserves my young nobleman from surfeiting of his parents, and weans him from the dangerous fondness of his Mother. It teaches him wholesome hardship; to lie in beds that are none of his acquaintance; to speak to men he never saw before; to travel in the morning before day; and in the evening after day; to endure any horse and weather, as well as any meat and drink.*

All of which serves as justification for the continued practice of travel in an age of declining pilgrimage. So just as Pausanias and Picaud assumed specific motivations for travel (i.e., historical appreciation and pilgrimage), so does Lassels incorporate the pulse of the era, the search for knowledge and experience, into his dissemination of guidebook-related advice.

The continued evolution of the genre, though, is clearly evident throughout the rest of the book. Similar to today's guidebooks, *The Voyage of Italy* begins not with the start of the author's journey but with a general introduction to the region's geography and culture. After a discussion concerning Italy's flora, fauna, and weather, Lassels explains that Italy's greatest asset (it's #1 attraction perhaps) is, indeed, its people—"Yes, yes, it's this great blessing of God, warm Sun, which hath so thoroughly baked the Italian wits, that while (according to the observation of Charles the V) the French appear not wise, but are wise; the Spaniards appear wise, but are not wise; the Dutch neither appear wise, nor are wise; the Italians only both appear wise, and are wise."

But the author's love affair with Italian culture is brief; most of the book describes a systematic journey through notable Grand Tour cities. And while the author's city synopses are often quite redundant—a brief history of the city, a checklist of sights that need to be seen—the style represents an *ars apodemica*-like system of categorization that perhaps signals the beginning of the structured guides we use today. His various discussions regarding the region's culture (i.e., how Italians get married, how they raise their children, how they serve dinner), for example, are clearly the genesis of the robust introductory sections—history, currency, weather, food—common in many modern guidebook brands. And Lassels's use of the book's margins to delineate certain monuments or themes (i.e., "The Inhabitants of Rome," "My Journey From Rome to Naples") portends the eventual arrangement of guidebooks by useful touristic categories such as Lodging, Food, and Attractions.

But despite these advances, *The Voyage of Italy* still suffers from the excruciatingly linear style encountered in previous guidebook iterations—"I went there, and then I went there, and then I went there." Perhaps mindful of his observational tendencies, Lassels, in the book's Preface, recognizes the criticism the book might face for its emphasis on sights with religious significance and for its dependence on "Ceremonies, and Church antiquities." This prediction bore out; it is nearly impossible to go a full page without the introduction and subsequent discussion of a new chapel or church. A search through the book's second part reveals church after church after church: on page 86—"Soon after I came to S. Pauls Church, here S. Paul was buried by Lucina a Roman Lady . . ."; on page 90—"In the third place stands the little Church of the Tre Fontane, so called because S. Paul was here beheaded, and where his head jumpt thrice, three fountains gushed out"; and on page 134—"Going on still, I came to the Church of S. Lorenzo in Miranda." This tedium persists even as the author describes S. John Laterans Church, "the mother-Church of all Churches in the world, and the Popes Cathedral," its significance muted by the sheer volume and intensity of ecclesiastical overload.

Exposure to religious artifacts was, however, only a small part of the impetus behind the Grand Tour philosophy. The primary justification for the elaborate journeys of these Grand Tourists was, of course, experience gained through exposure to the outside world. Until the middle of the nineteenth century, in fact, most travel *was* justified in some way, shape, or form, if for no other reason than to warrant both the significant time and money needed to pursue it. All that, however, would soon change. With the emergence of new technology, the world was about to get much smaller and therefore, much more accessible.

Two hundred years after the publication of *The Voyage of Italy,* the following review concerning an increasingly popular brand of guidebooks, the *Handbooks for Travellers,* was published in the *London Times:*

> *Into every nook which an Englishman can penetrate he carries his Red Handbook. He trusts to his Murray as he would trust to his razor, because it is thoroughly English and reliable; and for his history, hotels, exchanges, scenery, for the clue to his route and his comfort by the way, the Red Handbook is his "guide, philosopher, and friend." (Sept 22, 1859)*

The books for which this effusive praise had been written were the creation of the Murray family, the first publisher, according to Parsons, to fully "appreciate the need for comprehensive and practical guidebooks." By the time the above review was circulated, the Murrays had released around two dozen guidebooks and had established themselves as the preeminent authority on bourgeois travel. Their handbooks were so influential, in fact, that one historian relates an incident where no less an authority than the Queen of England "had expressed a wish to see what was written about Windsor . . . before final passing for printing" in the *Handbook for Travellers in Berkshire, Buckinghamshire and Oxfordshire.* There is no surviving evidence, unfortunately, on whether the Queen was allowed to make her requested edits.

This evolution of the guidebook spectrum from a scattered collection of verbose ramblings to a flourishing market of influential companies and brands was due to a change in both traveler motivations and travel opportunities. Advances in mass communication technology allowed for a greater dissemination of information; advances in transportation technology allowed for a greater dissemination of travelers. Formal education by travel, the philosophy promoted through the development of the Grand Tour itinerary, evolved into informal education through experience—people simply became curious about what lay beyond their village, their town, and their city. More importantly, many of these people finally had the means to pursue that curiosity. By the end of the century, with the development of the locomotive, steamship, and pleasure yacht, no destination was too remote; no curiosity was insatiable.

This increase in traveling opportunities was fittingly noted by Mariana Starke, an author anointed by one scholar as the first "professional guidebook writer," in the introduction to her book *Travels on the Continent*. Starke's guidebook, published by the Murray family in 1820, was notable for two reasons. First, it was a clear improvement, systematically and categorically, over the linear style utilized by writers such as Lassels. Of particular note was her use of exclamation points to delineate the importance of specific paintings and sculptures, a system that would evolve into "author's pick" type recommendations in today's guidebooks. Second, Starke emphasized the importance of firsthand exposure and experience in developing a coherent guide, an attitude that stood in contrast to those of previous guidebook authors such as Pausanias who too often advanced popular myths as facts.

One proponent of this on-the-ground approach was John Murray III, a descendant of the aforementioned Murray publishing house and eventual distributor of his own guidebook brand. As Murray himself said, "[Starke's] was a work of real utility, because, amidst a singular medley of classical lore . . . it contained much practical information gathered on the spot." The combination of a determined yet controlled focus on "where to go and how to get there" along with a succinct yet useful addition of "why to go" would be the great contribution of the Murray brand. No longer would guidebooks be weighed down with redundant paragraphs of trivial anecdotes and long-winded accounts of tedious details. Instead, they would be developed through objective descriptions, not to pedantically educate, but according to author Lynne Withey, to efficiently and effectively "[take] the uncertainty out of travel." From Murray:

> *Arriving at a city like Berlin, I had to find out what was really worth seeing there, to make a selection of such objects, and to tell how best to see them, avoiding the ordinary practice of local guide-books, which, in inflated language, cram in everything that can possibly be said—not bewildering my readers by describing all that might be seen—and using the most condensed and simplest style in description of special objects. I made it my aim to point out things peculiar to the spot, or which might be better seen there than elsewhere.*

Murray's diligence and ambition, combined with his family's publishing expertise and a perceptible marketing know-how (all the handbooks were the same size and color and were titled in a similar fashion—"*Handbook for Travellers in . . .*") produced a series of titles that would catch the attention of a German printer and bookseller named Karl Baedeker. Duly impressed with the product Murray had created—he called the Murray series of handbooks the "most distinguished guide ever published"—and recognizing the sizable demand for this new kind of product, Baedeker decided to enter the guidebook game himself, releasing German-language handbooks to Holland and Belgium in 1839. Karl Baedeker's goal was similar to Murray's—to create a guide that provided just enough information to get visitors where they needed to go and to appreciate what they were seeing but to leave the "aesthetic and emotional responses" to the visitors themselves. The style proved enormously successful and while much of the Baedeker success was due to the overall growth of the guidebook genre mentioned above, the emergence of the Baedeker brand as an indispensable tool in the independent traveler's suitcase was also the result of hard work (Parsons implies that the stress of keeping the guides up to date contributed to Karl's early death), dedication (an introduction to one of the guidebooks notes: "The entire contents of the book have been compiled from the personal experience of the editor, and the country described by him has within the last few years been repeatedly visited by him solely with the view of gathering fresh information"), and a sophisticated yet subtle mix of all three pillars of the guidebook structure.

Built upon the foundation developed by previous guidebook authors, this unique mix of guidebook elements can be seen in our fourth addition to the Guidebook Hall of Fame and the brand's first English-language title, *A Handbook for Travellers on The Rhine, From Switzerland to Holland,* published in 1861. To use just one example—while previous guidebooks had relied mostly on text-based instruction to outline the routes needed to arrive at certain destinations ("go here and then turn here and then go straight"), Baedeker, cognizant of the number of choices now available to independent travelers, improves upon the previous system by incorporating easy-to-read tables as well as a wide assortment of maps for regions, cities, and specific destinations. The inclusion of more visually pleasing components to the format mercifully ends the era of the linear narrative guidebook and suggests the beginning of a more fickle consumer—one who preferred to jump around the guidebook's information rather than digesting the entire text beginning to end. The addition of maps, so important to the guidebook structure today, is of particular note. As scholar Edward Mendelson notes, "Karl Baedeker and his sons always provided more and better maps than anyone else did; nothing less would adequately serve the traveler who wanted to move quickly and freely through medieval streets or mountain passes."

The Rhine's release signified the beginning of inexorable growth. With the death of Karl Baedeker in 1859, and with the brand under the stewardship of the founder's sons, the company grew quickly, directly challenging Murray with additional English-language guidebooks to continental Europe as well as with specific titles for London and Great Britain. But England was merely a stopover for the family's larger vision of world guidebook-domination. In the 1870s, as control of the company was passed to Karl's son Fritz, the firm, according to Mendelson, "began its great period of expansion," releasing guidebooks for such far-flung regions as the United States (1893), Constantinople and Asia Minor (1905), and India (1914). Parsons calls this era the "age of Baedeker," as the brand "achieved an absolutely impregnable position as market leaders." It also signaled the beginning of a new industry, one that continues unabated to this very day. Subsequent guidebook brands—Fodor's, Frommer's, Rough Guides, Rick Steves and Lonely Planet—owe much of their success, and much of their format, to the development and implementation of the Baedeker model. But before we turn to the final member of our Guidebook Hall of Fame, we must return briefly to the middle of the nineteenth century, to the beginnings of mass travel, as Murray and Baedeker continued to compete for the eyes of an increasingly mobile public—it is there where the seeds were planted for the final step on the professional guidebook's evolutionary ladder.

In the midst of the battle for guidebook supremacy in the 1860s, John Murray III, mindful of the high price of his handbooks (one scholar notes that the books had "an average price equal to an agricultural laborer's weekly wage"), and searching for a way to widen the appeal of his guidebook series, released a handful of more affordable "knapsack" guides to places such as Italy and Norway. The decision to publish these guidebooks is a telling one; it suggests that Murray anticipated the emergence of less affluent travelers. Unfortunately, the books bombed—the scale needed to sustain a discount alternative not yet possible—and were discontinued after only eight years. But Murray's vision proved to be a prophetic one. It took nearly a century and the conclusion of two world wars, but the rise of an independent segment of less prosperous travelers signifies the last ripple in our guidebook/traveler chronology.

By the mid-1960s, in fact, the means to travel outside one's own country became accessible enough for the United Nations to designate 1967 the International Tourist Year. For the multitude of travelers heeding this call—the slogan the UN chose was "Tourism, Passport to Peace"—choosing their "guide" became a most intimate affair. Choices abounded— one newspaper editor at the time mentioned that there would be more than four hundred guidebooks to Europe released in 1962 alone. And in a *Los Angeles Times* article written five years later, book editor Robert Kirsch suggested that "[c]hoosing travel guidebooks is a lot like selecting a spouse. You look for compatibility or incompatibility with the author. Anything between could lead to trouble."

For many, that spouse became Arthur Frommer. A Yale-educated lawyer stationed in Germany in the mid-1950s, Frommer's first foray into the guidebook world began when he produced a small pamphlet of travel tips designed for American soldiers interested in traveling around Europe. Energized by the success of this initiative, Frommer returned to Europe two years later to produce his seminal tome, *Europe on 5 Dollars a Day*, the first edition of what would become a multi-million-dollar guidebook publishing empire. The author's thrifty traveling style (never, for example, take a room with a bath) caught on quickly—one *New York Times* article claimed that one of every five Americans who made the trip to Europe in the late 1960s went off the guidance of the Frommer brand: "Not content to leave it at that, some 5,000 of them will write to Arthur Frommer. They will tell him they could never have done it without him; they will tell him they swear by him. Some will write 10-page, hand-written letters on lined paper telling Arthur Frommer every single hotel, restaurant, train, plane, bus and beaded bag that happened to them on their way through Europe." But while *Europe on 5 Dollars a Day* would be a worthy and deserved inductee to our admittedly subjective Guidebook Hall of Fame, the last spot at the podium has instead been reserved for the first ever publication of a guide with a similarly zealous base of devotees and disciples. It is also, perhaps, the world's most ubiquitous—and possibly most discussed—guidebook brand.

The celebrated soul of Lonely Planet developed sometime in the 1960s with the appearance of what came to be known as the "Hippie Trail," a 6,000-mile overland journey across Turkey, Iran, Afghanistan, Pakistan, India, and Nepal. Who initiated this journey? Young people, mostly, many of whom were "hacked off with the tired old ways and days," says Rory MacLean, author of the book *Magic Bus,* a re-creation of the decades-old journey (his own mini-pilgrimage one might say). These young travelers, weaned on the counter-cultural output of men like Jack Kerouac and Allen Ginsberg, were "a footloose generation devoted to the acquisition of experience and self-knowledge." So they set off for India, both spiritually and physically, because they could, and because the alternative, remaining in the West and following the path set down by the previous generation, was no longer the only option.

Tony and Maureen Wheeler, the founders of Lonely Planet, were a small part of this vast traveling migration. The couple left London in 1972, traveling east across Asia and eventually arriving in Australia approximately seven months later with, in what has a become a famous anecdote of guidebook lore, a mere twenty-seven cents to their name. The Wheelers quickly settled into part-time work, spending evenings and nights rehashing stories and answering questions about their long journey to Australia. In desperate need of funds, the Wheelers "began to think about selling this information instead of giving it away."

The result was a ninety-six-page pamphlet called *Across Asia on the Cheap,* the final addition to our Guidebook Hall of Fame. Unlike today's Lonely Planet guidebooks, which are filled with glossy photographs and exhaustive descriptions, *Across Asia on the Cheap* was focused primarily on instructing the traveler where to go, how to get there, and why they should go in the first place. In many ways, the narrative reads more like an opinion piece, or maybe a blog post, than an instruction manual, as the author supplements much of his advice with corny jokes and irrelevant anecdotes, many of which are amplified with a frequent exclamation point. Of traveling via bicycle, Wheeler writes: "Involving even less paperwork would be a pushbike—even that is getting to be a fairly common way of making the trip. We even heard of a couple of good European lightweights for sale in Kabul!" And of preparing for a lack of petrol en route, the author advises, "It is a good idea to carry a few spare gallons in case they've run out somewhere and are not expecting another delivery for a few weeks. We saw that once in Turkey!"

But the exclamation points are simply a reflection of the author's enthusiasm, a refreshing deviation from the cantankerous output of Picaud or the mundane guidance of Pausanias. Sometimes that enthusiasm is reflected in a youthful exuberance that would seem not only out of place, but also rather incendiary, in our modern politically correct culture. In a section called "Dope," for example, Wheeler suggests that the traveler "can get stoned just taking a deep breath in the streets." And in Bali, the "mushrooms go down well. . . . Afterwards, you can trip gently down to the beach and watch a truly unbelievable sunset."

In other sections, Wheeler's vitality is exemplified in his brazen attitude and outlook. When describing how locals might respond to the temptation of Western women through verbal or physical harassment, the author explains, "It's humiliating for the girls and frustrating for the would be protective guys. So if you can lay hands on one of the bastards take advantage of it and rough him up a little." He takes a far less rigid tone, however, in regards to the locals' religious customs: "The Hindu religion is such a comic book, Disneyland setup it is almost difficult to take it seriously." And, when discussing ways in which the traveler might replenish his or her bank account in Singapore, Wheeler says: "Chicks can pick up easy money working for the escort services—they're quite respectable."

But these musings were merely a reflection of their time, an era when travelers would respond honestly to new experiences without regard for political correctness or sensitivity. It was all wrapped up in the purpose of the hippie trail—to go, to see, to do, to react, to live. All things considered, Wheeler's attitude is remarkably conciliatory and friendly, and his enthusiasm for new experiences is reflected in the way he gushes, often redundantly, about the local citizenry: "Once in, Singapore is a very pleasant place and, as everywhere, the people are great"; "Malaysia is one of the most beautiful countries you'll pass through and its people are incredibly friendly"; "[Thailand is] a calm pleasant country with friendly people—we certainly found them so."

This approach, cultivated at a time when long-distance transportation was becoming increasingly affordable and mass communication was opening up international narratives to new worlds, led to remarkable success. Forty years after its debut, Lonely Planet had printed over a hundred million guidebooks in nine languages and was seen as one of, if not the, most influential voice in the history of the guidebook industry. But all success stories breed contrarians, and as Lonely Planet grew more successful, those who had once savored its unique voice in an otherwise bland industry began to deride its founders for venturing off the proverbial free and unshackled hippie trail. Its "shoestring" guide for backpackers, for example, was soon de-emphasized and by 2005 made up only three percent of the company's total sales. As one employee told *The New Yorker,* "Our Hawaii book used to be written for people who were picking their own guava and sneaking into the resort pool, and we were getting killed by the competition. So we relaunched it for a more typical two-week American mid-market vacation. That sold, but it didn't feel very Lonely Planet."

Today, many argue that Lonely Planet guidebooks have become so relied upon as to become almost antithetical to their original purpose of facilitating free and independent travel. As former Lonely Planet contributor Thomas Khonstamm writes, "You go to another country and rather than trying to understand the nuances and textures of that culture, you end up spending your time with a roving band of people like yourself." That thought, so common among fervent travelers today, is echoed wistfully by a main character in *The Beach,* a popular novel of today's backpacking generation: "I want to do something different, and everybody wants to do something different. But we all do the same thing."

The editorial shift that sparked much of this reflection—explained by one employee as a transition from a reliance on local history and economics to an emphasis on snappy highlights and digestible itineraries—suggests not only a changing guidebook industry but also a changing media landscape in general. To maintain relevancy in an increasingly dire print environment, Lonely Planet was forced to concentrate its efforts on its best-selling guidebooks, a strategy that continued a self-perpetuating cycle where destinations became popular primarily *because* they were Lonely Planet approved. By doing so, the brand began to launch travelers not toward fresh experience but instead toward everybody else. If the hippie trail embodied freedom, the Lonely Planet Trail, as it came to be known, embodied the complete opposite—rigid travel in a tightly structured environment. In 2007, the Wheelers, perhaps mindful of this shift, or perhaps simply weary of their brand's crumbling business model, ended their Lonely Planet journey, selling much of the company to the BBC and paving the way for the next evolution of the guidebook industry.

After a few relaxing nights in Lusaka at Chachacha Backpackers (where I did indeed pass the time "pleasantly enough"), I took an early morning taxi from the hostel to the city bus station. My goal was to take a minibus north to the town of Kapiri Mposhi, from where I could board a train to the Tanzanian city of Dar es Salaam. Although I had relied heavily on my guidebook's recommendations to that point, information on this particular excursion was limited. Besides a brief mention of the timetable and the cost, there were no additional details about tickets, stations, or amenities. I had, however, been fortunate to find a ticket window the previous day in Lusaka and had secured a cabin berth for the Tazara Railways Express all the way to my final destination. It was the strangest train ticket I have ever purchased, printed on what seemed like cardboard, and no bigger than the size of two postage stamps. But the clerk assured me it was legit.

I found a minibus headed to Kapiri Mposhi quickly and was the first to board, an unfortunate occurrence at an African bus station. I spent the next three hours battling the rising sun and making small talk (weather, sports, politics) with the man who had sat down next to me. By nine o'clock, the many touts who roamed the station began to drink, and the man who had quite literally pulled me from my taxi spent most of his time begging me to buy him a beer. After two hours, his tenacity had withered, the heat throttling his initial exuberance. When I asked if I was going to make the train, he averted his eyes and said quietly, "Please just buy me a beer." Shortly thereafter, three women with large canvas-wrapped packages approached the bus; they were taking the train to Dar es Salaam as well—would the driver be able to get them there on time? And just like that we were off, roaring north out of the capital and up to Kapiri Mposhi. We arrived at the station in plenty of time to board, and after discovering that my four-person cabin was already occupied by six boisterous male travelers, a train employee promptly led me to a second unoccupied cabin before holding out his hand for a small token of gratitude.

The journey took nearly forty-eight hours, with frequent delays and mechanical hiccups, but I would gladly do it many times over again. I spent the time reading my book and gazing out the window, watching the central African landscape slowly creep by. Food and beverage were never a problem. At each stop, women from the villages would come up to my window to sell fresh mangos and bananas; the dining car, meanwhile, was stocked with cold beers and sodas. At dinnertime, as the sun ducked behind distant hills and the dark clouds became framed against spectacular bursts of orange and red, a man brought me a plate of rice, chicken, and watermelon. I ate dinner alone in my cabin, repeatedly reminding myself how lucky I was to be in that exact spot, on that exact train, in that exact moment. The next day, another gift—the sight of a galloping giraffe making his way through the dry scrub of eastern Tanzania. I sat perched at my window for the next three hours, camera ready, until another sunset shrouded the animals in the absolute darkness of a rural African night.

The train journey from Kapiri Mposhi to Dar es Salaam would become one of the most enduring memories from my travels through Africa. On its face, it would seem to resemble an example of true guidebook-less travel, a side excursion launched away from the usual touristic trail and executed without the assistance of my print guidebook. And unlike at the Chachacha, where I had crossed paths with travelers from all over the world, I had seen only a handful of other non-Africans on the train, more evidence that the route existed "off the beaten path."

And yet I have not, admittedly, been entirely candid. While it is indeed true that my *Africa* guide contained little information about the trip—there was no indication of where to buy train tickets, no pictures of the journey, and no details on the boarding requirements in Kapiri Mposhi—I did not go into this journey unprepared. On the contrary, thanks to the latest and most important component of the guidebook evolution—the focus of the next chapter, in fact—I was as prepared for the railway excursion to Dar es Salaam as I had been for any trip I have ever taken.

INTERLUDE — LEWIS AND CLARK: EXPECTATIONS

One can only imagine what Thomas Jefferson, the United States' first true bibliophile, would have thought of my *Africa* guidebook if he were alive today. He certainly would have been fascinated with the way the book had been bound together and enamored with the color photographs sprinkled throughout its pages. But probably more than anything, he would have been astounded by the book's granularity, the remarkable level of detail by which an entire continent is dissected

within a single volume. Because beyond the book's dozens of
maps and hundreds of hotel recommendations lay thousands
of minute particulars—things like average regional tempera-
tures, relevant postal codes, currency conversions, and how to
say "What time does the bus leave?" in Swahili—invaluable
bits of information for even the most discerning of travelers.

It is this high level of detail to which the President aspired
with his proposed trans-continental exploration. In his famous
June 1803 letter to Meriwether Lewis, Jefferson stated the primary objective of the expedition—to find "the most direct
and practicable water communication across the continent for
the purposes of commerce." But while the primary objective
was singular, the purpose of the expedition was not; Jefferson, as one would expect from a man as curious as he, had
numerous requests to make of the explorers. He wanted, for
example, to learn more about the people who inhabited these
regions—the names of the tribes, their sizes, and their relationships with others. He was similarly interested in learning
more about the country through which the explorers would
pass and asked Lewis and Clark to describe the nature of the
soil, to catalog the diversity of vegetation, to track "mineral
productions of every kind," and to monitor the "proportion of
rainy, cloudy, and clear days." Jefferson also reached out to his
friends and colleagues, requesting a list of what *they* wanted
to know about the region. Dr. Benjamin Rush, for instance,
the main medical consultant for the expedition, wanted to
know more about the Indians' medicine, morals, and religion.
Among his varied questions were, "In what manner do they
induce sweating? How long do they suckle their children? Is
suicide common among them? Do they use animal sacrifices
in their worship?" What Jefferson had in mind for the expedition was not the creation of a coast-to-coast map but rather the
development of the first true pan-United States guidebook,

complete with detailed information on the region's food, culture, and weather.

Jefferson wasn't starting this "guidebook" from scratch. According to historian Donald Jackson, among the President's 6,000 printed volumes were many titles reflecting his fascination with North American geography and exploration: Daniel Coxe's *A Description of the English Province of Carolana*, Jonathan Carver's *Three Years Travels throughout the Interior Parts of North-America, for More Than Five Thousand Miles*, and Captain James Cook's *A Voyage to the Pacific Ocean*. From these titles, says historian John Logan Allen, "there emerged a group of images—patterns of belief about the nature and content of the land lying between the Missouri River and the Pacific Ocean." And from these images, part of what Allen routinely calls American "geographical lore," emerged a series of expectations that would guide the development and planning of the Lewis and Clark expedition.

First, there was the belief that the great Missouri River was the most direct path to the Pacific Ocean and, more importantly, that it was navigable to its source. Jean Baptiste Truteau, an explorer who had attempted (and failed) to reach the Pacific Ocean in 1794, supported this belief, writing in his journals that the river was navigable "from its mouth to its source . . . for the largest pirogues." In his own book, *Notes on the State of Virginia*, Jefferson himself noted the significance of the Missouri, describing it as more important geographically than even the mighty Mississippi. But where was the river's source? That point was highly debated—some accounts claimed its headwaters to be close to the Pacific Ocean, others said the source of the river was more inland. Allen has argued Jefferson and Lewis tended to believe the latter, believing (rightly so) that the source of the Missouri River was closer to present-day Montana.

The second component of geographical lore, described by one author as "the error that was to prove most durable of all," was the existence of a short portage from the east-flowing river (the Missouri) to a west-flowing river (called, at various points, the Oregon, the "River of the West," and the Columbia). Unlike the conjecture surrounding the Missouri's source, the concept of a short portage between two opposite-flowing rivers was based on actual observation, specifically Alexander Mackenzie's, who wrote of a "beaten path . . . over a low ridge of land eight hundred and seventeen paces in length" leading from one to the other. Mackenzie had, of course, been traveling in present day Canada, and the river he found on the other side had proven to be unnavigable, but Jefferson and Lewis adapted this information to conclude that a similar gap must exist farther south.

Complementing the idea of a short portage was the belief of a relatively low "pyramidal height-of-land" in the middle of the United States, a notion suggested by men like the war veteran Robert Rogers who observed several rivers in the western mountains and claimed that "by those rivers the continent is divided into many departments, as it were from a center." This notion also developed from an ignorance of the complexity and size of the Rocky Mountains. One of the most popular maps of the era, for example, pegged the Rocky Mountains far below their actual size, at "3520 feet high above the level of their base"; Jefferson and Lewis, meanwhile, maintained that the Blue Ridge Mountains were the highest on the continent and used their knowledge of that chain to envision the shape and alignment of the Rockies. If all these beliefs and assumptions were indeed true, then a potential trans-continental all-water route would involve neither a long portage nor a particularly steep ascent up the western chain of mountains.

The third and final component of geographical lore concerned what the expedition would encounter on the other side of the divide. In May 1792, Captain Robert Gray, on a mission from Boston to establish fur-trading contacts with inhabitants of the Northwest, sailed his boat, the *Columbia,* into a "great river which would henceforth bear her name." Unable or unwilling to proceed further, he passed on the coordinates of the river's mouth to Captain George Vancouver who, according to Allen, would "complete the image of the Great River of the West" by sending one of his lieutenants 100 miles upstream. Stopping at the present-day Columbia River Gorge, the lieutenant's account of "a magnificent mountain peak" (Mount Hood) would merge with Mackenzie's description of a similar range of mountains to offer the "near-conclusive proof of the possibility of a water communication across the continent." The expected path to the Pacific, and therefore the route for Lewis and Clark, was now clear: up the Missouri, over the mountains, and down the Columbia.

That was what the men expected to find in terms of terrain and travel; but what could they expect in terms of the people they would encounter? The Northwest may have been the great unknown, but it was far from empty—the land was populated with a native population as diverse as any region in the world. As historian James P. Ronda has written about the beginning of the expedition, "Perhaps the greatest uncharted space ahead was a human space." Little was known about these tribes, hence all the ethnographic questions concerning culture, food, and languages proposed by Jefferson and his friends. But the collection of these details always remained secondary to the main objective of Indian encounters—to establish American superiority and to convince the tribes to participate in Jefferson's system of trans-continental commerce. And according to Ronda, the President fully expected the Indians to kowtow to the men of the Lewis and Clark expedition, to "be properly impressed with the wealth and power of the new nation." As Stephen Ambrose has written of

Jefferson: "He thought of Indians as noble savages who could be civilized and brought into the body politic as full citizens." Adopting and adapting these beliefs from their leader, such was the arrogance (and ignorance) with which Lewis and Clark approached their native encounters.

But despite this aggregation of rumors, theories, conjectures, ideas, and attitudes, Lewis and Clark still lacked the single greatest determinant of any expedition's success: firm knowledge about the territory the men would be crossing. All things considered, the image of the Northwest remained, according to Allen, "a combination of fact and rumor, of theory and conjecture, with a sprinkling of hope added for seasoning." Historian Bernard DeVoto was less charitable, calling it "an area of rumor, guess and fantasy." This combination of truth and fiction allowed the men's minds to wander, and they often bought into the outlandish speculation of the era. For instance, there was a belief that a great mountain of salt existed near the headwaters of the Missouri River. There were also reports of volcanoes in what is now South Dakota, anecdotes so convincing that Thomas Jefferson felt it necessary to brush up on the topic, purchasing a copy of Claude Nicholas Ordinare's *Histoire naturelle des volcans* in 1802. Other rumors were even more peculiar—that mammoths and giant ground sloths still roamed the upper region of the Missouri River and that a group of Welsh colonists, descendants of the twelfth-century Welsh prince Madoc og Gwynned, had settled and lived happily among the Indians. And, as Ambrose correctly points out, "what was not known, or what was assumed but was badly wrong, was more important than what was known."

❧ ❧ ❧

CHAPTER 3

The Guidebook Evolution—
The Amateurs

I initially had only one clue as to what I would encounter on the train journey from Kapiri Mposhi, Zambia to Dar es Salaam, Tanzania. It was contained within my print guidebook's introductory description of Zambia:

> *Save Lusaka and Livingstone, this is the "real" Africa, so rare among the increasingly developed and Westernised parts of the region. . . . So if you like your travel easy and your wilderness neatly bundled into a homogenized and Westernised version of "Africa," then much of Zambia may not appeal. But if you enjoy a raw edge and an Africa with few tourists, Zambia is the place you're looking for.*

Since the train's route passed through a large swath of eastern Zambia, I felt that this report could perhaps be used to predict what my experience aboard the train would entail: a difficult journey (see: raw edge) with limited modern amenities and few tourists through—and this is the most important part—the "real" Africa. And since I had already spent time in the two cities, Lusaka and Livingstone, that ostensibly constituted the "non-real" component of Africa, I hoped to juxtapose that experience with a trip through its corresponding piece; who wouldn't, after all, want see the "real" version of the destination to which they traveled?

But what was the "real Africa"? I wasn't entirely sure. When I lived in New York, I often heard from friends and family who wanted to experience New York as a true New Yorker did. But as a true New Yorker, I often yearned to experience the city as tourists did. I wanted to be liberated from my crowded forty-five minute commute and unshackled from the small windowless cubicle in which I spent ten hours each day. On the rare occasion I was off from work on a weekday, I would do the most touristy things I could— visit museums, eat at restaurants that had long waits on the weekends, walk around Central Park. The "real New York" I knew was methodical, crowded, redundant. And so I wondered if the author of the Zambian introduction within my guidebook had perhaps erred—maybe the "real Africa" was more the "rough on the diamond" rather than the "diamond in the rough."

But in a world inundated with travel-related information, assumptions were unnecessary. And so when my print guidebook proved insufficient in providing details regarding my train journey through the "real Africa," I did what Lewis and Clark could not—I took my search online to dig through what has become a giant warehouse of comprehensive travel advice. It was on a popular train-related website, one I had used previously to plan train travel through both Europe and Asia, that I found information on where to buy a ticket in Lusaka, what time to arrive at the station, and what I could expect to see. Charts showed departing and arrival times for several stations along the route. Exhaustive first-person accounts of the journey included pictures of the cabins and scenery as well as information about the train's dining car and beverage service. And one ambitious couple had even uploaded an eight-minute travel documentary of their two-day experience aboard the train complete with tranquil narration and a subtle musical score: "It's been incredible. We've seen some beautiful country—hills, lakes, farms—and we've enjoyed every bit of it," the woman says as the film slowly goes dark. This was, apparently, the "real Africa" in all its high definition glory. The seamless availability of this information, then, meant that there were few surprises during my own trip; my glimpse of the giraffe, for example, was not unexpected but anticipated, due to one traveler's account of the train passing through a national park.

The absence of this material within my *Africa* print guide-book was not surprising; as I had learned on the train, few non-African travelers make this journey. And to include every possible side trip within the book would unnecessarily expand an already bloated volume. The solution to these edi-torial decisions, then, has traditionally been to release a niche guidebook, such as the ones described at the beginning of the previous chapter. Perhaps it would be called *Train Travel in Southern Africa* or *Zambia and Tanzania: Off the Beaten Path*. But print publishers have finite resources and there are sim-ply some destinations too obscure or activities too esoteric to warrant publication of these micro-focused guidebooks. And so it is within this discussion that we finally encounter the next stage of the guidebook evolution—the emergence of the Internet and its army of amateur guidebook creators. No lon-ger is travel advice limited to those with a publishing contract. No longer is thorough coverage restricted to the world's most popular destinations and routes. Instead, anybody can now say anything about anywhere—a capability that presumably enhances all three pillars of the guidebook structure for every destination in the world.

My train trip from Zambia to Tanzania was not the first time during my African travels that I had ducked into the amateur guidebook sector. At nearly every stop along my itinerary, I had used the Internet judiciously to supplement, confirm, or contradict the information within my larger print guidebook. I had validated hotel recommendations by checking online reviews, verified bus times with region-specific message boards, and frequented blogs to make sure I wasn't missing anything along the way. If my professional print guidebook was the trip's engine, the amateurs were the oil, a lubricant I intermittently applied to make sure everything was running smoothly.

The addition of the amateurs to the overall guidebook spectrum, it would seem, signifies a great new era of guidebook literature, capable of filling every niche for every location. But questions abound. What motivates these new guidebook creators? Is the information produced accurate, coherent, and useful? And, most importantly, what does this influx of new material mean for the traveler? To understand this important shift in the guidebook evolution, we must first look back many hundred years to the journeys of two men who, quite unknowingly, may have in fact been the world's first travel bloggers.

The story begins in the Middle Ages with two men, an Englishman and an Italian. The first is Sir John Mandeville, an English knight born in the town of St. Albans, who in 1322 set out "over the sea" on a pilgrimage to the Holy Lands. He returned thirty-four years later, having traveled not only to Jerusalem and its surrounding area but, in his words, to "Turkey, Armenia the little and the great; through Tartary, Persia, Syria, Arabia, Egypt the high and the low; through Lybia, Chaldea, and a great part of Ethiopia; through Amazonia, Ind the less and the more, a great part; and throughout many other isles." Few Europeans had ventured so far into the world; even fewer were motivated enough to chronicle their adventures for the general public. But Mandeville was ambitious. So he began to write, recording his adventures over three-plus decades and transcribing the eventual book into Latin, French, and English, so "that every man of [his] nation may understand it."

The stories that emerged from *The Travels of Sir John Mandeville* were remarkable. In one chapter, Mandeville describes the island of Lango, on which lives a princess in the form of a dragon, "a hundred fathoms in length," whose only hope to return to human form is to be kissed on the lips by a knight. In another, Mandeville discusses the wonder of Amazonia, "the land of Feminye," a place inhibited by all women, who, stubbornly, "will not suffer no men amongst them to be their sovereigns."

Mandeville saves his wildest anecdotes, however, for his tales of improbable island oddities. There is the island with snails so large that its citizens can lodge inside their shells, "as men would do in a little house." One populated with "serpents, dragons, and cockodrills" and another where the geese have two heads. There are also several islands where the inhabitants are cursed with gruesome deformities: one where the people have the heads of dogs, one in which the people have ears down to their knees, one in which the people have the feet of horses (allowing for them to be "strong and mighty, and swift runners") and yet another where the people have no heads at all, and instead have eyes inside their shoulders.

The stories made for fascinating reading, and from what historians can gather, the book was a marvelous success. The fact that over three hundred handwritten copies of *The Travels* still exist today, an unusually high number for a book of the Middle Ages, provides evidence of the work's widespread popularity. Even William Shakespeare found time to peruse its curiosities; in *Othello,* the main character speaks of the "Cannibals that each other eat . . . and men whose heads do grow beneath their shoulders," a clear reference to the motley characters inhabiting Mandeville's islands.

There was only one problem. None of it was true. Sir John Mandeville, in fact, never even existed. Instead, some scholars suggest that the book was a ruse concocted by a Flemish monk. It seems that the monk had mined his extensive collection of travelogues, reputed to be the best in the world, to create Mandeville's fanciful adventure, borrowing myths, legends, and rumors from other accounts to weave an intricate tale of adventure and exploration. What was his motive? Nobody is sure. Some have hypothesized that it was an attempt to ruminate on the merits of humanity. Others suppose it was little more than a publicity stunt. Unfortunately, the world will most likely never know since little else is known about the story or the man.

Much more is known about the second "blogger," a wealthy Italian merchant who traveled from Venice to Asia in 1271 with his father and uncle. The merchant was Marco Polo, and by making his name synonymous with exploration and discovery, history, unlike the disrepute it has showered on Mandeville, has paid him the ultimate compliment. Polo's *Travels*, the book that emerged from the adventure, endures today because of the author's unique ability to transcend the literal and monotonous accounts provided by previous explorers, or, as one author puts it, to mingle "fact and fantasy, personal experience and legend, all of it buttressed by straightforward assessments of the people and places he encountered, and all of it energized by his braggadocio." For an audience of Polo's era, however, his stories were understandably difficult to believe. And by including fantastical tales encountered through hearsay or legend, Marco infused an additional element of disbelief onto a narrative already regarded with skepticism.

The book includes several layers of believability. First are the anecdotes that, once viewed with uncertainty, are now confirmed, as the once mysterious objects described have become commonplace:

> *Of coconuts: The Indian nuts also grow here, of the size of a man's head, containing an edible substance that is sweet and pleasant to the taste, and white as milk. The cavity of this pulp is filled with a liquor clear as water, cool, and better flavored and more delicate than wine or any other kind of drink whatever.*

Then there are the anecdotes in which Polo's enthusiasm produced descriptions of people, places, and things that seem to be exaggerations but have subsequently been, at least to some extent, verified by other accounts and sources:

> *Of Kublai Khan's Palace: The sides of the great halls and the apartments are ornamented with dragons in carved work and gilt, figures of warriors, of birds, and of beasts, with representations of battles. The inside of the roof is contrived in such a manner that nothing besides gilding and painting presents itself to the eye. On each of the four sides of the palace there is a grand flight of marble steps, by which you ascend from the level of the ground to the wall of marble which surrounds the building, and which constitute the approach to the palace itself. . . . In the rear of the body of the palace there are large buildings containing several apartments, where is deposited the private property of the monarch, or his treasure in gold and silver bullion, precious stones, and pearls, and also his vessels of gold and silver plate.*

And finally, there are those tales that cannot be believed at all. Stories that Marco undoubtedly collected from fellow travelers yet still felt compelled to include in his narrative:

Of an extraordinary kind of bird: The people of the island report that at a certain season of the year an extraordinary kind of bird, which they call a ruch, makes its appearance from the southern region. In form it is said to resemble the eagle, but it is incomparably greater in size; being so large and strong as to seize an elephant with its talons, and to lift it into the air, from whence it lets it fall to the ground, in order that when dead it may prey upon the carcass. Persons who have seen this bird assert that when the wings are spread they measure sixteen paces in extent, from point to point; and that the feathers are eight paces in length, and thick in proportion.

It was with this collection of exotic stories that Marco Polo, back in Italy after twenty-four years on the road and finding himself imprisoned after a naval battle with Genoa, met the Italian writer Rustichello. Together, they put the tales to paper, immortalizing both the fact and fiction of Marco Polo's great adventure.

Both Mandeville's and Polo's books often read like journals, with biased opinions, tedious minutiae, and irrelevant digressions. In fact, the lack of linear structure or recurring storylines in relation to characters, places, and themes makes each work more analogous to today's travel blogs than to the purpose-driven narratives we now classify as "travel literature." And indeed, both pieces contain an element so intrinsic in modern day travel blogging that its appearance has almost become expected—that of embellishment. The degrees of exaggeration vary—in Mandeville's case, the entire work is fabricated; in Polo's case, only bits and pieces—but its underlying presence is a critical reason why the works can be compared to so much of the travel-related user-generated content that is created today.

A quick comparison of four relatively recent posts, keeping the destinations hidden, illustrates the importance of this connection:

#1—FROM A MESSAGE BOARD

"_____ is amazing, there is no other [place] like it. I miss it so much :(Life is so much better there, people are friendlier and aren't absorbed in their own world. They actually care about you!"_

#2—FROM A REVIEW

"_We spent almost 3 hours [there]. _____ is a sensory overload. Sites, color, sounds, smells—it's all in there. Amazing!"_

#3—FROM A TRAVEL BLOG'S "WALKING TOUR"

"_We are going to stop and take in all the sights and explore [its beauty]. Once we're done I think you'll agree that it is both exotic and beautiful . . . the architecture is outstanding . . . the shopping is some of the best."_

#4—FROM A TRAVEL BLOG

"_What I experienced in _____ is incredible and I will not fully be able to express it for years to come. My [experience] in _____ has been amazing and it is something I will take with me for the rest of my life. I may not ever be able to truly comprehend all that I've learned, but I hope I can find a way to share my experience with others."_

Each entry, typical among user-generated travel content, depicts a user grappling with the English language (i.e., amazing, outstanding, exotic, incredible) in order to adequately express his or her experience. But while the flowery language is comparable, the destinations are most certainly not. Excerpts #1 and #4 are taken from reports about trips to Morocco. Excerpts #2 and #3, on the other hand, are taken from reports about trips to the Moroccan Pavilion at Walt Disney World in Orlando, Florida.

In the same way that a reader may consider Marco Polo's description of a coconut histrionic amplification (after all, it's *just* a coconut), so might a reader consider #3's reaction to what many consider an over-commercialized fabrication of a country a significant exaggeration of the destination's worth. And yet only with the proper perspective (e.g., direct knowledge of what coconuts taste like or the experience of previous visits to Walt Disney World) would that reader be able to distinguish apparent embellishment from accurate portrayal.

There are, of course, various reasons why the traveler feels the need to embellish. One is bravado, as if the act of travel alone merits recognition—"I went far way, did something crazy, and would totally do it again." Another is justification, the enhancement of an experience or situation in order to justify the expense, time, and effort taken to get there. Yet another is elaboration for the sake of the audience—nobody wants to read about the author sitting on a beach.

But the most interesting one, at least for the purposes of this narrative, is the embellishment of the experience as it relates to the benign desire for understanding. Despite the resources available to us today—high definition television, digital image galleries, restaurants serving exotic cuisines— people often still choose to experience the real thing: to see the Eiffel Tower, to go on an African safari, to eat sushi in Japan. And when experiences either exceed or fall short of pre-trip expectations, travelers feel the need to relate their emotions to their family and friends and co-workers. Only when they sit down to write do they encounter the stifling limitations of the written word—hackneyed adjectives such as "amazing" and "terrible" and "remarkable" and "horrible" only go so far. And so they embellish, in the hopes that their exaggerations allow the reader to fully comprehend the magnitude, good or bad, of their experience. Forget Mandeville for a minute, whose entire account was fictionalized and whose motivations were unclear, but was the desire for understanding Marco Polo's objective when he took liberties with certain people, places, or things? It would seem so. At the very least, it played a significant role.

Laurence Bergreen, one of Polo's biographers, made exaggeration one of the central themes of his study of the explorer. "Unlike Mandeville," Bergreen argues in the epilogue of *Marco Polo: From Venice to Xanadu* "who set out to fabricate, Marco believed every word he dictated." And although *Travels* "contained puffery, it was not a fabrication, and [Polo] expected—in fact, demanded—that his audience believe every word." Polo "strained" to convince readers of what he saw and this burden reduced the merchant's prose to increasing amounts of bravado and embellishment. Bergreen asks: "Did any writer equipped with Marco's experience ever feel the need to boast as much as he did, or to plead with his audience to accept what he was saying as the truth?" And not only was Polo's tale restrained by the boundaries of the written word, it was also limited by the era's rudimentary technology. With copies having to be reproduced by hand, mass distribution of his narrative was impossible. In an attempt to secure his legacy, to convince the world that what he said was true, Polo often resorted to carrying around copies of his book, handing them out to important dignitaries and colleagues.

Oh, how far we've come. Today, a 300-word blog post can be available to millions of people within the span of a few seconds; a photo can be tweeted and shared in real time. And because of the ease of digital content creation, the phenomenon extends far beyond blogging with maps, reviews, itineraries, and other user-generated "destination-themed" content

spreading across the Internet as free and easy-to-access information available in dozens of languages all over the world.
These days, anybody can be Marco Polo, as intrepid travelers
venture out into the world and go online to tell their stories,
often embellished, to eager readers back home.

But before we begin to unravel the latest and most important element of the guidebook evolution, let's first return to
Polo's story, and specifically, to the aspects that made the distribution of his tale possible. The first is time—specifically,
the time the Italian was unintentionally afforded when he
was sent to prison. This period, undoubtedly difficult for the
peripatetic explorer, allowed Polo to exert his mind rather
than his body, and to carefully collect his thoughts, memories,
and recollections into clear manuscript form. The second is
means—specifically the specialized skills and advice provided
by Rustichello. Polo, despite being adept at so many things,
was a literary neophyte—even with the time and motivation
to create his book, Polo would have been lost without the
guidance of the Italian writer.

Time and means are both central themes of Clay Shirky's
Cognitive Surplus: Creativity and Generosity in a Connected Age,
an example-driven study detailing the birth and proliferation
of user-generated content. Shirky argues that, "Since the Second World War, increases in GDP, educational attainment,
and life span have forced the industrialized world to grapple
with something we'd never had to deal with on a national
scale: free time. The amount of unstructured time cumula-
tively available to the educated population ballooned, both
because the educated population itself ballooned, and because
that population was living longer while working less." Most
of this "surplus," as Shirky calls it, went toward television—
Americans watch somewhere around two hundred billion
hours of TV every year. The incredible amount of time spent
absorbing these programs, however, was rarely questioned.

Instead, it was assumed that human beings, now blessed with an abundance of disposable hours (at least compared to previous generations), wanted, more than anything else, to watch television. But Shirky argues that this assumption may be wrong: "But what if, all this time, providing professional content isn't the only job we've been hiring media to do? What if we've also been hiring it to make us feel connected, engaged, or just less lonely? What if we've always wanted to produce as well as consume, but no one offered us that opportunity?" If true, then all human beings needed was an outlet, an easy springboard to participation and collaboration.

That springboard would be the Internet, an accessible, well-connected network of billions of human beings from all over the world. For many would-be Marco Polos, the barriers to entry have been virtually eliminated, allowing for an increase in "amateur" contributions. Suddenly, travel anecdotes and trip photos can be seen by virtually anybody and sometimes, with the right amount of skill and luck, that content will gather an audience, turning what began as an arbitrary upload into, quite possibly, a new profession.

But as writer Jeff Howe argues, the rewards for this sort of content creation are often ancillary to the act of creation itself:

> [I]t's not about the money. It's about cred, or, to give that a more theoretical cast, it's about the emerging reputation economy, where people work late into the night on one creative endeavor or another in the hope that their community—be it fellow designers, scientists, or computer hackers—acknowledge their contribution in the form of kudos and, just maybe, some measure of fame.

It's about being good at what you do, getting some sort of credit, and going to bed knowing that you have, through your contributions, built up some measure of respect inside the community. As Shirky explains, "Evidence accumulates daily that if you offer people the opportunity to produce and to share, they'll sometimes take you up on it, even if they've never behaved that way before and even if they're not as good at it as the pros."

Many of these amateur contributions can be found in the travel blog universe, an amorphous collection of rambling tales from millions of travelers all across the world. The true invention of this form of travel expression (with apologies to Mandeville and Polo) is usually credited to a writer named Jeff Greenwald, author of *Shopping for Buddhas*, *Mister Raja's Neighborhood*, and *The Size of the World*, who, in a fit of middle-age angst in 1993, decided to "travel around the world—from Oakland, California, to Oakland, California—without ever leaving the ground." As he traveled from destination to destination, Jeff's already hefty backpack was weighed down even further by something new for travelers—a laptop computer, built to run on four AA batteries and brought along so the author could submit travel reports back to his publisher for distribution on an increasingly popular media outlet, the World Wide Web.

The end result of Greenwald's experiment was a fractured composite of colorful reflections, illustrating both the toils— "Got back to Senegal early this morning, after a total of eight days in Mali: an eye-opening but torturous side trip to a roasting, dusty land fraught with transportation nightmares"— and the joys—"No amount of 70-millimeter film or H-8 videotape, no collection of poems, no miraculous dance of globe-trotting megabytes can convey the beauty of Boudhanath on a full-moon festival night"—of long-distance travel. Since its publication, Greenwald's blog has spawned millions of imitators; there are now blogs on specific countries, blogs on specific cities, blogs on traveling as a female, blogs on traveling with a child, blogs on long-distance cycling, blogs on scuba diving, and blogs on basically every other possible style or feature of traveling.

But Jeff Greenwald and those who followed are but single travelers and their blogs, to be fair, are hardly the most efficient application of a technological achievement that has connected billions of individuals around the world. Among travel aficionados, then, there soon arose a great desire to marginalize the individual, to create a system where the sum of society's travel experiences became exponentially larger than its individual parts. One of the earliest applications of this system was the travel message board—collections of geographically and demographically dispersed users digitally congregating toward (and often passionately discussing) a specific travel-related interest. Recognizing the value these contributors can bring to the guidebook experience, the most innovative of the professionals have sought out collaborative relationships with the Internet's army of digital nomads. One popular professional guidebook brand, for example, uses its brand recognition to attract hundreds of thousands of eager advice givers and seekers. Comprehensive in its coverage, the message board funnels downward into approximately two-dozen destinations ("Americas—Cuba" or "Asia—Thailand") as well as into topic-specific threads such as health, technology, and diving. It is within these threads where amateur contributors flex their backpacking muscles, increasing their status within the so-called travel "reputation economy" through the dispersal of valuable advice. These kinds of forums, incidentally, are especially useful for travelers looking for answers to esoterically specific questions: I'll never forget receiving vital information on the procurement of a Russian visa from the pithy and condescending matron of the Eastern Europe board.

Even more indicative of the push to aggregate the world's travel knowledge was the emergence of the travel review website, digital communities where travelers' opinions of the places they visited could be combined into a single holistic ranking (e.g., "Five Stars" or 82%). It's a system, of course, that works well for highly trafficked destinations—renowned New York City museums or popular Parisian restaurants—but not so well for relatively unknown entities in less frequented locales, especially those who toil endlessly to create an amenable atmosphere only to be bludgeoned by the digital pen of a disgruntled diner or grumpy lodger. More than that, it's a remarkably strange system to use for destinations that traditionally have been recognized as the most popular attractions in the world. The reduction of these once-in-a-lifetime experiences to vague and perfunctory asides has led, at times, to an almost comical assessment of the world's wonders. On one popular review website, for example, the Taj Mahal and Machu Picchu are deemed worthy of pristine, five-star rankings, thanks to thousands of gushing reviews. The Pyramids of Giza, though, are only able to garner the support for a four-and-a-half star ranking, seemingly due to the unavoidable hassle of Pyramid touts and the oppressive heat of the Egyptian summer. Still, the Pyramid's less-than-perfect ranking remains a far better fate than the one granted the majestic Great Wall of China, whose rating is jumbled among reviews of restaurants with the same name, including popular versions in Ruidoso, New Mexico and Borehamwood, England.

The ubiquity and growth of these tools—and countless others—have subsequently made the Internet the ultimate agent of travel humility; no matter how grand your proposed trip has become, no matter how many countries you plan on entering or how many miles you plan on traveling, somebody, somewhere has not only gone further and farther but has also documented the journey for the entire world to see. And once that information is absorbed, no longer does the execution of your trip seem exceedingly complex and utterly far-fetched.

Instead, it is merely a quasi-imitation of a journey already completed, assessed, and written about by somebody else.

While nearly every destination on the planet has been catalogued and reviewed in some way or another, perhaps no place on earth elicits such a wide-ranging spectrum of opinion as Varanasi, an Indian city located on the banks of the Ganges River and considered by many to be one of the most spiritually significant places in the world. Varanasi's religious importance, however, has unintentionally fostered a different kind of reputation—that of a tourist hotspot. Every year, throngs of visitors flock to Varanasi for the can't-miss spectacle of the "burning ghats," an event where bodies are cremated and ceremoniously released into the water for eternal peace. This convergence of devotees and onlookers has both energized and strained the ancient city's fragile infrastructure, producing a frenzied atmosphere distinct from anywhere in the world. Advocates of Varanasi are quick to cite its spirituality and religious importance. Few destinations resonate with such resilient faith and devotion, they say, and to witness or participate in the ceremonies that line the river is to partake in an enhanced level of piety. Its detractors, however, dismiss the city as a squalid cesspool, polluted beyond repair and infested with touts looking to capitalize, monetarily and illegally, on Varanasi's fame.

Nowhere do these diametrically opposed opinions come to life more than in the ramblings of the digital world, where aspiring explorers immerse themselves in a city steeped in historical significance and return to their computers to record their stunning experiences. Those who embrace the city speak confidently and gush accordingly, often citing patience and an open mind as keys to unlocking its wonders:

FROM A MESSAGE BOARD: Just wanted to let all prospective travelers know that anyone contemplating a visit to Varanasi should absolutely come here. Awesomeness is the word. Have no words to explain this surreal place. Awestruck. Will write more about this captivating place. Watch out.

FROM A BLOG: I loved Varanasi to bits and still cannot get over having been there. I loved the people, I loved the narrow and narrower lanes, I loved the sounds, some of the smells and all of the sights, I loved the vibes, I loved everything about Varanasi. So much that I hope to go back for a few weeks every year.

But those who despise Varanasi are just as loud, often using a more tangible, less spiritual, argument. One particular blogger's rants, encompassing several thousand words, expose a petulant traveler unable to adjust to the city's manic pace and grimy facade. "The train station," she writes . . .

. . . was absolutely filthy and disgusting. Very smelly. Stench of urine. People pissing on the platforms or at the tracks. People sleeping and resting on the floor, everywhere. People everywhere. Show me the exit, please!

The next day, as she made her way down to the sacred river, the repulsion continued:

Kids swimming, diving and playing around in the water made me shiver of disgust. The water looked awful with its brownish color and all the debris floating around in it. After what I have read, seen and heard I would not touch that water with a stick even.

Harsh words, but the blogger's ruminations on the city were hardly unprecedented. No less an authority than the esteemed Mark Twain visited Varanasi (or Benares, as it was called then) in the nineteenth century, recording his experience in his classic travelogue, *Following the Equator*. In describing the same spectacle as the blogger above, Twain tells his readers, "I think one would not get tired of the bathers, nor their costumes, nor of their ingenuities in getting out of them and into them again. . . . But I should get tired of seeing them wash their mouths with that dreadful water and drink it. In fact, I did get tired of it, and very early, too."

The city proved difficult for the author to navigate, with Twain writing it was as

> *. . . busy as an ant-hill, and the hurly-burly of human life swarming along the web of narrow streets reminds one of the ants. The sacred cow swarms along too, and goes whither she pleases, and takes toll of the grain-shops, and is very much in the way, and is a good deal of a nuisance, since she must not be molested.*

So what's the difference between the bitter complaints of a frustrated blogger and Twain's tempered criticism? The easy answer is interpretation. Twain's book was a travelogue, meant to entertain the reader with a whimsical account of an intrepid journey. Like Marco Polo's narrative, it included several fantastical tales, intermingled with Twain's observations and travels, and was released to a public well accustomed to the author's literary style. Blogs, on the other hand, along with other amateur guidebook extensions, lack a similar, structured categorization. Instead, they appear anonymously in searches for destinations, often alongside information on plane tickets, hotel rooms, and tours. Unlike Twain's narrative, blogs have become, for better or for worse, an intricate component of the larger "travel advice" industry.

To which one might then inquire—what exactly, then, is the purpose of the modern day guidebook? Guidebook historian

Nicholas T. Parsons, for one, suggests the professionals have settled into an inherently objective role: "Nowadays a guidebook sees it as its task to dispel myths, however venerable, rather than propagate them, and lays claim to dispassionate accuracy." While this isn't always the case, the general rule is followed more often than not. But with the amateurs, emotion is often the primary motivation. Exaggeration and bravado, as we saw with Mandeville and Polo, tell only part of the story; as the comments on Varanasi show, there are also those circumstances, personal and largely irrelevant to other visitors, that can easily sway perspective. The traveler thinks, "I am going to go home and review this hotel because the owner was a jerk." In that case, the traditional guidebook function is lost, overridden by a secondary incentive. In some ways, it's an indication that we have come full circle in the guidebook evolution, similar to the days when guidebook authors (like Aymeric Picaud, who we met in the previous chapter) would describe locals as "badness and nastiness personified" or when angry English Protestants would disparage the great sights of Catholic Rome.

Just as important, however, is the fact that this type of opinion is everywhere. A bad online review, often instantaneously rebutted by a subsequent post, might serve little purpose other than to confuse the reader. A single message board thread on Varanasi, for instance, might contain a dozen drastically different opinions of the city, ranging from life-changing nirvana to nausea-inducing mayhem. Ignorant of the visitor's motivation and disposition, readers are forced to process this information, to separate the "grain from the chaff," as they attempt to plan their trip. And because of that, Varanasi does more to explain the significance of the "amateur's" effect on the guidebook evolution than any other destination in the world.

Over a hundred fifty years ago, Edgar Allen Poe warned the public of the possible dangers triggered by a burgeoning publishing industry. "The enormous multiplication of books in every branch of knowledge," said Poe, "is one of the greatest evils of this age; since it presents one of the most serious obstacles to the acquisition of correct information, by throwing in the reader's way piles of lumber, in which he must painfully grope for the scraps of useful matter peradventure interspersed." One can only wonder what Poe would say if he found himself on an Internet message board.

☙ ☙ ☙

I had spent much of the two-day train journey from Kapiri Mposhi to Dar es Salaam alone in my four-berth cabin. Occasionally, a young man would enter without saying a word and hop up into one of the top bunks for a quick nap. He carried no luggage; I guessed he was a train employee taking advantage of the open beds. After waking, he would hop down and exit, again leaving me alone. Most of the time, I appreciated the solitude—it allowed me to read and think and sleep. But the line between solitude and loneliness is thin, easily eroded by time, and by the end of the second day, as the train sputtered and moaned toward our final destination, I began to wander the hallways, peeking my head in open cabins and hoping to find someone to talk to.

It was through this search that I became friends with three women, one Zambian and two Tanzanians, who were traveling in an adjoining cabin. I had met the lone Zambian the day before. She was from just outside Lusaka, traveling by herself, and headed for a holiday on the island of Zanzibar. We had talked for a few hours about our travels and she had playfully chided me for using the word "exotic" to describe the surrounding landscape. I had countered that I simply used the word to imply unfamiliarity (I did, after all, live in New York City) and that if giraffes running past my window didn't warrant its use, what did? "Well then am I exotic?" she asked me. "Is this train exotic? Are these villages exotic?" The other two women, sisters from Dar es Salaam, were less critical of my observations and found the conversation quite amusing. They had been visiting family in the country's interior and were returning home with fresh produce. One was carrying a giant head of lettuce; other packages of vegetables were strewn around the cabin.

As we approached Dar, the conversation turned to Tanzania as a whole. We talked about the country's history and its government, about the languages spoken and the most tourist-heavy regions and cities. The women also mentioned that most people mispronounce the country's name. I had always pronounced it Tan-za-NEE-ah, with the emphasis on the third syllable—it's the only way I had ever heard it said. But these ladies pronounced it Tan-ZAN-ee-ah, with the last two syllables converging to almost make it sound more like Tan-ZAN-nyah. "That's how you actually say it," they told me.

When I finally reached a computer in Dar es Salaam, I searched the Internet to see if there was indeed a larger disagreement concerning the country's name. There was—I found nearly a dozen message board threads discussing the topic as well as links to audio and video files promising the proper pronunciation. But the responses were all over the place. Some posters suggested that the two women I had met on the train were correct and that the emphasis should be on the ZAN, rather than the NEE. Other contributors suggested that both ways are correct. Yet another poster recommended the pronunciation as Tan-zan-EAR, while a fourth cheerfully advised: "I think that as long as you say it with a smile you're fine with any of them." So which to believe? I had no idea. And if I wasn't able to utilize the amateur guidebook sector to find something as seemingly straightforward as the best pronunciation for a country's name, what were the chances I would be able to use those same guidebook extensions to efficiently plan a trip as intricate and as complicated as my African excursion? It was difficult to imagine.

One must conclude, then, that the obituary for the linear, structured, and well-categorized professional guidebook has perhaps been penned prematurely.

INTERLUDE — LEWIS CLARK: PREPARATION

Like so many travelers today, Lewis and Clark had their own pile of information to sort through. There were no guidebooks to the region they would be crossing, per se, but instead bits of theory and conjecture—"guess, rumor, and fantasy"—out of which had emerged a set of tenuous expectations. Lewis and Clark prepared for their journey with those expectations in mind, while at the same time leaving open the possibility (the guarantee?) that things could go off the rails at any moment.

First things first—how much would the trip cost? In an undated document from 1803, Lewis lays out an estimate "of the sum necessary to carry into effort the Missouri expedition." The total came to $2,500, the amount Jefferson would request (and receive) from Congress "for the purpose of extending the external commerce of the U.S." It was a comically low estimate—trip planning was still in its infancy and Lewis thought he would take only twelve men—but the document is telling in how Lewis appropriates the funds. Among Lewis's itemized costs were $217 for mathematical instruments, $430 for means of transportation, $696 for Indian presents (the largest expenditure) and $87 for "contingencies" which could include, one supposes, mammoth attacks or volcanic eruptions.

With the trip funded, the real preparation began. Many modern guidebooks contain introductory information—details on culture, food, and weather—designed to prepare the traveler for his or her trip. But with this information limited, it was up to Lewis (much of the preparation for the trip began before Clark was on board) to supplement his already notable experience as a frontiersman with a bevy of new knowledge and skills. The first stop was Thomas Jefferson and his friends, who, according to Stephen Ambrose, "gave Lewis a college undergraduate's introduction to the liberal arts, North American geography, botany, mineralogy, astronomy, and ethnology." One member of the American Philosophical Society, Dr. Benjamin Rush, provided consultation to the expedition with such (questionable) medical advice as "Flannel should be worn constantly next to the skin, especially in wet weather" and "Shoes made without heels, by affording equal action to all the muscles of the legs, will enable you to march with less fatigue, than shoes made in the ordinary way."

For instructions on surveying and astronomy, so that the men could accurately log their longitudes and latitudes, Jefferson called on Professor of Mathematics Robert Patterson as well as astronomer/mathematician Andrew Ellicott who, in his reply to Jefferson's appeal for help, wrote, "Mr. Lewis's first object must be, to acquire a facility, and dexterity, in making the observations; which can only be attained by practice; in this he shall have all the assistance I can give him with aid of my apparatus." Patterson also developed a custom cipher—a code—for the expedition, based on the key word "artichoke," so that Jefferson and the men could communicate safely over thousands of miles. Although the cipher was never actually used, one sample message sent before the expedition had departed remains as evidence that Lewis and Jefferson, like two school kids playing around with new walkie-talkies, eagerly tested it within the safe confines of Philadelphia. The sample message read: "I am at the head of the Missouri. All well, and the Indians so far friendly."

The explorers also benefitted from their time spent in St. Louis, the city on the edge of the great western wilderness. As Ronda wrote: "No other city could have provided Jefferson's explorers with such a range and quality of information about the Indians." Bowing to his experience as a structured military man, Lewis went about collecting information from the city's traders in the most systematic manner possible. In a long letter to Thomas Jefferson in December 1803, Lewis explained the details of his design: "In order therefore to avail myself as far as possible of their information under these circumstances, I drew out a form of paper containing 13 or 14 columns, which I headed with such subjects as appeared to me most important to be known relative to the Indians." In short, Lewis conducted a survey.

But although this education was crucial for the success of the expedition, Ronda argues that "perhaps no single phase of endeavor was quite so important as the assimilation of the most precise and up-to-date maps of the American Northwest then available." To this task was assigned Secretary of the Treasury Albert Gallatin who requested a mapmaker to . . .

> . . . *project a blank map to extend from 88° to 126° West longitude from Greenwich and from 30 to 55 north latitude . . . in this I intend to insert the course of the Mississippi as high up as the Ohio from Ellicot's, the coast of the Pacific from Cook and Vancouver, the north bend of the Missouri and such other of its waters as are there delineated from the three maps of Arrowsmith and from that of Mackenzie, and the Rio Norte and other parts of the Missouri from Danville and Delisle.*

It was, in essence, an aggregation of known geographical knowledge as well as an invitation to further the process: "Here is what we currently know; please connect the dots."

Next, Lewis drew up a packing list. There were no hotels where Lewis and Clark were going, no restaurants, no banks, no convenience stores. Instead, every item deemed necessary for success of the expedition had to be carried from the start. As historian Paul Russell Cutright explains, "It was no small task to anticipate all that he would need in the way of arms, food, clothing, camping paraphernalia, scientific instruments, and Indian presents for a party of still undetermined size that, for an indefinite period of time, would be out of touch with normal supply sources." And as could be expected for such an ambitious journey, Lewis quickly blew through his original estimate of $2,500.

The most important items on the list were rifles. They were of dual importance, integral for both hunting and self-defense. Lewis ordered fifteen of the U.S. Model 1803, a rifle that, according to Ambrose, "delivered a lead slug on target with sufficient velocity to kill a deer at a range of about a hundred yards." As a sustenance backup plan, Lewis purchased one hundred and ninety-three pounds of dehydrated "portable-soup," which he described as "one of the most essential articles in the preparation" of the expedition. The importance was reflected in its cost, $289.50, which, as Jackson points out, was about as much as Lewis had originally estimated for mathematical instruments, arms, and ammunition combined.

What else? For scientific purposes, Lewis brought two sextants, a chronometer, and a compass. He brought necessities such as cloth, shirts, and fishing hooks, as well as non-essentials such as salt, tobacco, and whiskey. He brought journals and ink, knowing his thoughts about the journey would be greatly anticipated, as well as oilskin bags, to protect the pages against the rain. He also brought plenty of gifts for the Indians, including beads, scissors, silk, paint, knives, and thimbles. To top it off, Lewis brought a collection of books, the closest approximation the explorers had to a guidebook. Included in the library were Antoine Simor Le Page du Pratz's *History of Louisiana,* a favorite of Thomas Jefferson's, *The Nautical Almanac and Astronomical Ephemeris,* which helped the explorers fix their location, Dr. Benjamin Smith Barton's *Elements of Botany,* in order to help catalog the territory's flora, and, of course, Alexander Mackenzie's *Voyages.*

Still, it was difficult for the men to adequately prepare for a region of which so little was known. And so on July 4th, 1803, Jefferson wrote to Lewis granting the men what Ambrose has called "the most unlimited letter of credit ever issued by an American president." It provided the men with a blank check, allowing them to spend the country's funds as they saw fit. Said Jefferson in his note: "I also ask of the Consuls, agents, merchants and citizens of any nation with which we have intercourse or amity to furnish you with those supplies which your necessities may call for, assuring them of honorable and prompt retribution."

Knowledge, supplies, and unlimited credit—as Lewis and Clark launched the most famous expedition in American history, it seemed they had prepared as best they possibly could for what would be a true guidebook-less journey. But although modern libraries are filled with information about the Lewis and Clark excursion, one aspect remains relatively opaque—as Jackson has noted, "The record gives us little by which to sense the excitement of the party as the day of departure approached." There was little discussion of the natural wonders they were bound to discover; no talk of the encounters they were expected to have. Instead, a single emotion pervaded much of the explorers' correspondence—that of confidence. As Lewis wrote in his June 1803 letter to Clark: "[S]hould nothing take place to defeat my progress altogether I feel confident that my passage to the Western Ocean can be effected by the end of the next Summer or the beginning of Autumn." Lewis and Clark would travel to the Pacific Ocean, they would return, and they would reap the benefits of their endeavor. It was as simple as that.

CHAPTER 4

❧ ❧ ❧

Guidebook Backlash

Although I still wasn't sure how to correctly pronounce Tanzania, my heavy reliance on the amateur guide-book sector during my two-day railway excursion from Kapiri Mposhi in Zambia to Dar es Salaam in Tanzania had served me well, accurately describing, among other things, where to buy tickets for the train, how to get food, and what to expect from the middle of the night border crossing. But upon alighting in Dar, my loyalties returned once again to my thousand-page print companion (which didn't, by the way, bother to wade into the Tanzania pronunciation conundrum) and, specifically, to its medley of trans-continental African "destination highlights."

One of the great drawbacks of being a serial guidebook adherent is the obsessive compulsion that accompanies the development of a trip itinerary. Through convincing rhetoric (like rating systems or Author's Pick connotations) and strategic imagery (such as glossy photographs), guidebooks often create a set of destination obligations—places a traveler simply *must* go when in the appropriate region. And despite the admitted absurdity of the practice, I have often found myself analyzing the success of my own trips by comparing their components to these guidebook suggestions ("Waterfall? Check. Palace? Miss"). To some, this is the epitome of lazy travel, akin to reading the first few pages of a novel before throwing it away. But to me, the comparison serves as an important measure of trip efficiency; travel is a costly and time-consuming endeavor and I have traditionally believed it best to maximize the number of destination highlights in order to increase a journey's worth. Checklist travel, I suppose, is an expected consequence of strict guidebook adherence.

Two of the fifteen highlights in my *Africa* guidebook were in Tanzania—Stone Town on the island of Zanzibar and Mt. Kilimanjaro. My intentions were to visit each, Stone Town for its historical significance ("Between the 12th and 15th centuries, Zanzibar became a powerful city-state, exporting slaves, gold, ivory and wood, and importing spices, glassware and textiles") and Kilimanjaro as a sort of pilgrimage ("At 5896m, Mt Kilimanjaro is the highest peak in Africa and one of the continent's most magnificent sights"). Both were on the way to Nairobi and since they commanded such prominent placements in my guidebook, I judged them essential components to a complete African itinerary, two quick checkmarks before proceeding north to Kenya.

I arrived in Zanzibar via boat from Dar es Salaam. Upon arrival, many of the boat's passengers scurried into awaiting vehicles, destined for the island's "unsurpassed collection of beaches." But I remained behind, having booked a room at a guesthouse within Stone Town itself. I dropped my bag off at the hotel and began to snake through the town's crooked corridors. Although my guidebook described it "as a historic wonder in itself that amply repays a few days of wandering through its narrow streets and alleys," I was bored with Stone Town after a few hours. The architecture may have been "fascinating" and I'm sure the buildings were a "photographer's dream," but I found the "lively street stalls" more akin to kitschy souvenir shops and quickly grew tired of tour agencies trying to sell me side trips to other parts of the island. I concluded that Stone Town was indeed worth a visit, but for a traveler like myself, one who enjoys moving quickly, an afternoon would have sufficed. The excursion also highlighted my continued over-reliance on the guidebook's advice—it had told me to schedule a few days in Stone Town, one of the "highlights" of Africa, and so I did.

After returning to Dar es Salaam from Zanzibar, I took a bus to Moshi, "a bustling town at the foot of Mt. Kilimanjaro" and close to the border of Kenya and Tanzania. My wife and I had plans to climb Mt. Kenya later that month and so I had stopped in Moshi to simply *see* the mountain, rather than actually climb it. Like many travelers, I was also hoping for the region's iconic photograph: a stoic giraffe or elephant, pausing momentarily under an arching acacia tree, framed against the backdrop of the hulking mountain, and capped by a small tuft of cloud circling Kilimanjaro's summit. If that's not "Africa," I don't know what is.

But if the guidebook can be conceptualized as a magnet, and if one pole of that magnet attracts groups of disparate travelers from around the world, then the other pole attracts people aiming to serve those travelers—travel agencies, tour guides, hoteliers, restaurateurs, touts, and swindlers. This was Moshi—a town built for invading armies of aspiring mountaineers and those wishing to capitalize on the craze. I arrived in town to find the mountain cloaked in a thick layer of clouds; I also arrived as a hot commodity, an unclaimed tourist defenseless from the advances of overzealous touts pitching trekking trips, equipment, and accommodation.

For the next few days I was trailed by an insistent man intent on selling me a slot on an expedition up the mountain. At my hotel, he remained in the lobby, waiting for me to finish showering or sleeping. At Internet cafes, he lingered outside patiently, waiting for me to log off the computer. And at restaurants, despite my continued protestations, he boldly sat at my table, peddling affordable trips up Africa's tallest peak.

He was impossible to escape, and I quickly realized that my vision of Moshi and Kilimanjaro would never materialize; my memories, instead, would be of this tout's face, smiling wildly and forever talking. After three days of reading in my hotel and checking my email, I bought a bus ticket for Nairobi. The clouds never lifted and I left the city without ever seeing the mountain.

While it might seem imprudent to condense a region as big and as diverse as Africa into fifteen "must-see" destinations, the publisher of my guidebook was merely following a centuries-old tradition—the distillation of large amounts of qualitative information into easily digestible, spoon-fed suggestions. This classification and organization of must-see attractions dates back to around 140 B.C. when Antipater of Sidon, a Greek-speaking epigrammatist, catalogued seven of the most impressive "wonders" of the world. By doing so, he sparked one of the most durable tourism-related marketing gimmicks of all time. About five hundred years later, another work emerged, wrongly attributed to a writer named Philo of Byzantium, but forever cementing the legacy of the Seven Ancient Wonders of the World. Although later lists make a few substitutions (such as the inclusion of the Lighthouse of Alexandria), the book's must-see attractions were as follows: the Hanging Gardens of Babylon, the Walls of Babylon, the Giza Pyramids, the Colossus of Rhodes, the statue of Olympian Zeus, the temple of Artemis at Ephesus, and the Mausoleum at Halicarnassus.

Often categorized as a "guidebook" by modern-day scholars, "Philo's" book was in fact a curious representative of the genre, as it chose not to help its readers get closer to the wonders, but to actually encourage them to stay away. Our favorite guidebook historian, Nicholas T. Parsons, notes the following from the book's introduction:

Everyone has heard of each of the Seven Wonders of the World, but few have seen all of them for themselves. To do so one has to go abroad to Persia, cross the Euphrates river, travel to Egypt, spend some time among the Elians in Greece, go to Halicarnassus in Caria, sail to Rhodes, and see Ephesus in Ionia. Only if you travel the world and get worn out by the effort of the journey will the desire to see all the Wonders of the World be satisfied, and by the time you have done that you will be old and practically dead.

According to the author, all that effort just wasn't worth it. Instead, foreshadowing the future success of coffee table pictorials and television documentaries, the author chose to satisfy the traveler's instincts with an alternative experience—detailed descriptions of the Wonders that would, in essence, eliminate the desire to see them in person. And not only would these descriptions satisfy the traveler's curiosity, but thanks to the extraordinary capacity of the human imagination, they would deliver an experience superior to actually being there: "[I]f a man investigates in verbal form the things to wonder at and the execution of their construction, and if he contemplates, as though looking at a mirror image, the whole skillful work, he keeps the impressions of each picture indelible in his mind. The reason for this is that he has seen amazing things with his mind."

Nearly two thousand years later, the acerbic American Mark Twain, during the same trip in which he visited the holy city of Varanasi, would arrive at the Taj Mahal in Agra, India. While ruminating on the effects of the proliferation of guidebook material, Twain seems to come to a remarkably similar conclusion, suggesting, perhaps, an inherent flaw in the second pillar of the guidebook structure—that of description. He begins the discussion by asking his readers to examine a few pieces of guidebook-related material:

I wish to place before the reader some of the usual descrip-
tions of the Taj, and ask him to take note of the impres-
sions left in his mind. These descriptions do really state the
truth—as nearly as the limitations of language will allow.
But language is a treacherous thing, a most unsure vehicle,
and it can seldom arrange descriptive words in such a way
that they will not inflate the facts—by help of the reader's
imagination, which is always ready to take a hand, and
work for nothing, and do the bulk of it at that.

Twain's suspicion of linguistic accuracy in describing the
monument stemmed from personal experience. Before his
first ever visit to Niagara Falls, the author's contact with
various pieces of guidebook material had contributed to an
enhanced level of anticipation that had ultimately clashed
with the eventual reality of the experience:

I had to visit Niagara fifteen times before I succeeded in get-
ting my imaginary Falls gauged to the actuality and could
begin to sanely and wholesomely wonder at them for what
they were, not what I had expected them to be. When I first
approached them it was with my face lifted toward the sky,
for I thought I was going to see an Atlantic ocean pour-
ing down thence over cloud-vexed Himalayan heights, a
sea-green wall of water sixty miles front and six miles high,
and so, when the toy reality came suddenly into view—that
beruffled little wet apron hanging out to dry—the shock was
too much for me, and I fell with a dull thud.

Only through recurring visits did Twain develop a genu-
ine appreciation of the Falls' beauty and therefore, an understanding of its place among the country's natural wonders:

Yet slowly, surely, steadily, in the course of my fifteen visits,
the proportions adjusted themselves to the facts, and I came

at last to realize that a waterfall a hundred and sixty-five feet high and a quarter of a mile wide was an impressive thing. It was not a dipperful to my vanished great vision, but it would answer.

Taking full blame for his distorted perceptions ("I am a careless reader . . . who overlooks the informing details or masses their sum improperly"), Twain wonders if he is not better off staying away from these destinations altogether, thereby eradicating the disappointment he feels upon encountering such objects, and instead allowing the inflated descriptions of the guidebook to serve as his enduring memory.

While it is probable that "Philo" was being sincere with his recommendation to remain at home, Twain, of course, was being sarcastic. Still, both commentaries, one written more than a thousand years ago, the other over a century ago, illustrate just one complaint in an ever-increasing catalog of guidebook-related criticism. This complaint, that the anticipation of the journey often exceeds the actual experience, is more prevalent than ever, as an increase in guidebook-related content, often enhanced through photographic re-touching or clever video editing, has replaced the limitations of the written word and has created a system of unrealistic and often unattainable expectations. Twain's initial dismay at the sight of Niagara Falls is no different than the reaction of a woman I encountered on a trail in Nepal's Khumbu Valley, who, annoyed by the incessant lines of backpack-burdened visitors and equipment-laden yaks (often absent from majestic Himalayan-related imagery), and apparently oblivious to the remarkable snowcapped peaks that surrounded us on all sides, angrily turned around and stormed back to the lodge, exclaiming that the highway to Everest was "the most disappointing experience of my life!" What she expected to see or encounter, I was not sure. But in this case, perhaps Twain was right—she would have been better off staying home.

While these anecdotes prove that this type of guidebook condemnation is actually as old as the genre itself, it is also clear that amplified rancor has appeared only as a result of an ever-expanding guidebook industry. As we saw in the first half of this book, not only is there more travel information about every conceivable destination, but with the emergence of the amateur sector, it is also becoming increasingly difficult for the traveler to know whose advice to trust. Complaints have followed. The guidebook is a crutch. The guidebook only leads to other travelers. The guidebook hinders discovery. The guidebook ruins destinations. In short, the guidebook evolution has clearly changed, and continues to change, where we go, how we get there, why we go, and how we ultimately feel about the destination.

Because of this evolution, the guidebook, even in a world inundated with intrusive electronic devices, often remains the most controversial item in a traveler's suitcase. Cynics argue that travel should be spontaneous and liberating, and that those tourists who ramble itinerary-free, leaving the world's preconceived notions and opinions at home, are rewarded with the truly unique travel experiences. These detractors further suggest that the inconveniences and confusion associated with travel sans guidebook are eclipsed tenfold by the unsullied perspectives and enlightening experiences the traveler aimlessly happens upon.

Many of today's travel writers agree. In Paul Theroux's *The Tao of Travel,* author Dervla Murphy, when asked to provide the readers with a few traveling tips, says, "Choose your country, use guidebooks to identify the areas most frequented by foreigners—and then go in the opposite direction." And Rory MacLean, during a particularly stale journey through the once tourist-heavy streets of Kabul, Afghanistan, openly opines in his book *Magic Bus,* "Perhaps the only way to experience real wonder and freshness today is to travel without a guidebook."

Murphy and MacLean's views were enthusiastically shared by Albert Camus, the French philosopher, writer, and traveler. In his *Notebooks,* Camus famously sentimentalized (albeit unintentionally) the intrepid and guidebook-less traveler when he wrote:

> *What gives value to travel is fear. It is the fact that, at a certain moment, when we are so far from our own country . . . we are seized by a vague fear, and an instinctive desire to go back to the protection of old habits. This is the most obvious benefit of travel. At that moment we are feverish but also porous, so that the slightest touch makes us quiver to the depths of our being.*

Could the protection of old habits that the traveler runs back to be the consultation of a Lonely Planet guide or an online message board? Is it the comfort of a well-reviewed hostel or the peace of mind of an expat filled bus route? And if true, does this mean that these old habits are easier than ever to return to and Camus's "obvious benefit" of travel is quickly disappearing?

In 1910, *The New York Times* published an article entitled "Baedeker's Great Britain: The Guidebook as it is To-day and the Guidebook as it Would Be in Utopia." In it, the author bemoans the current state of the guidebook evolution by using the famous Swiss mountain, the Matterhorn, to demonstrate the inability of the genre to produce truly unique traveling revelations. When a friend remarks that the Matterhorn is surprising, the author agrees:

*For the Matterhorn is surprising; that is its essential quality
as a sight. As you are bouncing along in a wagon, meditating
on immortality or the number of eggs you will eat for sup-
per, you suddenly round a corner, and the Matterhorn strikes
you in the face. You are not overcome by its height; you are
not overwhelmed by its proximity; you are merely astounded
that it is there.*

But this astonishment, argues the author, is severely tempered by the evolution of guidebook literature. The genre,
in this case *Baedeker's*, does a disservice to the visitor by providing too much information—information that effectively
diminishes the experience. Instead, the traveler is better
served encountering these attractions unprompted:

*And that explains the quintessence of sightseeing, which is
this: that mountains and rivers, cathedrals and towns were
all made by God or man to be come upon suddenly, and not
to be sought out by train or trolley. For you never truly see a
thing until you see it of a sudden, caught round the corner of
a street or from the window of a passing train.*

The guidebook evolution has unfortunately eliminated
many of these sudden, grandiose encounters. On the contrary,
entire vacations are often organized around seeing those objects
which would most "surprise" the traveler if their existence had
been otherwise unknown: week-long treks to Machu Picchu in
the Andes or dusty, multi-day car rides to Uluru (Ayers Rock)
in the Australian Outback. These attractions are immensely
popular precisely because they are so well known. And yet one
can only imagine the magnitude of these experiences without
an already embedded base of knowledge and imagery. Picture driving through China and unexpectedly running into
the Great Wall. Or hiking in the United States and suddenly
coming across the Grand Canyon. Those encounters, already

amazing in their own right, would undoubtedly reach another level.

In his revealing *The Art of Travel*, Alain de Botton laments the emotional advantages the world's early explorers, such as Lewis and Clark, had compared to the modern day traveler. As evidence, he presents the case of twenty-nine-year old German Alexander von Humboldt, who left home for South America in the summer of 1799, intent on furthering the world's knowledge in a variety of scientific and geographical disciplines:

> *He travelled fifteen thousand kilometres around the northern coastlines and interior, on the way collecting some sixteen hundred plants and identifying six hundred new species. He redrew the map of South America based on readings supplied by accurate chronometers and sextants. He researched the Earth's magnetism and was the first to discover that magnetic intensity declined the further one got from the poles.*

Impressed by Humboldt's accomplishments, and in an effort to demonstrate the futility of modern "exploration," de Botton contrasts Humboldt's journey with one of his own, a tame weekend sojourn through the Spanish capital of Madrid. As he sits alone in his hotel room upon arrival, de Botton pouts, describing to his readers a strange urge not to explore, but to inexplicably and unexpectedly return home:

> *On the desk lay several magazines provided by the hotel, offering information about the city and two guidebooks that I had brought from home. In their different ways, they conspired to suggest that an exciting and multifarious phenomenon called Madrid was waiting to be discovered outside. . . . And yet the prospect of those enticements, about which I had heard so much and which I knew I was privileged to be able to see, merely provoked in me a combination of listlessness*

and self-disgust at the contrast between my own indolence
and what I imagined would have been the eagerness of more
normal visitors.

The author's growing apprehension and trepidation are
quickly justified as he is forced from his room (by the hotel
maid no less) and begins to explore the "must-see" itinerary of
the city. At one point, as he stands beneath a statue of Carlos
III, de Botton is surrounded by an animated throng of camera-
wielding tourists and wonders, "with mounting anxiety, What
am I supposed to do here? What am I supposed to think?"

As the trip continues, de Botton is clearly flummoxed by
his own motivations and becomes increasingly resentful of
Humboldt's "imaginative freedom": the ability to discover
the destination on one's own time and in one's own way. The
German explorer, de Botton explains, was "free to think that
everything, or perhaps nothing, might be interesting," a luxury often not afforded the modern day traveler. Instead, he
surmises, today's travelers are restrained by a system of prede-
termined and increasingly uniform opinions: "Where guidebooks praised a site, they pressured a visitor to match their
authoritative enthusiasm, and where they were silent, pleasure or interest seemed unwarranted."

Throughout my own travels, I had developed a similar
interest in this concept—what de Botton explains as Humboldt's ability to "think that everything, or perhaps nothing,
might be interesting." But this notion, one promoted fever-
ishly by the anti-guidebook crowd, clashed directly with my
overriding dependence on guidebook-related material. I owe
much of my traveling happiness to the advice gleaned from
both professional and amateur guidebook material and I have
learned to tolerate the results of strict guidebook adherence—
the disappointing experiences (such as Stone Town or Mt.
Kilimanjaro), the noisy hostels, pre-packaged bus routes, and

overpriced breakfasts—by regarding them as small bumps on the proverbial open road.

But the time had clearly come for me to break away from the guidebook, to explore a part of the world without the meticulous preparation and absolute reliance that had accompanied nearly every one of my trips since I was a child. Pulling my inspiration from the great American explorers Meriwether Lewis and William Clark, I decided that it was time to set off as if there *were* no material available on my chosen destination—no restaurant recommendations, no bus timetables, and certainly no glossy photo galleries of country highlights. For an obsessive-compulsive guidebook adherent, the idea of guidebook-less travel was undoubtedly daunting. But people were disconnecting and experimenting all around me—some from their phones, some from social media—espousing on the many virtues of removing themselves from their previous fixations. And for someone who had traced the evolution of the genre and had slowly become disillusioned with the near ubiquity of biased and subjective information about seemingly every destination on the planet, this kind of exercise seemed not only appropriate but necessary, the logical progression of my traveling resume.

Since I was an academic by trade and had designated this exercise a guidebook *experiment*, I felt it prudent to develop my own set of hypotheses concerning guidebook-less travel. My near-complete reliance on guidebook information to that point in my life, of course, meant that I was somewhat ignorant of the benefits and detriments of this approach. But just as Lewis and Clark had used various sources to develop a few theories about what their journey would entail, my experiences had provided me with a few clues as to what I could expect to find. And no place had provided more hints as to what this journey would involve than a country I believed was unlike anywhere in the world.

※ *※* *※*

My disgust toward India formed like an encroaching virus, slowly spreading throughout my body as I made my way through the country for the first time. During my first few days in Delhi, as I stumbled through the touristic obligations of the Red Fort (check) and the Jama Masjid (check), I began to develop persistent headaches, my head throbbing both from dehydration and the relentless bustle of the Paharganj neighborhood in which I was staying ("popular with back-packers!"). As I made my way west into Rajasthan ("camels and forts!"), the virus spread to my stomach, and it became impossible for me to eat anything but plain white toast and juice. By the end of two weeks, as I snaked through Ahmed-abad and onwards to Mumbai ("India's most exciting city!") by cramming my battered body into the third level of non-air conditioned railway cars, I felt an overwhelming sense of mental and physical exhaustion unlike anything I had ever felt before. This exhaustion quickly sapped my usual enthusi-asm and as the journey continued, I began to hide in my room, brooding over the feeling of entrapment I felt in such a fre-netic country and shooting off angry emails to my girlfriend, chiding the Indian people for their garbage filled streets and intrusive public demeanor. I craved solitude and cleanliness and silence and health, and when I finally emerged from the unbearable squalor of the Indian streets after a flight to Europe, I felt invigorated, cherishing my pristine bathroom, Western-style breakfast spread and a nighttime temperature that dropped below eighty degrees. I fired off a few more mean-spirited emails, thrilled to have India in my rear-view mirror and looked excitedly toward the rest of my trip.

And yet a funny thing happened—India stayed with me; the virus proved benign. My mind often returned with remarkable detail to specific episodes and people I had met in the streets or on the train or at the temples. My initial disdain was replaced with a bewitching intrigue; what followed was an insatiable desire to learn more about the place—to find out what made India so maddeningly alluring. In *Video Night in Kathmandu,* the writer Pico Iyer describes a similar hypnotism when a Chinese photographer stumbles into his hotel room one night and begins ranting about his own India experience:

> *He had just arrived, he said, from the land of my forefathers. 'Varanasi,' he said, spitting out the name. 'They call it a holy city. But it is a filthy city, a stinking city, a city full of shit!' He had had enough, he said, more than enough of 'silk men' and a holy river that was only a large-scale bathroom. He had had enough of cosmic dirt. He had had it up to here with the world's most persistent touts. He had had enough of being hounded and harassed. He had been taken, he said, for $350. He had been in India for six weeks, he went on, and six weeks was enough—no, more than enough. He could stand it no longer. And he wanted to go back, and he could talk of little else.*

Memories of that trip today, which in totality encompassed thousands of miles and several continents, nearly always focus on my time in India. With ample reflection, it is now easy to see what made that segment so memorable, what made those recollections so much clearer than, say, my time in Sydney or Beijing or Moscow: India is the most guidebook-proof destination in the world. This designation, of course, suggests two conflicting characteristics. On the one hand, it implies that no matter how much travelers read beforehand, no matter what kind of opinions or perceptions they develop through months or preparation and pre-trip planning, most travelers will be unprepared for the complexity and sensory assault of their first India experience. On the other hand, the idea of a guidebook-proof destination also offers the opportunity for unrestrained discovery, a place where one can savor the traditional appeal of true exploration and where the unexpected should not merely be tolerated but gleefully embraced.

Consequently, this guidebook-proof distinction does not simply evaporate with repeated visits. While most return travelers learn to patiently cope with the sensory and emotional hurdles posed by Indian travel, one can never fully anticipate or prepare for what may be even the most modest journey through the subcontinent. Large India guidebooks (mine was more than a thousand pages) may tell you where to go, how to get there, and what it's going to be like. But they are laughably inadequate in preparing you for the crowds as you board an Indian train, the heat of the Indian summer, or the smells from an Indian market. This characteristic, this guidebook immunity, is what makes India such a unique and rewarding destination; while other countries undoubtedly have guidebook-proof elements, only in India is this attribute so salient, so dominant, so persistent. On my first visit, I was too overwhelmed and frustrated with an inability to dictate my own path to fully appreciate these unique India-only moments. But repeated visits have taught me to tolerate the many difficulties of Indian travel and to savor those incidents for which I am unprepared. And so if I were to use my Indian experiences to develop a simple hypothesis concerning guidebook-less travel, it would be as follows: guidebook-less travel is tremendously difficult, filled with tangible and emotional obstacles, but if those difficulties can be tolerated, it can also be exceedingly memorable.

A final thought. Think back to the last time a friend or family member told you about a trip or vacation. What did they say? What did they remember? What did they feel were the most tale-worthy parts of their trip? My guess is that the narration of the journey involved incidents where things did *not* go according to plan—a flat tire, an unexpected encounter with a stranger, or, a travel story favorite, unforeseen airport delays ("And we were stuck on the tarmac for two hours!"). One rarely hears about the destination highlights—the Eiffel Tower, the Great Wall—most likely because there is an implicit understanding that the listener already knows what those incidents involved. And so the narrator, whether consciously or unconsciously, scans his or her memories for those events which made the trip *unique*, those incidents which diverged from the guidebook-aided plan, in order to buttress the account of their journey.

But what if there was no plan to begin with? Wouldn't that increase the percentage of memorable experiences? That, I believed, would be the great contribution of guidebook-less travel.

ぶ   ぶ   ぶ

Experiences had provided me with hypotheses concerning guidebook-less travel; now I needed a destination. To find one, I opened the simplest online world map I could find, careful to shield myself from unexpected exposure to unwanted guidebook material, and scanned its topography. Beginning my search in the Western Hemisphere, my eyes slowly gravitated to the northeast corner of South America, to the countries of Guyana, Suriname, and French Guiana, a region rarely discussed in even the most ambitious of traveling circles. Closer to the United States than more popular destinations like Peru and Argentina, and only miles away from the well known island getaway of Trinidad and Tobago, this cluster of small countries seemed like a perfect place to launch my experiment.

I pulled up an online ticket-booking agent and found that the only way to access those countries via New York was through the Guyanese city of Georgetown. Luckily, and somewhat surprisingly, the flights were affordable, direct, and fairly consistent throughout the week. A preliminary route began to emerge after an unsuccessful search for additional in-region airline tickets (including the startling discovery that the quickest way to French Guiana via New York was through Paris). I would fly into Georgetown and head east overland, following a fairly straightforward path through Suriname and French Guiana. I would allow ample time to explore inland, away from the ocean, and eventually backtrack using a similar course, returning to Georgetown for a flight back to the United States. It was the most basic itinerary possible and I knew that it would eventually evolve into something much different than I had originally planned. But wasn't that the point?

To my delight, the route also resembled the path of Meriwether Lewis and William Clark. Both journeys involved overland travel to a relatively unknown part of the Americas, both had the goal of reaching a specific landmark (for me, the French Guiana city of Cayenne and for Lewis and Clark, the Pacific Ocean), and both involved backtracking to their original departure point. I believed that these logistical similarities would be helpful in finding connections between the two trips and would assist me in developing shared themes concerning guidebook-less travel. And through this process I hoped to capture but a small glimpse, a mere inkling, of what it must have been like for these men to travel across the United States without a guidebook.

In terms of my expectations, it is probable that Lewis and Clark knew more about the western part of North America than I did of these South American countries; to say there were considerable gaps in my knowledge of Guyana, Suriname and French Guiana would have been a tremendous understatement. I knew so little about the region that I wasn't entirely sure what language was spoken in any of the three countries (although French for French Guiana seemed an obvious guess). The knowledge I did possess was trivial— that is, it was useful only for specific trivia questions. For instance, I knew that Guyana was a part of the West Indies cricket team. And that Guyana was the site of the famous Jonestown cult. I also knew that a large population of Guyanese expats lived in Jamaica, Queens. But that was the extent of it; I knew practically nothing about Suriname or French Guiana.

My inspiration to visit the region, in fact, was derived from this dearth of knowledge; what better way to understand the effects of the guidebook than to visit a group of countries I knew nothing about? And yet, I did not go in blind; no explorer ever does, certainly not Lewis and Clark. Instead, the minimal information and assumptions with which I began my trip were deduced from both the general knowledge I had of the world (climate, geography, etc.) and from the map I had purchased of Guyana, Suriname, and French Guiana, before I left. As historian John Logan Allen has written, "[M]inds can fill blank spaces on maps with amazing facility. When little is known of an entire area, the little that is known or partly known is put to good use." Here are the conclusions I came up with.

In terms of weather, since the countries were so close to the equator, and since I would be traveling in July, I knew it would be hot, sometimes unbearably so, and that it was most likely the rainy season. The region's latitude also helped me postulate on its topography, which I assumed to be lush, wet, and hilly. Because most of the roads on the map hugged the coast, and because the countries' southern borders essentially ringed the northeast edges of the Amazon, I guessed that the interiors of the countries were impassable, and primarily consisted of dense jungle. I saw only one railroad line, from Georgetown to New Amsterdam in Guyana, and assumed that most of my travel would be either by road or, very likely, by river, since the highway system seemed to dissolve the farther south one went. Finally, the capital cities, two of which were broken out separately on the map, looked tiny, which led me to question both their attractiveness as a tourist destination and their overall level of importance to the region as a whole.

I developed a few other random conjectures. Judging from Guyana's proximity to Trinidad, I assumed that its food would involve a mixture of Caribbean and Indian flavors; I had no guess as to what I would eat in either Suriname or French Guiana. Since all the countries were so close to both Venezuela and Brazil, I wondered if there was any semblance of an oil industry. If so, I figured I'd encounter cities far larger and far glitzier than I expected. The names of the places on the map led me to believe that English was spoken in Guyana, Dutch in Suriname, and French in French Guiana, but I surmised that these were only the official languages, and that other dialects dominated the interior. Finally, because I had encountered so few people who had ever visited the region, I speculated that the tourist infrastructure in each country would be vastly underdeveloped, and that I would have difficulty planning and executing my various excursions.

My assumptions about the region helped form my packing list. To keep my clothes and other valuables dry, I brought a rain jacket and a rain cover for my backpack. Unaware of what kind of accommodation would be available, I brought both a sleeping sheet and a lightweight sleeping bag. To protect against the unrelenting attack of jungle mosquitoes, I brought both insect repellant and a small bug net. To protect against the harsh equatorial sun, I brought sunscreen, a long sleeve lightweight shirt, a baseball cap and sunglasses. And not knowing what currency was used in each country, I went to the bank and secured a large stack of crisp, multi-denomination, U.S. bills.

The final item on my packing list was a small moleskin notebook, specifically reserved for daily reflection. This was uncommon; I have not traditionally kept a journal during my past travels. But one of the reasons I was able to adopt the Lewis and Clark expedition as a guidebook-less exemplar was because of the explorers' painstakingly detailed account of their journey. Stephen Ambrose has gone so far as to call the Lewis and Clark journals "a national literary treasure," explaining that "their adventure is accessible in a way that . . . the experiences of the other great explorers are not." To *not* keep a journal during my own trip, then, would have been nothing less than sacrilege.

In the end, I was prepared for only a handful of scenarios— blistering heat, torrential rain, obstinate mosquitoes. For all other developments, I would have to rely on my traveling experience, my decision-making, and not least of all, luck. While I was in no way as educated as Meriwether Lewis or as savvy as William Clark, I felt I was sufficiently prepared through years of travel for nearly anything the region would throw at me. With no guidebook to help me find a hotel or calculate currency conversions or recommend a place to eat, I would have to be.

For many years, I worked in an office building next to one of the larger bookstores in New York City. During lunch, I would linger in its travel section, diligently collecting every bit of information I could about destinations to which I would be traveling in the near future. I would write down names of hotels and restaurants and check their reviews when I returned to my desk, flag specific tour companies in order to contact them for prices, and sketch sample itineraries using the store's abundance of maps. I never viewed this practice as monotonous trip preparation; it was rather something I thoroughly enjoyed. My time spent poring over this guidebook information, in fact, often augmented my enthusiasm for upcoming trips, temporarily transporting me from a gloomy cubicle to the mountains of Patagonia or the islands of the South Pacific.

All of which makes the buildup to my guidebook experiment a rather distinct experience. While Lewis and Clark tirelessly gathered every piece of information they could about the region through which they would be traveling, I purposely avoided sullying my experiment with unsolicited exposure. And so I refused to read anything about the three countries, staying away from the bookstore I had so often visited, avoiding online review sites and message boards, and using only the simple map I had purchased to visualize potential experiences. The Guianas, then, remained mostly invisible, a rough amalgamation of the various conjectures and assumptions noted above.

As the date of the trip approached, my usual enthusiasm was supplemented by mild trepidation. This was unknown territory for me, quite literally in fact. I wasn't sure how to feel—should I be excited? Scared? Nervous? In a July 2nd, 1803 letter to his mother, as he prepared to leave for the first leg of the expedition, Lewis wrote the following:

> *The nature of this expedition is by no means dangerous, my route will be altogether through tribes of Indians who are perfectly friendly to the United States, therefore consider the chances of life just as much in my favor on this trip as I should conceive them were I to remain at home for the same length of time. . . . For its fatigues I feel myself perfectly prepared, nor do I doubt my health and strength of constitution to bear me through it.*

Lewis's tone was meant to placate. He knew the journey would be difficult, more difficult than anything he had attempted to that point in his life. But the confidence he exuded with his words was real; he *knew* he was the right leader for the expedition and any apprehension he may have felt was buried underneath an impenetrable layer of will and conviction. He had been building toward this expedition his entire life.

I am not trying to equate the dangers of my own trip to those of the Lewis and Clark expedition; in that sense, the trips are incomparable, laughably so. But our emotions on the eve of our respective journeys were similar. While I was indeed nervous, something I probably hid from my own wife and family, I was also confident, knowing that I was finally ready to dissolve my guidebook addiction and to remove myself from the limitations of guidebook-dependent travel. I was living in a hyper-connected world, a place where we allow other people to tell us what movies to see, what music to download, and what restaurants to eat at. I was tired of the guidance; I was finally ready to start exploring.

Truthfully, I had no idea what would happen. The best outcome would be a sustained series of unexpected, euphoric experiences—the type explorers Hiram Bingham and Antonio da Madalena must have had when they turned the corner and saw, respectively, the perched ruins of Machu Picchu and the majestic sprawl of Angkor Wat. The worst outcome would be the exact opposite—constant boredom, unexpected danger or illness, heightened frustration, and perpetual discomfort triggered by shoddy hotels, indigestible food, and the mind-numbing aggravation that can only be caused by the endless advances of a country's touts, swindlers, and opportunists. Those were the extremes, of course, and I theorized that the real experience would fall somewhere in the middle.

On the day of my departure, I woke up, had breakfast with my wife, finished packing, and ran a few errands around town. After lunch, I picked up my backpack, which, for the first time ever, did not contain a guidebook, and walked out the door of my apartment, on my way to South America.

CHAPTER 5

❧ ❧ ❧

Georgetown

I once read that the measure of a society is revealed in the way it queues. If that's true, the boarding process for the overnight flight to Georgetown, Guyana, one of the most disorganized and anarchic procedures I have ever witnessed inside an airport, was revelatory. There was no regard for the announcements, no concern for seat numbers or baggage allowances. And there was no actual queue; upon hearing the notice that we were about to board, all passengers streamed forward to form a huddled mass, congregating next to the ropes and thrusting their boarding passes at the nearest available employee. Although zone instructions were repeated ad nauseam ("Ladies and gentlemen, we are boarding by zone numbers only. Please do not try to board until your zone number has been called."), the mass pushed ahead.

This was it, the beginning of my guidebook experiment and my first tangible impression of the Guianas. If this had been a traditional journey, I would have spent some time at the airport scanning my guidebook material for last-minute information about the region, perhaps memorizing currency rates or mapping out potential breakfast stops for our early morning arrival. I'd be mentally removed from the sterile glow of the Terminal 4 waiting area. But because I had spent the last few weeks avoiding all material about the Guianas, the passengers heading to Georgetown provided the first clues as to what this trip would entail. And so my senses were heightened, my curiosity piqued. To where, exactly, was I going?

My fellow travelers were a diverse lot, an assorted mix of shapes, sizes, and colors. Earlier, as we waited for our flight to board, I had observed their movements and conversations with the empirical diligence of a trained ethnographer. I looked for clues on food, but few people were eating; on currency, but all I saw were U.S. bills; and on weather, but it was hot and humid in New York, so most were dressed in short sleeves and jeans. And while I heard several languages—Spanish, French, Hindi—the most distinct, and the only one I could fully understand, was the language of hip-hop. "We gonna git into the studyo. We gonna make some monee," said one lavishly dressed woman to her friend, as her two cackling children darted in and out through the rows of seats.

While the mass of people heaved forward, I lingered toward the back and waited until most passengers had filed in. When I reached my seat, I found it already occupied by a fidgety Guyanese man staring out the window. He asked if I'd like for him to get up—I said I would and he begrudgingly rose to take his proper place in the middle next to me and a young girl, no older than seven or eight, who was apparently traveling on her own. Uninterested in the carry-on luggage chaos erupting in the aisle, disturbed by the near-anarchic conditions by which we had boarded the plane, and increasingly anxious about what the next day would bring, I put my headphones on and was asleep before we took off, knowing that for the first time in my life I would wake up in a part of the world I knew virtually nothing about.

My second impression of the region came several hours later and only a short distance out from landing in Georgetown, when I woke up and drowsily slid open the airplane window

shade to reveal a sea of unbroken forest canopy, topped errati-
cally by patches of billowy white clouds. I had anticipated
that the interior of these countries would be covered in thick
forest, but to see such density so close to the capital city was
alarming and made me wonder how far inland, realistically, I
would be able to travel.

We landed shortly thereafter, and the disorder that had
begun the trip repeated itself, only in reverse, with people
ripping their luggage from the overhead compartments and
fighting to exit the plane. I was unhurried, with no immediate onward plans, and was the final passenger to enter the
customs line at Cheddi Jagan International Airport. I used
the downtime to explore the waiting area and to continue my
search for information about the region. The "Tourism Information Booth" was closed but the posters and photographs
lining its exterior provided a handful of telling images. The
most prominent was a large, frayed poster for Kaieteur Falls,
described as "The highest single drop waterfall in the world."
It was an odd proclamation—it seemed rather forced—and I
imagined a group of tourism ministers sitting around a table,
deliberating the most appropriate way to classify this waterfall
as the best of *something, anything*. But the execution was con-
fusing; I wasn't even sure what "single drop waterfall" meant.
The other photographs were mostly of animals—a bird called
"Cock of the Rock" and the "Harpy Eagle—The Largest
Eagle in America and the World's Most Powerful Raptor,"
suggesting that Guyana's must-see attractions perhaps lay
within its jungle interior rather than on its coast or in its cities.

Compared to the frenetic boarding process, immigration
was a relatively organized procedure and I was officially
stamped into Guyana within an hour of arriving. I exited
the airport and was quickly claimed by a taxi driver named
Madho, an older Indian man, wearing slacks and a long sleeve

button-down shirt. He encouraged me to sit up front and as we pulled away from the curb, asked where I was from.

"New York," I said. "I live in Queens."

He perked up. "Queens? I have family up there. My daughter lives on 125th St. in Jamaica." It was very close to a previous apartment of mine. "She runs a car wash. Right on Atlantic Ave." I told him that I had most likely passed it on many occasions.

This kind of dialogue would be repeated many times throughout my stay; nearly every Guyanese seemed to have at least two or three relatives living in Queens. But I already knew about the Queens connection; it was everything else about the country that I needed to learn. And so I used the rest of the taxi ride to substantiate or refute several of the assumptions with which I had arrived. The food in the region, according to the driver, was indeed a mix of Caribbean and Indian flavors, with "curry, chicken, and mutton" ranking among his favorites. There used to be a railroad between Georgetown and New Amsterdam but it was long gone by the time I came through. And the one thing I had to do while I was here was take the boat ride to Venezuela.

"How long does that take?" I asked.

"Oh, about twenty-four hours," he answered.

The advice I really needed, however, was of a more short-term variety. "Can you recommend any hotels in Georgetown?"

He paused. "Sure, I can bring you to two places."

"What's the difference?"

"Well, the nicer one is a hotel. It's about $30 a night."

"And the other?"

"More of a guesthouse. About $15 a night. But people only stay there for a short time."

"Short time like a day? Or short time like an hour?"

"More like an hour," he said.

I chose the former and we pulled up to a place called the Sleep-In International a few minutes later. The hotel was three floors and divided into several sections, with a large pool and an open-air restaurant and bar. The lobby was clean and tidy, with wicker chairs and potted plants positioned neatly around a flat screen television. And although the room ended up costing $55, not $30, it was clean and cool, a wall-mounted air conditioner comfortably supplying refuge from the day-time heat.

I had traditionally been quite wary about arriving in a new city without having at least a rough idea of where I would be staying, be it a specific hotel or general neighborhood. But the Sleep-In was fine, a comfortable option in what seemed, at least according to the cab driver, to be the heart of the city. I paid my bill and settled into the room, pleased with the driver's recommendations and exhausted from the overnight journey.

JOURNAL ENTRY — GEORGETOWN

Day 1—Georgetown, Guyana: My guidebook experiment has begun and all is well. For dinner, I sat poolside at the Sleep-in International in Georgetown, Guyana eating a bowl of chicken curry and watching small children frolic in the water. I could have been anywhere in the world—Mumbai maybe or even Miami. In that sense, the experiment so far has been rather tame, devoid of the kind of moments for which the Lewis and Clark expedition is so fondly remembered—tense Indian encounters, terrifying grizzly bear attacks, exhilarating buffalo hunts. But it's only been a day . . .

As I sat by the pool, flicking mosquitoes off my table, I thought of Meriwether Lewis's famous journal passage in which he "reflected that [he] had as yet done but little, very little indeed, to further the happiness of the human race or

*to advance the information of the succeeding generation."
In a way, my own journey was similarly altruistic—to
understand how the proliferation of guidebook material has
changed the way we travel. Will my inquiry and subsequent
findings prove to be as socially and culturally valuable as
the exploration of an entire half of a continent? Well . . .
of course not. That was never my intent. And to suggest
otherwise would be bravado of the highest order. Instead,
I hope only to contribute to what I believe is an important
and timely conversation and to help people assess, ponder,
and consider their own level of guidebook reliance.*

*Regardless of the social significance of my experiment,
though, this trip—only a day old but several months in the
making—has so far revealed much about myself. In short, it
has helped me realize that my desire to travel stems not from
a need for adventure, as people close to me have previously
suggested, but rather from a need for accomplishment, an
extravagant way to check things off an intricate to-do list.*

*Travel, I have realized, is not a disruption of a methodical
and systematic way of life but rather a robust and rewarding
extension of it. This could perhaps explain why I abhor sed-
entary beach vacations and enthusiastically embrace overland travel—bus routes, train trips, hiking. These kinds of
journeys provide a series of checkpoints along the way by
which I can measure my progress: "Today, we will advance
to this campsite" rather than "I wonder what we will do
today?" Each trip I take is subsequently segmented into a
series of distinct and measurable accomplishments—make
it to a certain city, visit a specific museum, eat at a well-
known restaurant—hence my fierce loyalty to the neat and
orderly advice within the guidebook spectrum.*

*And so what to make of my first day in Guyana? There
is still a feeling of accomplishment—I had made it to the
city and to a serviceable hotel. And in a way, the feeling is*

*amplified because I did it without the help of a guidebook.
But from here my route is murky and while the journey does
indeed have an overriding objective—I'm hoping to make
it to Cayenne, French Guiana—it lacks the usual series of
checkpoints by which I can measure my progress. What I
envision, then, is a more dynamic journey, one in which
accomplishments are of the short-term rather than long-term
variety. If I had brought a guidebook, I would have exited
the plane with the singular goal of reaching my pre-booked
hotel. But without it, my objectives were more immediate,
more precise: get through customs, convert currency, find a
taxi, gather information from driver, find a hotel. There is
no off-switch for this kind of travel, no coasting through the
day knowing that a guesthouse driver is waiting for me at
the airport. For someone who embraces accomplishments,
however small, perhaps that is a good thing. Maybe, in fact,
this kind of travel will be even more fulfilling than the usual
guidebook-aided variety. We will see.*

The first impulse for many travelers arriving in a new city is
to seek out its main attraction. First time visitors to Paris no
doubt scan the horizon for signs of the Eiffel Tower; visitors
to Sydney make a beeline down to the harbor to watch the sun
set against the Opera House. But I had no idea what image
graced the cover of the Georgetown guidebook, no clue as to
its premier attraction, and so, using the only bit of knowledge
I had so far received, turned left out of my hotel and walked
toward what my taxi driver had called, "the busiest market in
Georgetown."

But Stabroek Market was not really a market; it was a party,
a raucous one. The frenzy was concentrated around a long
red and white building extending across several blocks and
crowned by a tall clock tower. This was the actual commercial

hub of the bazaar, an enclosed, gloomy maze of pocketbooks and purses, mangos and cucumbers, chicken and fish. A more primitive version of the typical American shopping mall, these labyrinths exist all over the world, and I thought back to the countless warnings I had read in guidebooks about similar places over the years—"Take care in [enter city name here]'s Central Market; it's a pickpocket's dream."

But the energy of the market was not contained inside; instead, it extended outwards, into the adjoining streets and parking lots, where groups of people blended together, laughing and shouting and drinking, to form a chaotic mass of revelry and jubilation. Music exploded from portable, wheeled, DJ booths with names like "Big Time Hustler" and "Sounds of Life," as their owners pushed the speakers around the streets hocking bootleg CDs. The shops and stands, brimming with goods, were open, but the proprietors were noticeably unmotivated: "Come on, buy a scarf mon. No worries," one said to me.

The scene, remarkable in its own right, was even more so when viewed against the backdrop of the city's notable architecture. Georgetown was an old city—several of the structures surrounding Stabroek Market exhibited obvious signs of colonial influence. It was easy to imagine rich Europeans perched high upon these terraces, sipping scotch and staring longingly into the sea. But now, those buildings were the property of the Guyanese, and they seemed as much a part of society as the beer and the music. Strictly speaking, they embraced the celebration. City Hall, for example, while unoccupied on the day I passed through, still took the time to authoritatively instruct its citizens to "Abstain. Be Faithful. Condomise."

After a few hours in the market and its surrounding extensions, I wandered away from the main square, onto a mellower side street where an excited man with jumbled teeth approached me, asking my name and where I was from.

"First time in Guyana mon! Guyana a beautiful country!" It was both a statement and a question.

His name was Marvin, "Marvelous Marvin," and he was selling a collection of carved masks and glass bottles. The bottles, he explained, were old liquor flasks from the colonial days, left in the country by its former conquerors. He held one up for me. "See this? From the British. Very old. Great souvenir. And this one, Dutch. Over a hundred years old!"

"Interesting. But I just arrived, don't really need any souvenirs yet," I told him. Instead, I said, maybe he could recommend a few sights around the city?

"Have you been to St. George's? You have to go to St. George's!" The cathedral was one of the city's premier attractions, he said, a picturesque church located just a few blocks from here. I promised him I'd go there shortly.

"So, the market, is it always that crazy?"

He grinned. "Just people havin' a good time mon. They just hangin' out and havin' fun. You know, in Guyana, there are no laws. There are no rules."

Heard in a vacuum, Marvin's words could have been worrying—a lawless, binge drinking town is no place for a tourist. And it was true that I had just spent several hours walking around the city without seeing a single other visitor. But my experience during that time, when I had been treated not with aggression or hostility but with a startling level of indifference, had aroused a different kind of fear. While grateful for the breathing room, I viewed the apathy as a bad sign for my future travels. Persistence is the result of competition, competition is the offshoot of success; nobody had tried to get me to take their brochure, to ride their bus, or to sign up for their tour—did that mean that those services didn't even exist? Was I on my own here in Guyana?

I left Marvin and followed his directions to St. George's Cathedral, a hulking wooden church occupying its own block in Georgetown's grid of streets. Despite its stature, it looked abandoned, and I had to search for a way inside. There was only one other family, an anxious mother with her two young sons, quietly kneeling, saying their prayers. I walked around the interior, through the pews and the altars, unbothered. Decaying pillows, meant for the benches, were scattered around the floor and loose wires dangled from the unplugged fans bolted to the wooden columns. Fluorescent lights lined the walls but they were turned off, allowing for the afternoon sun to filter in through the building's stained glass windows. Soon, the family left, and I was alone, left to marvel at Georgetown's primary tourist attraction all by myself. St. George's would be filled the next day, I was sure of that, as the carousers I had seen in the market tried to atone for their sins—wash, rinse, repeat. But on that Saturday afternoon, the church was empty, if not a bit eerie, and I embraced the tranquility for a few more minutes, sitting comfortably on a splintered back pew, a lone visitor, set to discover a country unknown.

I woke up the following morning, a Sunday, to the gentle sounds of church music emanating from a nearby chapel. The change in music from the previous day matched the change in mood; everything seemed much calmer, even sluggish, and when I went downstairs for my free continental breakfast, the employees seemed unprepared for my arrival. I was the first guest inside the air-conditioned buffet room and with the dishes still full, I hungrily helped myself to a Sunday feast: eggs, pineapple, watermelon, and three kinds of bread. I poured myself a cup of tea and sat down next to the pool, unfurling my map across the table.

My goal for the day was to head south, to Kaieteur Falls, the only destination worthy enough to warrant its own poster in the Georgetown airport. That distinction had led me to believe that it was Guyana's primary tourist highlight; it was also the only destination in the country I knew anything about—"The Highest Single Drop Waterfall in the World!"—so I figured it was as good a place to start as any.

According to my map, the falls, and the National Park in which they were located, were around two hundred miles from Georgetown. There seemed to be two viable transportation options: by river, down one of the country's largest waterways, the Essequibo, to one of its branches, the Potaro; and by road, south out of Georgetown, through Linden, Mabura Hill, and Mahdia, and terminating at a riverside village named Pamela's Landing. Knowing nothing about either route, I decided to pursue the road option first; it seemed the more practicable (that comforting word Jefferson, of course, had used in his instructions to Lewis and Clark) and, based on previous experiences with privately chartered boats, probably the more affordable. Judging from my interactions with the hotel employees over the past twenty-four hours, I was skeptical I'd be able to find any information at the Sleep-In International and so I folded up my map, finished my breakfast, and went outside to search for clues.

It was early, so the sun and the heat were still tolerable. I turned left out of my hotel, onto Brickdam Street, passing both the police station and the government buildings, and re-traced my steps to Stabroek Market, where, the previous day, I had seen large numbers of minibuses congregating haphazardly, patiently waiting for the appropriate number of passengers to justify departure. While the insanity of the market area had subdued significantly, it was still noticeably crowded—this time with a more transactional and goal-oriented Sunday crowd—and I wandered around the activity, searching for some sort of direction. The arbitrary organization of buses had led me to believe there was no primary depot, no information booth from which I could gather the necessary fare and schedule info. Each bus, however, conveniently listed both its departure and arrival destinations along with a corresponding number, and so I scanned these names, hoping to find one that aligned with the southern route I had outlined on my map.

After twenty minutes, I turned up a quiet side street and saw three buses idling on the side of the road, their destination clearly outlined in stenciled yellow letters: Mahdia, one of the final towns on my proposed route and located only a short distance from what I believed to be the water-borne gateway to Kaieteur National Park, Pamela's Landing. Surrounding the bus was an assortment of touts, vegetable peddlers, and one shirtless old man, clamoring uncontrollably. Hesitant to unveil my intentions to the scavenging vendors, I sidled up to a nearby security guard positioned in front of a fenced-in government building.

"So these buses go to Mahdia?"

"Yes," he replied.

"Does it take long?"

"No, not long." He was now grinning; I don't think these were questions he heard every day, much less from an American tourist.

"Are there any hotels down there?"

He pondered the question. "Yes, nice hotel. Right in middle of town."

I nodded, thanked him for his help, and walked down the cracked sidewalk, back to my hotel. How long it would take to get from Mahdia to Georgetown was anyone's guess; too much depended on the number of stops, the quality of the road, the condition of the vehicle. Still, it was my first real lead, so I grabbed my backpack, checked out of my room, and returned to the cluster of Mahdia-bound vehicles.

With bag in hand, I had transformed into a potential customer and was soon surrounded by a herd of opportunistic
touts, aggressively pushing me toward their respective vehicles. They were all talking rapidly, promising quick rides and
comfortable seating. I picked out the fullest bus, and therefore
the one most likely to depart first, tore my backpack away
from the grips of the other men, and hustled up to its driver.

"How much to Mahdia?"

"Cheap—$7,000," he answered, equal to about thirty-five
U.S. dollars and about the price I paid to get, via bus, to a destination 200 miles from New York City. Skeptical, I looked at
another passenger, already seated on one of the three bench
seats and asked, "How much did you pay?"

"$7,000."

"Everybody here pay the same!" came the screeching reply
of a woman sitting in the front seat. I handed my backpack over
to the driver, who crammed it under one of the backseats, and
climbed into the already crowded, Chinese-made, Toyota Hiace.

All the window seats were occupied so I took one in the
middle, between two men who looked to be in their twenties.
Besides a few women and one old man, the passengers were
mostly young males, wearing jeans and plain t-shirts. The
van, on the other hand, was garishly decorated; hip-hop decals
and replica Guyanese flags lined the interior. Above the door,
in green-stenciled lettering, was the command, "Only God I
Trust, All Others Pay Cash." A few minutes after I sat down,
the driver started the engine, signaling a soon-to-be expected
departure and igniting the high wattage stereo system that
would be our brash companion for the next nine hours. But
it was early, I was eager to get moving, and the initial sound
of Bob Marley exploding through the scratchy speakers made
me giddy: *"Don't worry . . . bout' a thing . . . cause every little
thing—is gonna be all right!"*

Outside, there was a minor ruckus, and our entire bus looked to the left to watch a potential customer being shoved toward the vehicle. The young man to my right started laughing, shaking his head in disbelief: "They fightin' over the fuckin' bag mon!"

Our final three seats were taken by ten cases of beer, stacked artfully and arranged systematically throughout the van—a design meant to maximize room and minimize potential damage. Loading the passengers' bags on top of the bottles, the driver slammed the back door, climbed into his seat, revved the engine, and slammed his foot against the gas pedal. We were on our way to Mahdia and through the vibrating speakers, Freddie McGregor bid us farewell:

"Big ship sailing on the ocean . . . we don't need no commotion."

INTERLUDE — LEWIS AND CLARK: TRANSPORTATION

My objective as I left Georgetown was clear: get to Kaieteur Falls. Thomas Jefferson's directions to Meriwether Lewis were similarly unambiguous: find a continuous, all-water route through the United States and to the Pacific Ocean. This clarity was expressed in the letter Lewis had written to Clark, asking him to join the expedition as co-commander:

> *My plan is to descend the Ohio in a keeled boat of about ten tons burthen, from Pittsburgh to its mouth, thence up the Mississippi to the mouth of the Missouri, and up that river as far as its navigation is practicable with a boat of this description, there to prepare canoes of bark or rawhides, and proceed to the Missouri's source, and if practicable pass over to the waters of the Columbia or Oregon River and by descending it reach the Western Ocean.*

In hindsight, the simplicity of the paragraph is almost laughable; he made the journey sound so easy. Lewis's vision was based upon the handful of geographical fallacies mentioned previously—that the middle of the country rose into a pyramidal height-of-land, that the Missouri ran down one side, and that the Columbia or the Oregon ran down the other. A cross-country route in Lewis's mind, therefore, would consist of a paddle up, a walk over, and a paddle down. If this vision of topographical symmetry seemed too good to be true, it was also too irresistible to ignore.

As it turned out, most of the travel was indeed done via watercraft. The expedition began with three vessels—two small pirogues and a larger keelboat, custom built for the expedition in Pittsburgh. Fifty-five feet long and capable of carrying twelve tons of cargo, the keelboat has been described by historian Donald Jackson as a "useful but ungainly craft," one that turned into a "little warship" when armed with a swivel gun and a gunman. It was practical for transportation and protection yet very difficult to move upstream. When there was wind, the men ran up the sail, benefitting from Mother Nature's generosity; if the wind was particularly strong, they could make twenty or so miles per day. But without the benefit of a breeze, the crew strained to use brute force, pushing the boat manually with iron-pointed poles. It was exhausting and dangerous work, compounded by the bevy of obstacles they faced on the Missouri River—whole trees, branches, sandbars, whirlpools.

After spending the 1804-05 winter at Fort Mandan, located in present day North Dakota, Lewis and Clark sent the keelboat and a small crew back toward St. Louis, while the expedition continued westward with six canoes and two flat-bottomed pirogues. The captains' plan was to use these boats until they reached the Great Falls of the Missouri, where they would abandon the larger pirogues and walk around the falls with only the lighter and more manageable canoes. Once past the rapids, Lewis would finally unveil his "Experiment," a collapsible iron frame boat that the expedition had been carrying since the beginning of the trip. The boat's skeleton, developed during conversations with Thomas Jefferson, weighed less than 200 pounds; when covered in animal hides, however, it was a veritable cargo ship, able to transport an astounding 8,000 pounds. Back on the water, the crew would be able to continue upstream confidently, no longer solely dependent on the smaller and less sturdy canoes.

Unfortunately, those plans never materialized. While the Indians at Fort Mandan, according to historian John Logan Allen, "had assured Lewis and Clark that the portage around the Falls was no longer than a half-mile," the true distance was far greater, and the navigation around the falls became, in Clark's words, one of the most "perilous and difficult" parts of the expedition. As the men hauled the crew's gear around the rapids, Lewis scrambled to prepare his iron frame boat for launch on the other side. While he was able to secure the animal hides necessary to cover the frame—thanks to twenty-eight elk and four buffalo—he had encountered an unfortunate arboreal setback. There were no pine trees in the region, meaning there was no way for Lewis to obtain the pitch pine needed to bind the hides together. His attempts at improvisation failed, and when the boat was tossed in the water, "she leaked in such manner that she would not answer." With wounded pride, Lewis acknowledged his miscalculations and reluctantly abandoned the boat; the Falls had already taken longer than expected and they needed to keep moving: "To make any further experiments in our present situation seemed to me madness; the buffalo had principally deserted us, and the season was now advancing fast."

In early August, the expedition, now traveling by canoe, reached the point at which the river they had been following began to change. It was shallow, it moved quickly, and its banks were crowded with dense brush. Pulling the boats upstream was grueling work and the men were forced to balance precariously on the slippery rocks lodged into the river's bed. Most of the crew "wished much that navigation was at an end that they might go by land," Lewis wrote in his journal. On August 10th, Lewis finally concurred, writing of his decision to abandon the boats and to proceed with the expedition on foot: "Here I halted and examined those streams and readily discovered from their size that it would be vain to attempt the navigation of either any further." Two days later, he climbed Lemhi Pass and viewed, for the first time, the western side of the Continental Divide and the seemingly impassable mountains that came with it. With that view, says Stephen Ambrose, "went decades of theory about the nature of the Rocky Mountains, shattered by a single glance from a single man." More immediate than the nation's geographical understanding, however, was the issue of transportation—how would the expedition cross these mountains? As Allen explains, "The short portage, fixed for so long in geographical theory, simply did not exist, and with this realization came the prospect of a long overland journey to reach navigable waters."

But there would be no complaining, no wallowing in grief or second-guessing or self-pity; the expedition's captains would not allow it. The Rocky Mountains were simply another obstacle, albeit a rather large one, standing between the expedition and its primary objective, and if the men couldn't float through the mountains, then they would have to walk over them. There was little panic or apprehension with Lewis and Clark, only a remarkable ability to "resolve the increasingly obvious disparities between what they expected to find and what they really found."

On August 13th, Lewis held the party's first meeting with the only people who could help—the Shoshone Indians and

their chief Cameahwait. As the captain explained in his journal: "I still observe a great number of horses feeding in every
direction around their camp and therefore entertain but little
doubt but we shall be enabled to furnish ourselves with an
adequate number to transport our stores even if we are compelled to travel by land over these mountains." A few weeks
later, the Lewis and Clark expedition, a Shoshone guide
named Old Toby, and twenty-nine horses set out over the
Bitterroot Mountains. The roads were, according to Clark,
"some of the worst roads that ever horses passed." One expedition member called the mountains "the most terrible mountains I ever beheld." The men grappled with the bitter cold of
the mountain air (Clark wrote: "I have been wet and as cold
in every part as I ever was in my life") while the animals struggled to find proper footing, often slipping and falling on the
icy slopes. Ambrose calls September 16th "the worst day the
expedition had experienced to date," with relentless snowfall
from dawn to dusk and steep terrain through which the men
had to maneuver an entire caravan of horses and gear. The
journey was a sharp departure from what Lewis had termed
a "practicable" route from the Missouri to the Columbia in his
initial letter to Clark; this route wasn't practicable, it was near
death-defying, through a region so demanding that much of
it remains rarely traveled even today.

And yet for any dedicated traveler, regardless of pace of travel
or vehicle of choice, there are few greater feelings than simply
making progress, be it up the mountain, through the forest, or
down the river. No passage illustrates this joy better than Lewis's
April 7th, 1805 journal entry as the crew packed up their belong-
ings after a long winter at Fort Mandan and prepared to resume
their journey west. Their fleet may have been small, the region
that they would be crossing may have been unknown, but the
Lewis and Clark expedition was moving on. And because of
that simple fact, they were happy:

Our vessels consisted of six small canoes and two large pirogues. This little fleet although not quite so respectable as those of Columbus or Capt. Cook, were still viewed by us with as much pleasure as those deservedly famed adventures ever beheld theirs, and I dare say with quite as much anxiety for their safety and preservation. We were now about to penetrate a country at least two thousand miles in width, on which the foot of civilized man had never trodden; the good or evil it had in store for us was for experiment yet to determine, and these little vessels contained every article by which we were to expect to subsist or defend ourselves. However, as the state of mind in which we are, generally gives the coloring to events, when the imagination is suffered to wander into futurity, the picture which now presented itself to me was a most pleasing one. Entertaining as I do, the most confident hope of succeeding in a voyage which had formed a darling project of mine for the last ten years, I could but esteem this moment of my departure as among the most happy of my life.

CHAPTER 6

✽ ✽ ✽

Mahdia

*T*en minutes into our journey from Georgetown to Mahdia, our bus got a flat tire and we pulled into a dusty mechanic's shop to get it fixed. After a half hour of standing in the blistering sun, watching the other Mahdia minibuses fly by, we rode off once again, and the canals, restaurants, and two-story wooden dwellings that had lined the road out of Georgetown slowly began to disintegrate into a dense layer of impenetrable bush that would remain our scenery for the rest of the trip. At noon, we reached Linden, a town I had initially targeted as a potential stopover on the way south but had dismissed due to its proximity to Georgetown. Our brief passage through its streets confirmed my decision; it looked like nothing more than a tourist-unfriendly commercial hub, with large Norwegian freighters lining the edges of the river.

Soon after Linden, we crossed the Wismar/Mackenzie Bridge, a modest span over the Demerara River that marked the end of the modern concrete highway we had been driving on since Georgetown. From here, only two hours into the trip, the road would get progressively worse and our progress would be slowed accordingly. Just after the bridge, the highway, still fairly wide, changed from concrete to clay and dirt, and the driver was forced to negotiate the potholes by weaving the bus left and right, often hugging the extreme edges of the road like a skier searching for the best snow.

Nothing changed for the next several hours as we bounced over the cratered road, and the only sight we had was of the thick jungle stubbornly trying to re-take the land by creeping onto the makeshift highway. We eventually reached Mabura, the next town on my map, where an ominous sign indicated that we were "entering the interior." The bus stopped and everyone was asked to check in at a one-room police station. There, a bespectacled man carefully wrote down both my name and nationality; we were on our way only a few minutes later.

Shortly past Mabura, we arrived at the banks of the Essequibo, the massive river I had noticed on my map earlier that morning. Pulling into the Mango Landing Ferry Crossing, our driver, guided by two shirtless teenagers, backed our bus onto the ferry to join the other cars. As we chugged across the river, I leaned over the railings of the boat, digesting my first real glimpse of the jungle's scale while the other passengers circled our vehicle, searching for a modicum of shade from the midday sun. I saw no villages, no signs of life whatsoever, and the monotony of the view quickly became apparent—green thickets of forest, gently leaning over the brackish water, continuing for miles both up and downriver.

After a half hour, the ferry spit us out onto the western bank and we packed back into the bus. The road was now much narrower, and the intruding branches and palm fronds made it feel as if we were driving through a dark green tunnel. The shallow potholes in the road were now giant inverted moguls, and the driver was forced to slow down to a near stop as the bus tipped into and out of the massive cavities. Twenty minutes later, we turned left onto a similarly dented path and drove up to a wooden building where the driver unloaded the ten cases of beers. I saw only two people at the site; it seemed odd to think they would be able to consume so much alcohol.

"It's a shop," said one of my fellow passengers.

"And they're able to go through that much beer out here?"

"Well," he said, "You know. Two beers here, two beers there. And then it's all gone!"

His answer, of course, was no help. But I had a guess. Throughout the trip, our bus had occasionally passed narrow clearings made by small roads weaving through the tangled branches, and leading to the glaring sight of giant, tree-felling machinery. While I had seen numerous logging trucks heading the opposite way, I had yet to see any men using this equipment to pillage the forest's valuable centuries-old trees. I assumed the process had progressed from the outside in and that the timber immediately off the road had been sufficiently stripped down years before, forcing the workers to venture even deeper into the opaque bush. And I assumed the beer was for them, during breaks, on the weekends, a taste of freedom in an otherwise dangerous, lonely, and demanding profession. My guess turned out to be partially correct—timber, in fact, was only part of the equation.

As we backed away from the shop, a one-legged man hopped out and climbed aboard a motorcycle. He teetered for a second, gaining his balance, and started the engine while motioning for a woman, who had also appeared from the building, to jump on behind him. They sped ahead of us, in the direction of the main road, but our bus soon caught up and as we rode past, we saw the motorcycle spinning its tires, stuck in a deep gummy mud pit. They were still trapped, unsteadily trying to will the bike up a hill, as our bus drove away, spraying the two riders with a cloud of coarse dirt.

Our arrival in Mahdia, the town I believed to be the proper gateway to Kaieteur National Park, resembled a kind of practical joke, a staged performance designed to juxtapose and contrast the natural scenery with an almost comic view of humanity. After eight hours of tedious landscape, mile upon mile of jungle, broken only by the fleeting sight of tiny, tranquil villages, we drove up a steep dirt hill and entered the frenzied energy of a boisterous celebration. Men and women wandered the streets, sipping beers and strolling through the rows of decrepit shacks that lined the road. Shopkeepers sat in dusty plastic chairs, standing guard over their wares— vegetables, toiletries, and alcohol. Children, some naked, scurried through the alleyways unsupervised, kicking empty soda bottles and teasing the feeble, feral dogs that picked through the garbage. And it was all accompanied by a bass-heavy soundtrack reverberating through the town, along with the periodic declarations of a baritone DJ and the feverish screams of an indulgent audience.

It was in the middle of this frenzy that I exited the bus and stared upwards at a sign that said, "RH Hotel and Restaurant." Earlier, the driver had asked me what hotel I was staying at; I had told him I wasn't sure and so he had dropped me here, in the middle of the town. For the second day in a row, I feared I would quickly become the center of attention, the only outsider foolish enough to wander through this chaotic village. But, like in Stabroek Market, I was once again left alone, and as I walked down a skinny alleyway toward my hotel, I received only perfunctory looks, glances that were soon averted elsewhere to more interesting and livelier subjects.

The RH Hotel and Restaurant was a pink and white two-story building, fronted by a spacious open-air lobby. Two bar-size pool tables flanked the entrance, surrounded by potted palms and cropped shrubbery. An empty, algae-speckled fish tank lay off to one side, while a fully stocked bar dominated an opposite corner. Two women sat in straw chairs. One watched the flat screen television that flickered on the wall while the other was hunched over a large accounts book, counting money. I approached the one with the book and inquired about a room; she bristled at the interruption.

"We have two rooms—$5,000 and $12,000," the woman answered curtly.

"What's the difference?" I asked.

Looking up, her large cheeks puffed out as she spoke. "The $12,000 is nicer." She paused, deciding whether to elaborate. "It has air-con."

Because of my limited funds, and the obvious lack of a bank (or cash machine) in this town, I chose the cheaper of the two. She handed me a key and waved me toward the spiral staircase rising upward from the front of the lobby. The people in the streets had been remarkably indifferent to my arrival, as if I had been dropped off unseen, an invisible outlier with white skin and a backpack. But this woman was different— she clearly did not like me.

I climbed the stairs, walked down the hallway, and unlocked the door to my room. Rows of ants scurried away upon my arrival. The room needed a proper scrubbing—the paint on the walls was cracking and the floor tiles had a shallow coating of perceptible grime—but the bed sheets looked clean and it had its own bathroom. It would do.

I dropped my bag and walked out to the balcony to get a better sense of the area. Looking to my left, I discovered the source of the town's soundtrack: a modern DJ booth, built at one end of a crowded pool, next to a building that looked like an updated version of my hotel. It was three stories instead of two, had similar colors but fresher paint, and its wooden doors had a shiny new layer of glistening varnish. A large crowd mingled around the pool, dancing and swimming and singing along with the music. Opposite the DJ booth was a covered pavilion, where a young woman with an ice-filled cooler served a large line of waiting customers. Adjacent to the pool was an enclosed trampoline packed with agile children bouncing off the walls, off the floor, and off each other. Empty beer bottles littered the area. It was a massive party, inexplicable due to its remoteness, and I asked a man who had joined me on the balcony if they did this every night.

"Nah. Only Sundays."

"What's it for?"

"You know," he said shrugging, "people are just enjoying themselves." It was an echo of Marvin from the previous day.

Turning away from the party, I looked down the alleyway from which I had come. Inside the perimeter of the hotel's fence was a small teal shack, no larger than the size of a starter's hut on a golf course. Written in crooked black paint were the words "Tattoo/Barbershop." In front of the hut, seven or eight teenagers stood around a folding table, throwing money into the center and playing what looked like a game of dominoes. Past the hut, enclosed in a chain link fence, were some chickens and a few goats, standing among scattered piles of refuse. To the right of my hotel, I could see several other buildings, including a school, a bar, and one two-story shack, its closed doors illuminated with the faint flicker of red light bulbs—the unmistakable calling card of the town brothel.

I looked outward, past the party and the dominoes and the chickens, trying to make sense of it all. Massive cliffs covered with bush lay just beyond the town's limits, heaving upwards to form rolling hills blanketed by forest. Compared to Mahdia, Mother Nature was silent, the usual cackling of the jungle drowned out by the insurmountable drumming of the DJ. It seemed impossible for this city to be here, so loud and so obvious, in such a remote part of the country. But it was.

With the sun quickly setting, I decided to do a lap through town to find dinner. I had assumed that nearly everyone was at the pool party, but I was wrong, and as I wandered through the town's rubbish-filled streets, I passed dozens of Mahdians relaxing on their stoops—blasting their own music, drinking their own beer, enjoying their own party. As before, they paid me little attention, and I continued my blatant voyeurism unmolested. I walked past carousing couples, Chinese-run convenience stores, and the town hospital, a ruffled banner on its fence advertising "World TB Day, March 24 2008." There seemed to be little order to this town—no configuration, no rules, no police, and certainly no tourist infrastructure.

Unable to find any open restaurants, I returned to my hotel, and desperate for food, asked the woman who had checked me in where I could find something to eat. She shooed me around the back of the building where next to the trampoline, I found a large building labeled "Kitchen Corner." Inside, a smiling old lady sat quietly, slowly rocking to the music. I asked her, pleadingly, if she had anything to eat. She nodded and fishing the food out of giant pots scattered throughout the kitchen, handed me a plate of fried chicken, rice, and macaroni. I paid her and stood at the counter, scarfing down the meal and watching the party unfold.

Kids did backflips into the pool, couples grinded seductively in the water, and groups of men sat contentedly, their tables full of empty bottles. As I finished my dinner, I attempted, once again, to digest Mahdia. On my way down, I had expected to find a quiet jungle outpost, a lazy backwater village with a hotel, a few simple restaurants, and a relaxed demeanor from which I could arrange and launch my trip to the waterfall. What I found instead was a scene out of a Las Vegas nightclub, an apparently lawless town run by villagers, indifferent to the arrival of potential tourists. I wanted to go to Kaieteur, but I also knew that I would have little chance of organizing anything today. So I bought some beer and retreated to my room, resigned to wait out the revelry.

JOURNAL ENTRY — MAHDIA

*Day 3—**Mahdia, Guyana:** My room in Mahdia is small and hot. I've positioned the fan against the window to circulate the air but it doesn't seem to be working. The jungle critters are relentless—I can't keep the ants off my backpack and just before I went in for the night, I saw a moth the size of a sparrow perched on the wall outside my bedroom.*

I've been to my share of strange towns but Mahdia might just be the oddest of the bunch. I can't help but wonder what the guidebook has to say about this place or whether it's even in there at all: "Enjoy Mahdia's nighttime booze-fueled parties; wander the streets playing cards and getting tattoos; end the night at its renowned brothel!" But if my map-reading skills are correct and this is indeed the way to Kaieteur Falls, then I would assume a certain number of travelers do pass through this town. It's also possible, of course, that I'm completely wrong, that there are other more direct ways to travel to the falls, and that I'm the only non-Guyanese visitor this town has seen in years. I have no idea.

For whatever reason, Mahdia intimidates me. And this intimidation is undoubtedly amplified by my lack of guidebook-related information—I know absolutely nothing about this place or the people who live here. Although I had been generally left alone as I wandered through the streets tonight, I'm still uneasy around this much energy, this much alcohol, in a town I know to be cut off from the rest of the world by miles upon miles of endless jungle. It's one thing to be so far from home, that much I can handle. But it's quite another to be ignorant as to how to get home if I so desired—I have no idea if it's easy to return to Georgetown, the only Guyanese city I know to have an international airport. Perhaps buses run every hour from Mahdia; perhaps they run once a week. Regardless, tomorrow I will try and

*find my way to Kaieteur Falls. If that proves impossible, I'll
attempt to backtrack the way I came.*

*I've only been here for a few hours but I know that I
will never forget Mahdia. Arriving here was one of the most
unexpected and memorable traveling experiences I've ever
had. But I also can't wait to leave.*

I could still hear music when I woke up, but like the previous
day, the thumping bass had been replaced by the lofty inspiration of Christian soul. I pulled the curtain away from the
window and realized that the house from which the music
was coming was located a mere ten feet from my room. The
view from my window was straight onto their balcony, where
a naked baby toyed with a frisky brown puppy.

My plan for the morning was to move fast, figuring out
the quickest and most efficient way to Kaieteur Falls. Walking past the hospital I had stumbled upon the previous evening, I was grateful to see a few signs of normalcy returning to
Mahdia's streets. Energetic children, in full uniform, skipped
to school alongside their friends while toothless old women
picked up beer bottles and swept the area in front of their
stores. Just past the hospital were four large buildings positioned around a circular grassy knoll—the apparent business
center of Mahdia proper. The first of the four, a gray two-
story structure, was labeled "Police Station." The downstairs
door was ajar, so I walked in and found two men sitting at a
table, each one of them holding a mobile phone and casually
glancing at the television to their right. They squinted toward
me warily, avoiding direct eye contact.

"Morning," I smiled. "I wonder if you can help me—I'm
trying to get to the falls."

They barely moved. "Which falls?" one of them asked. *So
much for the country's iconic landmark*, I thought.

"Kaieteur. I was hoping to get a guide to take me there."

The officer turned his attention back to the television. "You need an aircraft."

"An aircraft? From Georgetown?"

"No, from here."

This surprised me; I hadn't seen a landing strip or a helipad anywhere. "I can take an aircraft from here? Like a helicopter?"

"No," the second officer replied brusquely. "An aircraft."

Aircrafts were usually pretty expensive, chartered aircrafts even more so. I tried a different method. "Well, what about a boat? Can I take a boat?"

"You can take a boat. You need to go to Pamela's Landing."

The landmark I had seen on my map next to the river; this was progress. "So I can rent one there?" I asked.

"Yes." Their eyes were now both directed toward the table, their hands rapidly typing on their phones.

"Great. Can I walk to the dock?"

"No, you have to take a taxi."

"How long is it?"

"About forty-five minutes."

"And the boat takes me to the falls?"

They exchanged looks and mumbled a few sentences in Creole. "No, you need to walk to the falls." The second officer's phone rang, and he turned away from the table to take the call. Left alone, the first officer decided to wrap it up.

"It's better to arrange from Georgetown," he said, the abruptness and finality of the declaration effectively ending the conversation. I stood there momentarily before turning around and walking out of the door.

I left the police station discouraged, fearing I would have to retrace my steps all the way back to Georgetown only to return to Kaieteur in a chartered airplane. The process seemed like a tremendous waste of both time and money. While it was still early, it had been an inauspicious beginning to the day. Passing by a wooden building labeled "Kitchenette," I decided to interrupt my search with some breakfast and to consider my options.

The restaurant had only three tables. A woman and a child sat at one of them, wearily watching an English-language DVD playing on a television crammed in the corner. *"This is the Water Life Cycle,"* it blared, before launching into a song, *"PHO-TO-SYN-THE-SIS!"* I slid my way past a few chairs, and asked the man in the kitchen if he had any breakfast. He waved his hand over the plastic-encased food that rested on the kitchenette's counter. I asked him what he recommended and he pointed to a mound of fried fish, his hand shooing away the flies that danced around the pile. "Fish and mashed eddoe," he said smiling. "Power breakfast!"

I sat down at one of the open tables and the man brought me my meal. The fish reminded me of Chinese sweet and sour chicken, the eddoe looked like mashed potatoes but tasted more like cassava, and the sugary tea, scalding hot and smoking, had bits of dehydrated milk floating on its surface. As I picked translucent fish bones out of my teeth, I asked the woman seated at the other table if the fish had been caught in Mahdia. "No," she said, chuckling. "It's sent from Georgetown. It's too hard to catch fish around here."

The woman turned out to be the wife of the owner and the mother of the seated child; she was also the first truly helpful person I had met in Mahdia. The family seemed unbothered by my presence, and so I lingered in the restaurant, sipping my tea, chatting with the woman about my trip, and watching the DVD. The program was called the "Guyana Learning Channel" and it starred an enthusiastic American volunteer reciting basic schoolbook concepts. *"Remember, 30 days have September, April, June, and November!"* I asked the woman if she knew how to get to the falls.

"Which falls?" she asked.

"Kaieteur," I said.

She breathed deeply and rolled out of her seat, snatching her mobile phone from a kitchen shelf. "Let me try something," she said. After a few calls, she sighed again. "All voicemails," she announced. Her final recommendation came after a moment of thought: "Have you tried the regional office?"

I had seen the regional office earlier that morning—it was the largest building of the four located around the grassy circle—but discouraged by my experience at the police station, had chosen not to enter. Now, energized by my meal and encouraged by the woman's advice, I decided to give it a try.

The building stood across from the police station, and with its fleet of vehicles and eight-foot-fence, exuded an aura, at least relative to the rest of the neighborhood, of administrative power. There was, however, no guard, and I walked unhindered into an open door labeled "Accounts." The interior looked like a bank, with partitioned glass windows separating the customers from the employees and their desks. One woman stood at the window to the left, conducting her business with another young woman behind the glass. When both turned to look at me, I apologized for the intrusion and asked if they could help me get to the falls. The woman behind the glass thought for a minute before directing me outside and up the stairs, indicating that a different division of the regional office might be able to help.

Upstairs, inside the "Superintendent of Works" office, I found two smartly dressed men, busily scribbling on a stack of hole-punched papers. They quickly dismissed my inquiries, directing me next door, to the "Personnel Division," where four additional workers were lined up in a row of contiguous desks. All four stopped working and looked up as I entered the room.

"Good morning," I began as they all stared at me. "I was wondering if you could help me get to Kaieteur Falls." They began to chat amongst themselves, discussing various options, until a wiry Indian man, dressed in baggy slacks and a blue button-down shirt, turned to me and said decidedly: "You need to talk to Gottfried." There was certainty in his statement, as if this was the only option, and the rest of the workers nodded approvingly, returning to their work. I asked the man if he could help me locate this Gottfried and he agreed, motioning me to follow him downstairs and out into the street.

The sky had turned dreary and it began to drizzle as we walked back into the main part of town. The man walked fast and I hustled to keep up. He looked like a classic paper pusher, someone who would have blended seamlessly into any company's accounting department. He was also a man of few words. To break the silence, I asked him if the town received a lot of tourists. "Oh yes," he said. "We had one just last week."

We hurried up to the town's only gas station where a gray pickup truck was parked on the street in front of the tanks. My companion tapped on the tinted window of the driver side door until it slowly lowered, revealing a hefty black man with pockmarked cheeks, gold teeth, and a flat-brimmed baseball cap. He stared straight ahead, through the windshield, as my escort explained the situation. As the sky darkened and the rain increased, the office worker excused himself, while the stoic man behind the wheel motioned for me to enter: "Get in," he said, and I climbed in through the passenger side door.

The man's name was Trevor. He spoke confidently yet tersely, and his answers to my questions always contained the minimum amount of necessary information. While we talked, his head remained on a constant swivel, his eyes scanning the people congregating outside, as if a better, and more profitable, conversation was just around the corner. His presence was designed to project swagger—through his hand motions, through his designer sunglasses, and through the rolls of money tucked visibly into the truck's middle console.

The experience should have been intimidating, that's what he would have wanted, but the exaggerated delivery made it comical instead.

"So I was hoping to find somebody to take me to the falls," I said. "Do you know Gottfried?"

One of his hands remained on the steering wheel; the other held a mobile phone. Unlike the paper pusher, who had a slight British twang, Trevor spoke in severely broken English, and his thick accent made it difficult to understand. "You need a guide mon. And a boat."

"Okay. Can you help me get them?" I asked.

"You need to charter the boat, a private trip. I can help—it will cost you $20,000." He paused, probably to gauge my interest. But I stayed silent. "I don't know about the guide—we need to talk to him."

"Okay, so where's the guide?" I asked.

Trevor indicated that his house was fifteen minutes away, down the road toward Pamela's Landing. I asked how I was supposed to get there. "I can take you," he replied.

We pulled out from the gas station, passed the police headquarters, and drove down a heavily cratered mud road. These were Mahdia's suburbs, sporadic houses situated well off the main path. After fifteen minutes, Trevor pulled the truck to the side and honked the horn. A compact shirtless man come scurrying out from a lopsided dwelling about a hundred feet away, shielding his eyes from the rain and jogging up to my window. Unlike Trevor, he had Indian features, and his accent was even more pronounced.

"I am Soldier," he said to me, before rapidly exchanging words with Trevor about the opportunity. They explained the route to me as follows: We'd go down to Pamela's Landing where we'd take a boat to a jungle village called Amatuk. From Amatuk, we'd take a different boat to the bottom of the falls. From there, we'd hike to the top of the mountain for a view of Kaieteur. Where we'd sleep would depend on our timing and the weather—there was a guesthouse on the top of the mountain that could accommodate us but if we moved fast enough, we might be able to sleep back at Amatuk. The whole trip would take less than two full days.

After conferring with Soldier, Trevor explained that the guide service would cost $30,000—about $150 U.S. I tallied the costs so far, wanting to make sure that, through all this back and forth, I understood everything perfectly. Throughout the entire negotiating process, my biggest fear was that I would run into unexpected but unavoidable costs. There was no way to get money in Mahdia, and I still needed to buy a bus ticket back to Georgetown.

"Okay," I said. "So that's $20,000 for the boat and $30,000 for the guide, right?"

"Yes," said Trevor. "And $8,000 for gas."

"And the $20,000 includes the boat to Amatuk and from Amatuk?"

"No, you have to pay for boat back."

"And how much is that?"

"Around $4,000." That made no sense; the boat there was nearly fives times as much as the boat back.

"And what about the boat from Amatuk to the base of the falls?"

Trevor looked at Soldier, asking him the question in Creole. "No charge," he said.

"And the boat from the base back to Amatuk?"

"Same," Trevor said. "No charge."

"So $20,000 for the boat to Amatuk, $30,000 for the guide, $4,000 for the boat to Pamela's Landing, and $8,000 for the gas. And that's it? No other costs?"

Although they both shook their head, I remained skeptical, and as I tried to figure out if I had enough money to proceed, I worked in additional budget to compensate for unforeseen expenditures. I had brought about $500 U.S. down to Mahdia, in a combination of U.S. and Guyanese dollars. Nobody took credit cards and from what I had seen of the town, there would be no way for me to get additional money. I had already spent some on food and lodging and Trevor and Soldier were quoting me prices that totaled up to around $310. Besides the additional costs I knew would pop up, I would also have to get a room when I got back, eat, and pay for the minibus back to Georgetown. Going to Kaieteur would leave me with limited funds, but it had been the reason I had traveled all this way; it was pointless to turn around now.

It was now pouring, the rain clattering on the top of the truck, and they both wanted an answer. "Fine. I'll do it," I said.

Fifteen minutes later, Trevor, Soldier, an unknown passenger we picked up, and I were lumbering down the jagged path to Pamela's Landing. Halfway through, as expected, Trevor mentioned that while he was happy to take me to the dock for free, I would have to pay another $5,000 for Soldier. Angry, but unwilling to derail the entire trip, I relented and paid the fee. Content (and possibly surprised) to have gotten extra revenue from the deal, he agreed to pick me up the following day for no charge.

Shortly thereafter, we arrived at Pamela's Landing. The grand entrance to Guyana's premier tourist attraction was little more than a rugged patch of riverbank downhill from a collection of half-built buildings. In the water bobbed a small fleet of weathered boats; on the shore stood a few curious loiterers. One man, holding a small toy car that doubled as a stereo system, provided the music, while two others stood to the side, attentively studying a newspaper. Down below, attending to a modern outboard engine, was the enigmatic Gottfried. Soldier explained to me that he was Trevor's father-in-law. He was also my boat captain.

I stood on the banks of the river, watching Soldier and Gott-fried load up the boat. Only a little more than $100 remained in my wallet, and I couldn't help but feel a bit anxious about the return journey. Without the use of a guidebook, I had fig-ured $500 would have been plenty for a few days' excursion, or that there would be some way to pay for this trip using other means. At the very least, I knew I should have haggled. Unfortunately (for me), haggling was a tactic I vehemently abhorred. It's not that I had never negotiated while traveling; I had done so many times. It's just that I hated the ambiguity of the practice and was often fearful, almost always irrationally so, that these frequently contentious negotiations would lead to a disruption of the trip. Disruptions led to diversions, diver-sions led to missed opportunities, missed opportunities led to a suspension of the original, carefully structured itinerary. In Mahdia, there seemed to be only one way to Kaieteur Falls; Trevor and team, then, held all the cards. When he said the boat cost $20,000, I should have said, "How about $15,000?" But I didn't. I suppose I was afraid (again, irrationally so) that Trevor's retort would have been, "Forget the whole thing," and so I simply nodded in agreement. My reluctance had clearly been a mistake; I hoped I would not regret it.

As we pulled away from the dock, Soldier pointed ahead, to a curved summit boldly emerging behind the rows of green hills. "We sleep on that mountain tonight," he whispered.

INTERLUDE — LEWIS AND CLARK: TRADE

Lewis and Clark's own monetary miscalculations, unlike my own, were somewhat offset by the unlimited letter of credit that had been provided to them by Thomas Jefferson. As they traipsed across the continent, the explorers used this letter of credit freely and often, racking up debts that far exceeded the government's initial estimate for the journey. And although it is difficult (if not impossible) to calculate the exact cost of the expedition, one document sent to Lewis in July 1807 by a government accountant pegs the total expenditures at nearly $40,000—approximately sixteen times the original estimate of $2,500. Regardless of its success, it had undoubtedly been an expensive journey.

Before leaving, Lewis and Clark did their best to secure what they believed to be the correct form of currency (or currencies), namely, items or goods that could help them trade their way through the continent. To that end, nearly seven hundred dollars of the initial $2,500 estimated for the trip had been specifically earmarked for "Indian presents," gifts meant to placate, both politically and economically, the tribes they would meet along the way. And thanks to his shrewd understanding of previous Indian encounters, what historian James P. Ronda describes as an impressive "grasp of frontier economics," Lewis had some specific ideas about what to bring. At the top of his list were blue glass beads, an item that was "far more valued than the white beads of the same manufacture and answered all the purposes of money." Brass buttons and red-handled knives were next, as were axes, tomahawks, tobacco, and face paint. These items were then separated into twenty-one individual care packages, each one assigned to a specific tribe or chief along the way. And yet, despite Lewis's supposed knowledge of the frontier market as well as the careful organization of the goods, the explorers, as they set off from St. Louis in May 1804, remained leery about the size of their haul. As Clark wrote in one journal entry, the inventory was "not as much as I think necessary for the multitude of Indians through which we must pass on our road across the continent."

He was right. As the expedition made its way toward the Pacific Ocean, trade supplies dwindled and the men were forced into constant haggling. At first, those involved found the bargaining amenable, with both the Americans and the Indians benefitting from the transactions. Lewis's journal entry on August 18th, 1805, as the expedition bartered for horses with the Shoshones before crossing the Continental Divide, reflects this reciprocity: "I soon obtained three very good horses for which I gave a uniform coat, a pair of leggings, a few handkerchiefs, three knives and some other small articles the whole of which did not cost more than about $20 in the United States. The Indians seemed quite as well pleased with their bargain as I was." The sellers, however, would prove to be quick learners. As Ronda explains, "Shoshoni traders soon learned that they could get much more if they bargained more sharply. . . . With the rate of exchange for horses now changing, Lewis was compelled to offer a battle-axe, a knife, a handkerchief, and some paint for one horse. For a Spanish mule, valued for its surefootedness, the American had to add another knife and some clothing."

Unfortunately, the economic climate would only get worse. Many of the Indians located on the other side of the mountains (i.e., closer to the Pacific Ocean) had traded with Europeans for years; they had therefore become skilled negotiators, adept at monetizing demand. Prices offered by these Indians were often two or three times the item's actual worth. And it's not like the expedition had quality goods with which to barter. Ronda again: "Gone were the calico shirts, brass combs, and 'small cheap looking glasses' that so charmed the Indians up the big river and across the Great Divide. What remained was a motley collection of fishhooks, brass wire and armbands, moccasin awls, worn files, and beads of various colors." The inventory was so lean, in fact, that many expedition members began ripping the brass buttons off their own clothing, having recognized the value the items could fetch on the open market.

When it came time to pack up and return east, then, the expedition found itself at the mercy of a fickle and demanding commercial partner. A series of journal entries by Clark in the middle of April 1806 illustrates the difficulty the expedition had in securing the horses needed for the return journey over the treacherous Rocky Mountains. In one entry, William Clark, renowned war veteran and one of the greatest explorers the world has ever seen, is reduced to a cheap market peddler, laying his goods out on a rock in preparation for a long day of negotiation:

> *I rose early after a bad night's rest, and took my merchandise to a rock which afforded an eligible situation for my purpose, and at a short distance from the houses, and divided the articles of merchandise into parcels of such articles as I thought best calculated to please the Indians, and in each parcel I put as many articles as we could afford to give and thus exposed them to view, informing the Indians that each parcel was intended for a horse.*

When the men weren't peddling their goods, they were hawking their talents. During the expedition's winter stay at Fort Mandan in 1804-5, a brisk blacksmith business run by Private John Shields proved to be the antidote to the camp's shrinking meat supply as the Indians traded corn for the mending of their hoes and blades. When that business dried up, the men capitalized on demand for a line of coveted battle-axes. Lewis summed up the contribution of Shields and his colleagues in a February 6th, 1805 journal entry: "The blacksmiths take a considerable quantity of corn today in payment for their labour . . . I believe it would have been difficult to have devised any other method to have procured corn from the natives."

In another journal entry, Clark demonstrates his own economic improvisation, channeling his modest medical experience—something he would do frequently over the next few weeks—to soothe the back pains of a certain chief's wife (described in the passage as "a sulky Bitch"): "This I thought a good opportunity to get her on my side giving her something for her back. I rubbed a little camphor on her temples and back, and applied warm flannel to her back which she thought had nearly restored her to her former feelings." Recognizing the gratitude of both wife and husband, Clark used the opportunity to trade the chief for two horses.

But the expedition's patience with these kinds of negotiations eventually grew thin and the men—short on currency, far from home, and unable to flaunt their unlimited letter of credit (the promise of U.S. government remittance meant nothing to most Indians)—succumbed to uncharacteristically devious measures. In a March 17th, 1806 journal entry, Lewis rationalizes a particularly brutish incident—the theft of a canoe from the Clatsop Indians—by referencing an episode in which the Indians had reportedly stolen elk from the Americans' camp: "We yet want another canoe, and as the Clatsops will not sell us one at a price which we can afford to give we will take one from them in lieu of the six elk which they stole from us in the winter." Calling the decision "at worst criminal and at best a terrible lapse of judgment," Ronda chides the explorers for their decision, suggesting that patience rather than deceit would have been more fitting for men of their supposed high character: "The essential honesty that distinguished Lewis and Clark from explorers like Hernando DeSoto and Francisco Pizarro had been tarnished."

What had led to this unexpected moral lapse? Most likely it was the desperation of travelers worried about the absolute essentials—food and transportation. As Lewis wrote several months after this incident, "Having exhausted all our merchandise we were obliged to have recourse to every subterfuge in order to prepare in the most ample manner in our power to meet that wretched portion of our journey, the Rocky Mountains, where hunger and cold in their most rigorous form assail the wearied traveler." It's not that the men had brought the wrong kind of currency—the Indians were more than happy to trade for blue beads and tobacco—it's that they simply had not brought enough. And when their inventory ran out, Lewis and Clark did whatever it took to keep their journey alive.

CHAPTER 7

❦ ❦ ❦

Kaieteur

I had chartered a boat to take me from Pamela's Landing to Amatuk, the village situated immediately before the route's first impassable set of rapids, but it turned out to be more of a shared taxi, and after twenty minutes of steady progress, our boat sputtered into a sloping dock to drop off the man who had been traveling with us, his three rubber hoses, and his two sacks of fresh vegetables.

Only forty minutes later, we reached Amatuk, and Gottfried turned the boat back downriver and sped away, his lucrative job finished, while Soldier and I grabbed our equipment and scrambled up the dock's hill. "We have to get an engine," Solider said as we entered the tiny settlement. He led us up toward the town's largest building, said a few words to the woman sitting on a chair outside the door, and motioned me to come inside. "In here, you buy something to eat," Soldier advised as he crouched down to examine an idle outboard engine.

It was a surprisingly tidy house, neatly swept, with rows of children's shoes placed obediently next to the living room's circular rug. But it was also a store, with a shop window built directly into the living space immediately to the left. I walked over to the counter and saw long shelves of dusty nonperishable goods for sale—soda, biscuits, rice. Unaware of the plan for food, I bought a packet of chocolate biscuits, enough to get me through the next two days if necessary.

Soldier emerged from the house with the 150 pound, twenty-five horsepower outboard motor slung over his shoulder. "Let's go," he said. "Take the bags." Grabbing both our backpacks and the container of fuel, I followed Soldier down a narrow dirt path through the jungle, watching as he struggled to keep the engine balanced between his arm and head. Midway through, he stopped, panting, and leaned the engine against a tall dirt mound. He instructed me to hold it steady while he hustled back to Amatuk to enlist additional help for the difficult portage. He returned five minutes later with a man from the village who hoisted the engine onto his shoulder and continued confidently down the trail. Soldier and I divided the equipment I had been carrying and followed behind.

We caught up with the man at the end of the path, a primitive sandy landing dotted with empty soda bottles and frayed clumps of rope. Soldier and the man dragged a canoe down from a small ledge and into the water, attaching the engine to its stern. I did my part by tossing our bags and the fuel into the boat, making sure to avoid the puddles of rainwater that had collected on its floor. Soon, we were on our way once again.

As we progressed farther upriver, the scenery began to change. The uniform walls of dark green jungle that had flanked the route to Amatuk had been replaced by rocky cliffs looming threateningly above dense thickets of forest, their coarse outlines reflecting sharply off the shimmering surface of the river. Just as I began to settle in, watching the birds flutter from one side of the river to the other, Soldier pointed to a cracked wooden sign, hung uncertainly on a thick tree trunk and partly shielded by the sprawl of the jungle's growth. It said, "Welcome To Kaieteur National Park."

We glided into another makeshift dock and Soldier instructed me to repeat the process we had performed earlier—bags out, engine off, find another boat. We had

arrived at the Waratuk ranger station, the apparent entrance
to the National Park, but it looked deserted and we continued
past the building to a small landing on the other side of the
rapids. "This is the National Park boat," Soldier said, pointing to a metal canoe angled up onto the shore. "It's the only
one here—we have to take it." Returning to the first landing,
Soldier again heaved the engine onto his shoulder, and carried it to our new ride; I dutifully followed, carrying our bags.
Second portage completed, Soldier revved the engine, and we
zipped away from Waratuk.

My first glimpse of Kaieteur Falls came only moments later
when, rounding a bend in the river, Soldier pointed ahead to a
barrage of green cliffs. Above the trees, I saw the topmost section of the waterfall thundering down into an unseen canyon
below. My first view of Kaieteur! But the moment was fleeting and Guyana's (supposedly) greatest tourist attraction was
soon cloaked once again by the towering cliffs and opaque
bush. Shortly thereafter, we arrived at Tukei, a man-made
clearing from which visitors began the hike up the mountain
to the top of the falls. Soldier tied the boat to a tree, hid our
extra fuel in the woods, and pointed to a dirt path that rose
crookedly into the forest. We strapped our bags to our backs
and begin the climb up.

The route was steep and damp, and I struggled to keep my
balance over the slippery, moss-covered rocks. The humid-
ity of the enclosed jungle, combined with the weight of my
pack, was a dewy combination, and my entire body was soon
covered in a thick layer of sweat. Soldier hadn't told me how
long we would be walking and the unfamiliar forest mock-
ingly transformed into a perpetual tease; I would often think I
heard the falls, only to stumble upon an inconspicuous creek,
pounding audibly against a handful of boulders. An hour and
a half in, Soldier mercifully told me that we had reached the

top of the mountain, and that the route, from there on out, was flat.

Apart from the poster in the airport, and my momentary peek from the river, I had never seen an image of Kaieteur Falls. So, when we turned off the main trail and emerged onto a clearing overlooking a torrent of water billowing down a 700-foot cliff, it was the closest thing I would ever come to "discovering" one of the world's natural wonders. It was an extraordinarily rewarding sight, especially after the minibus, the taxi, three boat rides, two portages, and a two-hour hike, and I crept to the edge of the cliff slowly, trying to interpret the scene's scale and magnitude. The indigenous name of Victoria Falls, another of the world's most famous waterfalls, is translated as "the smoke that thunders." But I thought Kaieteur had more of an incessant whooshing sound, its root beer colored water plummeting over the edge to create small wisps of placid fog.

Mostly, I marveled at the solitude. Rarely do travelers arrive at a sight as spectacular as this, unprompted and unaware of what they are going to see or what they are going to discover; even more rarely does that experience occur alone, the entire panorama revealed to them specifically. It was a real moment, the kind many travelers yearn for, and as I stood at the top of the falls, I watched the water race down the canyon to the navigable portion of the Potaro River, tracing the route we had traveled to get here.

Dark clouds began to dim the once bright sky and Soldier indicated that we needed to get moving. I followed him away from the cliff, through the trees, down a different path than the one from which we had come. Just as the heavens began to open, we arrived at the Kaieteur Guesthouse, and Soldier and I scrambled up the stairs to its covered deck as the scenery behind us exploded into a thunderous afternoon rainstorm.

Soldier hurried around the back of the building, unlocking the front door from the inside out, and I dragged both our bags into the guesthouse. The front room was unexpectedly spacious and surprisingly welcoming. There was a large dining room table with straw placemats aligned symmetrically around its edges. In the corner was a smaller reading nook, where a guestbook lay open among scattered tourism brochures. A large map of Guyana hung on one wall, while posters of regional animals hung on another. I brought my bag into one of the bedrooms and changed into dry clothes. When I returned, Soldier was waiting with a fresh pot of hot water, a bottle of instant coffee, powdered milk, and a jar of sugar.

As I sipped my coffee, a young man appeared, introduced himself as Rubin and explained that he was the ranger of the Kaieteur Falls guesthouse. After struggling to speak with Soldier for the past several hours, I was grateful to discover that Rubin not only spoke perfect English, but also knew more about Kaieteur Falls than anybody I had met up to that point. He sat down at the table, and acknowledging the tranquility, I asked him if it was a particularly quiet day.

"Yeah, we usually get some visitors via airplane from Georgetown. They fly in, stay the night, and return the next day. But overland trips, like yours, are a bit more rare—we get maybe two or three of those a month," he explained.

I related my surprise at finding such a spacious lodge so close to the falls. "How many people can sleep here?"

"Probably around thirty," he said, pointing out the various places where visitors have hung hammocks. "But they'd be packed in like sardines!"

"How long has it been here?"

"Oh forever," he said. "It was built back in 1975. The Canadian Prime Minister told our government that he wanted to visit the falls. Since we didn't have anywhere for him to stay, they decided to build a guesthouse. They renovated it in 1999, adding a few rooms and updating the kitchen."

It was a strange story, and when I tried to verify it later, I couldn't find any information about the Canadian Prime Minister's trip to the falls.

The conversation turned to my vacation—why I had come to Guyana and how I had ended up at Kaieteur Falls. I explained that I had arrived overland through Mahdia. He laughed. "You know why they call it that right?"

"What, Mahdia? No why?"

"Because people go mad there," he said smiling. "It's a crazy place." He explained that the entire town was built upon the region's mining industry. Guyana was rich in both gold and diamonds and market prices were at exorbitant levels. There had therefore been a mini Guyana gold rush, with people flocking to jungle towns to set up shop and try their luck with the big mining companies. The party I had seen in Mahdia was a way for these men, forced to spend difficult weeks slogging away in the mountains, to unwind before going back to their laborious work. There were even some mines inside the boundaries of Kaieteur National Park.

"The park is actually one of the oldest in South America—it was established back in the 1930s. The government reduced it to 4.5 square miles in the 1970s to accommodate all the companies that wanted to set up mining operations. Then, in 1999, it was expanded to its current size of 224 square miles. But the mining companies were already here, so they were allowed to stay." The compromise made sense, both politically and economically—it had allowed the park to expand beyond its comically insufficient size in the hopes of attracting more tourists, while maintaining one of the country's only legitimate revenue streams. But having a practice as environmentally intrusive as gold mining inside a national park still seemed bizarre.

He asked where I planned on going next. "Not sure," I answered. "Have any suggestions?"

I unfolded my map of the region and handed it to him. He pointed to a spot just southeast of Mahdia. "Iwokrama is very expensive, but very nice. Lots of things to do there."

"How can I get there? Can I take a bus from Mahdia?"

He thought for a second. "No, I don't think so. You have to arrange from Georgetown I believe."

I saw Rubin glancing outside the borders of Guyana, to Brazil, Venezuela and beyond. I asked him if he knew what Suriname was like. He shook his read. "I don't. I've never been there."

It was getting late, the sun was setting, and the only food that Soldier and I had was the pack of biscuits I had purchased in Amatuk. Rubin explained that there was a small settlement built for the miners about twenty minutes away—Menzi's Landing, because only "men can find it"—where we could buy the ingredients for a simple dinner. He agreed to come with us, and as we walked, he became my de facto tour guide for the region.

The path was uneven, filled with murky puddles, and as we skipped from rock to rock, Rubin mentioned that I should keep my eyes peeled for snakes. "The ones that like to hide on this path," he said, "are poisonous. They can bite you four times before you even realize what's going on." As I scanned the ground with my headlamp, I asked him what other kind of wildlife lurked among the trees. "Oh, all kinds," he said. "Deer, foxes, tapirs. And jaguars, of course. There are six kinds of jaguars here at Kaieteur—but only three are danger-ous. One particular kind travels in packs, six to ten at a time, and they don't let anything get in their way. If a human is blocking their path, they'll attack it, all together."

Twenty minutes later we reached Menzi's Landing, a large, open-air building that once again demonstrated the remarkable Guyanese ability to turn any situation, no matter how desolate or how isolated, into a party. Four men were gathered around a pool table, drinking beer, while multi-colored disco lights flashed around the walls. American pop music blared from a large tube television, propped up on a cart at the far end of the room. In the corner was a giant cooler, filled with ice and several cases of bottled beer. Behind the television was the store, where I could see various items arranged neatly around the interior of a cozy kitchen.

Rubin lingered at the entrance to the building while Soldier and I bought rice, bouillon cubes, an onion, and a packet of something called "beef chiplets," described on the packaging as a "meat substitute." The total came to $1,700 Guyanese dollars and when the proprietor, Sammy, mentioned she had no change, I relented and dipped into my already limited funds, buying beers for Rubin, Soldier, and myself, and perhaps prioritizing camaraderie over fiduciary responsibility.

We took a different route back to the guesthouse, a path that found us walking down the concrete airstrip I had heard so much about the past few days. It was an idyllically clear night, with a perfect temperature, and being on the top of the mountain with only a few other people, surrounded by the jittery sounds of the encroaching jungle, was exhilarating. We walked side-by-side, sipping our Guinness, and I swiveled my headlamp into the shallow depths of the forest, asking Rubin to identify the different eyes shining back in our direction. I mentioned how much fun this was, this night safari, and how relaxing the experience was after the madness of Georgetown and Mahdia. "It's true," said Rubin pensively. "It's great to be up here—breathing the clean air of the mountains once in a while."

"So how did you end up here?" I asked him.

He shrugged. "I'm from a tiny village down by Iwokrama. I saw the opening for a tour guide in a newspaper and applied. I went to a few interviews and eventually got the offer. There were two years of training and then I was sent up here, to take care of the guesthouse and help visitors."

"How long ago was that?"

"Well, it's only been a year for this current assignment. But I was here before. I had left, done my time, and then they called me up and asked if I could come back. I figured why not."

I asked him what he thought about everything I was seeing—the National Park, Guyanese Tourism, the sustainability of Kaieteur Falls. He talked about visibility and accessibility, and how Guyana remained off the radar for all but the most determined visitors. "Kaieteur Falls is unknown to everyone except in a few countries, it's almost like a secret." The statement was neither a complaint nor a boast; it was simply an intelligent assessment.

We reached the guesthouse and Rubin wished us a good night, heading back to his own building a few dozen meters away. Soldier and I went to the kitchen to start dinner. I chopped up the onion while he prepared the rice and chiplets. While cooking, I thought about Rubin's situation. He had been one of the few people I had met in Guyana who understood tourism, sustainability, and conservation. He could articulate different aspects of the flora and the fauna, and he was truly interested and invested in the work. And yet the government isolated him in a house on the top of a mountain instead of in a more visible position, promoting the country and its tourism potential. The lack of visitors suddenly made a lot more sense.

JOURNAL ENTRY — KAIETEUR FALLS

Day 4—Kaieteur Falls National Park, Guyana: I can barely hear the waterfall from my room at the Kaieteur Guesthouse but it seems close, thick moisture hangs in the air. The sounds coming from outside are of the usual jungle variety—chitter chatter, chitter chatter, croak, groan, croak—and as I lie on the bed, I see streaks of moonlight illuminating the panels of wooden floorboard.

The events of the day keep me awake. I am fortunate to be here—fortunate to have had the opportunity to see a natural wonder as stunning as Kaieteur Falls, especially one I hadn't even known existed before this trip. I can only assume that it's a Guyana guidebook favorite—perhaps the cover photo— and that similar to other world wonders, it had received a pristine 5-star rating on various travel review websites.

What would I have rated Kaieteur? I have no idea—and what a ludicrous question anyway. What makes a waterfall worthy of a 5-star rating? Its height? Its seclusion? The volume of water pouring over its ledge? In all three of these categories, Kaieteur impressed—but trying to rank it among other waterfalls (Niagara, Victoria) or destinations (the Great Wall of China, the Pyramids) seems fruitless, irrelevant, and insufficient.

Still, extraordinary experiences unfailingly conjure similarly extraordinary experiences and as I lie awake atop this Guyanese mountain, the rain water from the wet clothes draped around my room creating a nostalgic ambiance— drip, drip, drip—I can't help but reminisce about other memorable traveling moments, all of which are, in the end, invariably compared to the greatest thing I've ever seen.

It occurred 18,000 feet up the Nepalese mountain Lobuche East during one of my (very) amateur mountaineering excursions. Our team of five was climbing alpine-style—no fixed ropes—and moving quickly after an early morning start from a camp halfway up the peak. Three and a half hours into the climb, exhausted and out-of-breath, we approached a ridge where a panorama of early morning Himalayan light engulfed the jagged horizon of snow-capped peaks in a spectral display of violet, magenta, and fuchsia hues. I stopped; we all stopped. And as I balanced on the ridge, my crampons dug tightly into the snow, I uttered under my breath: "That's the most amazing thing I've ever seen."

I think about that moment a lot, mostly because it's the only time in my life that I felt it necessary to verbally declare the almost unfathomable exceptionality of an experience (even today, it seems strange that I said something aloud—but I did). Part of what made the moment so indelible was its suddenness—for over three hours, I had been focused solely on moving my body up the mountain, staying in step with the rest of my team— left foot, right foot, breathe, left foot, right foot, breathe. So when we ascended the ridge and were granted a view of the horizon from which the sun had risen, the scene was abrupt, encompassing, immersive. The landscape through which we were traveling had undoubtedly provided similar jaw-dropping panoramas during the previous few weeks—hell, the entire Everest Base Camp trek is itself a giant panorama of mountain goodness—but this one felt different. It was an unforeseen and unforgettable prelude to the summit of Lobuche that, in retrospect, far exceeded any other moment of the climb.

And so part of me wonders if our first view of Kaieteur— when Soldier had rustled me out of a daze and pointed upstream to the waterfall peeking out behind the mountains— was perhaps more memorable than our time spent wandering around the top. Sure, the view had been brief, but I had been unprepared at that moment for even a fleeting glimpse. It was an unexpected tease, a small taste, but also, in a way, a confirmation of the worthiness of my trip.

I am reminded of Clark's exclamation upon seeing what he believed to be the Pacific Ocean for the first time— "Ocian in view! O! the joy!" And yet the expedition was not actually at the Pacific Ocean—they were at the Columbia

River estuary, twenty miles from the coast. But that, of course, wasn't the point.

All of which makes me wonder about travel and expectations and preconceptions and surprises and discovery. It also makes me wonder if maybe, just maybe, the way we approach travel—with our 5-star rankings and destination highlights—is inherently inefficient and that perhaps anticipated grandeur, the kind we so often expect, can in fact be surpassed, and often is, by the abrupt glory of an unexpected glimpse.

I woke up the next morning to find Soldier in the kitchen, warming up what remained of the previous night's dinner. Unable to stomach a chiplets encore, I declined the offer of leftovers, accepted the offer of coffee, and finished off the remainder of my biscuits.

During our time together, I had learned what I could of Soldier's life. He had served in the Guyanese army, hence the nickname, but had become a tour guide soon after his service had ended. The first company he had worked for had taken advantage of him, pilfering most of the profits, and paying him only $5,000 ($25 U.S.) for two days of work. Unable to feed his wife and four children with this paltry income, he packed his bags, moved to Mahdia and began work in the mines. After only six months, he had made enough money to build his own house, which he constructed on an open plot just outside the main town. At some point, he agreed to continue work as a guide, this time for a different company and at a salary six times the previous rate. I had found him between assignments, and he had quoted me a per-trip price similar to the one he was paid by the tour operator. Since I had met Soldier, I had been searching for an appropriate word to describe him. He was respected, but not revered, friendly, but not endearing. Sometime that morning, I stumbled on the word that I had been searching for: capable.

While drinking my coffee, I leafed through the building's guestbook. It went back several years, and I noticed that even though I had found the place empty, the guesthouse had seen its fair share of visitors from all over the world. There were frequent mentions of two tour operators in particular, including the one that Soldier had said he currently worked for. But there were also a few visitors who wrote that they had done the trek "independently" and I wondered if their experiences had been similar to my own. One ironic theme infiltrated nearly every comment—the desire to keep the area around Kaieteur pristine and untouched by tourism.

While I scanned the comments, Rubin walked into the room and sat down in the chair next to me. He wished me good morning and asked if I had slept well. Then he got down to business. "I have to ask you a question," he said to me. "Did you come here with a guide service? Or did you come on your own?"

I sensed trepidation in his voice and admitted that I had hired Soldier alone, from Mahdia. "Okay, I thought so," he sighed. "That means that you need to buy a ticket to the park. People usually buy it in Georgetown, but since you're already here, you can buy it from me. And you also need to pay to stay in the guesthouse for the night. Together, it comes to $6,000."

It was another hit to my already deflated wallet, but I knew I had to pay. It was the right thing to do. Here was a guy trying to abide by the seemingly loose Guyana Tourism regulations, and he looked almost apologetic having to ask me for the fee. I filled out the necessary paperwork and he handed me a receipt, the first I had received since leaving Georgetown. We shook hands and I thanked him for the hospitality.

In the guestbook, I had read about a handful of Kaieteur Falls "must-sees," regional animals or particularly unique sights that were regularly encountered on the standard tour, and I asked Soldier to point them out to me, if possible, on the way down the mountain. We found one of them, the golden frog, almost immediately, sheltering next to a shallow pool of water inside a giant palm frond. We were less successful with the Cock of the Rock, a distinctive bird endemic to the region, but known to be more elusive. Perhaps recognizing his lack of guidance on the way up, Soldier continued the commentary voluntarily, pointing out the howl of a spider monkey, the footprint of a tapir, and the fresh droppings of a tree-dwelling sloth (although we somehow failed to spot the notoriously sluggish animal in the canopy).

Our boat was waiting obediently for us at Tukei and we jumped in, retracing our steps back to Waratuk and beyond. At the next stop, Amatuk, there was no sign of Gottfried (who Soldier had said would come and pick us up), so we paid the owner of the store $8,000 to take us back to Pamela's Landing. Midway through the journey, the skies blackened again, unleashing a brutal rainstorm far worse than the one we had walked through the previous afternoon. Our driver, determined to power through, sped the boat through the choppy water, forcing Soldier and me to crouch down in front, our heads between our knees, the sharp rain pelting our arms and legs.

Pulling up to Pamela's Landing, I was shocked to find Trevor already there, his pickup truck backed up gently to the edge of the water as he used the rain to power wash the mud-caked vehicle. We waved hello and scrambled uphill to the nearest covering, waiting out the rest of the downpour. When the rain finally subsided, Trevor drove by to pick us up. I noticed that his demeanor had changed significantly, from tough guy intimidator to concerned taxi driver, and on the ride back to Mahdia, he asked me multiple times if I had enjoyed the trip. I told him I had; it had been an exciting, albeit unorthodox tour.

As Trevor dropped me off at the hotel, taking the excursion full circle, I began to wonder how the guidebook would have steered me toward the falls. Did it recommend the uncomfortable mini-bus to Mahdia? Or Trevor's charter service to Pamela's Landing? It was unlikely. I guessed that the most recommended route involved one of the two tour services I had found in the guestbook. The most luxurious route would of course be the "drive-by" of the falls via the "aircraft" from Georgetown. But regardless of how circuitous or lengthy it may have been, my route, the one I had stumbled into, had been a success. It had allowed me to "discover" Kaieteur without significant preconceptions or buildup, and I knew I would remember the experience for the rest of my life. I could only hope that my subsequent guidebook-less forays would be as seamless and as rewarding as this one.

❧ ❧ ❧

Georgetown Again

*H*ow wonderful it was to be back in Georgetown, I thought, as I exited Minibus #42 and made my way toward the Sleep-In International. How nice it was to return to the comfortable environs of a city I had already navigated, one in which I could simply retrace my previous route. This segment would be a bit of a sojourn from my experiment, I decided, a brief lull in my commitment to guidebook-less travel.

And it was a break I desperately needed—it had been a brutal ride back. We had left Mahdia with only two other people and I had been able to secure a coveted window seat, comfortably positioned away from the constant stream of new passengers. It was a decision I would come to regret several hours later, however, when I was forced to choose between keeping the window open, and exposing the bus to mini cyclones of whirling sand, or slamming the window shut, and drowning us all in the suffocating heat of the Guyanese summer. The driver, meanwhile, had crammed the vehicle full of passengers—four people occupying each bench seat instead of the customary three. And when we finally arrived in Georgetown ten hours later, my arm was sore from holding on to the window's lever, my legs were cramped from angling them around the cases of beer, and my clothes were covered in a caked layer of mud.

After paying for a room and showering, I left my hotel in search of dinner. During my previous stay in Georgetown, I had stumbled upon an inconspicuous food cart, hidden among the side streets only a few blocks from my hotel. It was a humble operation, decorated with typical Rastafarian adornments—an Ethiopian flag, a Damien Marley poster, a frayed black and white picture of Haile Selassie. I had asked the owner to make me a plate of the day's offerings and he had filled a Styrofoam container with a generous pile of yellow rice, black beans, stringy beef, and mashed pumpkin. The meal was delicious, rich and filling, and I had been craving a repeat encounter during the entire bus ride back from Mahdia.

Unfortunately, I had failed to write down the cart's location and was forced to rely on my memory for directions, a strategy that failed miserably. I tried to visualize the route (left turn, right turn, left turn) but was soon lost, aimlessly wandering the roads between my hotel and Stabroek market. My surroundings grew increasingly grim, the setting sun making Georgetown, an already shadowy city, even more intimidating. And as I snaked through the narrow streets, all I heard was the faint drawl of Creole, the conceited roar of car engines, and the clink and clatter of empty beer bottles.

I knew the cart had been close to a building spanning an entire block and surrounded by barbed wire (a jail maybe? or a school?), but I began to realize that almost every building in Georgetown was, in fact, surrounded by barbed wire. After twenty minutes of searching, I found myself at least a dozen blocks from my hotel and decided to turn around, hesitant to venture too far and spooked by the emptiness of the night. Turning down a dark alley, back toward the general direction of the Sleep-In, I was approached by a young man on a bike.

"Yah buddy, where you goin'?" he asked, whispering. I ignored him and continued to walk. He tried again, a bit louder. "Yah buddy—where you goin'?"

"Back to my hotel."

"Where's that? Where's that?" he asked as he rode in circles around me. I walked faster, trying to piece together the quickest route back to my hotel. He circled a few more times before finally speeding ahead, disappearing around a corner. I exhaled and quickened my pace, turning onto a noticeably busier block where dim neon lights from the facades of rundown row houses flickered on groups of men drinking beer and listening to music. I was not supposed to be here, I thought, alone among the shady nighttime crowds of crumbling Georgetown. But I was, disoriented and noticeably vulnerable. About halfway down the block, I recognized the man who had approached me earlier, now off his bike, standing a few dozen feet ahead. Aware that abruptly turning around would attract unwanted attention, I decided to keep going, keeping my eyes peeled straight in front of me and maintaining a steady and confident stride.

But it was too late—as I attempted to slide past, the man grabbed both my arms and pulled them behind my back, motioning for his friends to come over and help. Struggling, I wriggled free from his grasp but was immediately grabbed again, this time by multiple men. The first attacker swung and hit me with a glancing blow across the face, telling me to be quiet, which I did, allowing the group that had gathered to rifle through my pockets, taking whatever they could find. One man slid his hand into my right pocket and ripped out my wallet, another pulled my left pocket inside out, dumping a few receipts and my hotel key onto the ground. And before I could compose myself, the men were running away back down the street, into the shadows, disappearing as quickly as they had appeared. I stood there, stunned, my heart racing, as the old homeless men, who had been sitting on the street a mere ten feet away, snickered.

After taking a few seconds to catch my breath, I hustled to the end of the block where I dishearteningly realized that the robbery had occurred a mere two blocks from the Sleep-In International and, shockingly, directly behind the main branch of the Georgetown police station. I jogged back to my hotel, exploded into the lobby, and began describing the incident to the two receptionists. Remarkably, the women actually stopped what they were doing this time to listen to my ramblings—but I knew their interest derived more from shock value than from actual concern, a kind of robbery rubbernecking. This presumption was confirmed only a few minutes later when, after explaining that I needed to make some calls to cancel my bank and credit cards, they insisted that I pay for a calling card with my few remaining dollars instead of using the main hotel line.

After canceling my cards, and knowing I had to report something to somebody, I reluctantly made my way next door to the police station, walking freely through the open barbed wire gates. It was only eight-thirty, but much of the station looked vacant. To my left, I saw a solitary officer standing guard in front of a cramped holding cell. To my right, a dim light illuminated an administrative office. I went inside and found several plainclothes officers seated at desks behind an elevated counter. Some of them were talking or texting on their mobile phones, the rest were conducting interviews. Nobody noticed when I walked in.

"Excuse me, I need to talk to someone. I've just been robbed," I said to a woman lying across two stools, her back propped up against the back wall. She looked up from her phone, aggravated by the interruption.

"You'll have to wait," she said, waving to the occupied workers at the desks. She motioned for me to take a seat against the wall but I declined, and instead asked her to find me outside when somebody was ready to talk.

I took a seat on a small concrete block and stared up into the black, starless night. Twenty minutes later, I was called back inside. "Somebody can help. Go upstairs," the woman said, pointing toward the back of the station where a door led into a faintly lit staircase. As I climbed the stairs, a young, baby-faced Guyanese police officer passed by, followed by three scantily clad teenage women. The officer's disheveled appearance, his shirt unbuttoned down to his midsection, and the giddiness of the women suggested the encounter had been something other than official police business.

The room upstairs was even dimmer than the office below. The space itself was large, with several partitions and half a dozen doors, but most of the desks were either unoccupied or permanently dormant. Only two of the doors were labeled—one, the "Listening Room," and the other, "Interview Room." The open windows allowed a faint breeze to flow through the otherwise dusty interior while a small television gently hummed with the sound of American hip-hop videos. Two men sat at desks, lazily flipping through tall stacks of paper. I stood in the doorway, waiting for directions, until one of the officers instructed me to sit down. Without looking up, he mumbled for me to begin.

I rehashed the story from beginning to end—where I was, what they had taken, what the men had looked like. As I talked, he repeatedly asked what I had been doing in the area. My answer, "It was only two blocks from my hotel and I was looking for dinner," was shrugged away. "They thieves mon. That the ghetto." Yes, I said. I understand that now.

As I wrapped up my tale, the officer slowly pulled a single piece of lined legal paper from the stack, picked up a disposable black ink pen, and asked me to start again from the very top—my name, my address, why I came to Guyana. From there, he proceeded to transcribe the entire experience, writing in a jumbled cursive that I found impossible to read. When finished, he picked up the paper and began to read: "I, David Bockino, of Jackson Heights, NY . . . was looking for the tofu cart . . . was approached by three Negroes." I nodded my consent, signed the document, and followed him downstairs to a waiting pickup truck; we were going to revisit the scene of the crime. "You never know," said the officer.

Both front seats were already occupied, so the policeman motioned for me to sit in the back, flanked by two additional officers. I led the way as we pulled out of the station, directing the driver around the corner and toward the exact location of the robbery. It had been only an hour and a half, but the streets had transformed—they were much quieter, sort of eerie, and the only sound I heard was the rumble of the truck's engine as it crept slowly down the narrow side road. Everybody had left the area except for four men in tattered clothes, sitting on a curb, drinking bottles of beer. The officer who had taken down my story opened the door and approached them. With the low light and gloomy facades, it looked like a scene from ghetto film noir, and I imagined the officer, silhouetted under a hazy light post, interrogating one of the frail drifters: "But I didn't see nothin' mon!"

The operation was unsuccessful, and after driving deliberately around the block, scanning the dark houses for clues, we returned to the police station. It had been a long day and I was exhausted. I asked if there was anything else that needed to be done; the officer told me that if they heard anything, they would find me at the hotel. I shook his hand and thanked him for his help.

JOURNAL ENTRY — GEORGETOWN

Day 6—Georgetown, Guyana: *It's karaoke night at the Sleep-In International, an irritating (and unavoidable) epilogue to the events of the past few hours. After my visit to the police station, I had used one of the hotel's calling cards to call my wife. I said I had been defeated—I had no money,* *no credit cards, no idea where to go for help—and was ready to abandon the experiment. But she convinced me to stay, to march on through this methodological hiccup, and so here I am, in my hotel room, penniless, listening to the grating melodies of 1980s American pop ballads.*

It was easy to link the robbery to my lack of guidebook material. Although I had earlier stumbled upon a culinary highlight—the Rastafarian food truck ("off the beaten path!")—I had failed to document its location. This lack of information led to the folly of idle wandering—idle wandering led to calamity. Lewis and Clark, being the efficient travelers they were, would have been disappointed in my actions, or lack thereof; they, obviously, would have taken celestial observations to mark the food truck's exact location.

But what happened today was not the guidebook's fault (at least not completely)—it was mine. Wandering through an unknown neighborhood in an unknown city past sunset, with a wallet full of cash and both my credit cards, was little more than a reckless decision. What the hell was I thinking?

I have been a remarkably lucky traveler, despite having had my share of risky encounters. In Kathmandu, a Nepalese man threw me through a door after he objected to something I said during a game of pool—a friend thankfully prevented the situation from escalating beyond a few haymakers. In Saint Petersburg, I narrowly avoided a pummeling after my two inebriated Dutch companions provoked a bar filled with unruly Russians. Other close encounters were less my doing—in Ahmedabad, India, I passed through a train station a mere twelve hours before a bomb took the lives of nearly sixty people. All these incidents occurred while traveling with a guidebook; only luck or quick thinking—not guidebook-related information—prevented them from being worse than they actually were. And although many guidebooks include sections on "Safety" and "Precautions

To Take Before Travel," advising the traveler what not to do in a certain region, they also include information on cities and countries the traveler may have never attempted to visit without their guidance in the first place. One guidebook, then, may tell me to protect my possessions on the New York City subway while another highlights the top destinations in Somalia. So there I am, preventing pickpockets by straddling my backpack and yet planning a trip to one of the world's most dangerous countries—"this Mogadishu hotel has a pool!"

In the end, I'm not sure what this robbery tells me about guidebook-less travel. It remains to be seen, for instance, what the guidebook spectrum has to say about the neighborhood in which I was robbed; although the policeman had called it "the ghetto," to say I would have avoided it entirely if the guidebook had been similarly hesitant is simply conjecture. Besides, I have more immediate concerns than analyzing my fateful decision—like paying for my hotel room. And so the only conclusion I arrive at tonight, as my cheek throbs with pain and my ears bleed from the piercing shrieks of amateur vocalists, is that perhaps I had simply reached the end of my traveling luck.

And with that, the experiment continues . . .

I spent the next few days cleaning up the mess, trying to piece together everything I had lost. Besides a slight bruise on my face, I wasn't injured, which was reassuring, but I was indeed broke, which necessitated my wife wiring me some money to continue my trip. My enthusiasm following a successful excursion to Kaieteur, a journey I had been able to execute sans guidebook, had been drained, and the apathy shown by the hotel employees was disheartening and frustrating. Even when I finally figured out the procedure necessary to make a collect call from Guyana, my hotel refused to help me dial, saying that to use the phone, I would first need to buy a calling card. "Doesn't that defeat the purpose of a collect call?" I asked. It was clear I needed some inspiration, some motivation to offset the momentary setbacks. Without a guidebook, I wasn't sure where to find it.

At some point during this process, while waiting for a callback from my wife at the hotel, I had picked up a brochure for a company called Wonderland Tours. It was a simple publication, with goofy font, low-resolution pictures, occasional typos, and inexplicable upper case letters. Their most popular tour, for example, was marketed as follows:

> *"A Tour to Kaieteur Fall is one of the enjoyable one-day trips anywhere in the World. Kaieteur's breath-taking single drop of 741 feet, the highest in the World. It's located in the herat of the Rainforest on one of the World's largest sandstone plateaus."*

Later that day, I stumbled upon the company's headquarters, a second floor office located a few blocks north of my hotel. Craving both an emotional pick-me-up as well as directions, I decided to see what Wonderland Tours had to offer. I opened the door, walked in, and for the first time since I had arrived in Guyana, felt like an actual tourist.

"Hi!" The woman behind the desk was beaming; her smile was infectious. "I'm Alisha. What can we do for you?"

"I'm actually looking for a way to Suriname," I said. "To Paramaribo."

"Oh, not a problem, not a problem at all, come on in," she answered, motioning for me to sit down on a chair next to her desk.

Alisha was twenty-eight years old, with a kind Indian face, a warm demeanor, and an enthusiasm for both her job and her country. She ran Wonderland Tours with her husband Mario but was joined in the office that day by her brother Cleveland, who was quiet but pleasant, offering his own subtle interjections whenever the conversation permitted it.

"You can book everything through here—one price. Our minibus—tourist friendly of course—will pick you up at your hotel at 4 A.M. He'll drive you down to the river where you'll have to cross the border and take a ferry. You'll pay for that yourself. I think it's about $25. Then, a different driver will pick you up in Suriname to take you the rest of the way to Paramaribo. The whole thing takes about twelve hours, including several hours waiting for the ferry to arrive. The cost is $50."

Considering it had cost me $35 to get down to Mahdia, it seemed like an acceptable price. I paid for the ticket with my recently acquired cash, explaining what had happened to me during my search for the food cart. They were genuinely disgusted but also not terribly surprised.

"Georgetown can be a rough city. There's a fine line between the acceptable areas and the ghetto," advised Cleveland. "Anywhere in Guyana, really. I was robbed in my own village!"

"Our grandma was robbed too. Right here in Georgetown," said Alisha. "They took everything—her money, her jewelry, her bank card. Everything except her passport." She explained that the thieves were not evil; their actions were merely a survival tactic. "The economy is bad here in Guyana, there are no jobs. Many people get by on only $5 a day. So they steal in order to pay their rent, to buy food, to buy clothes." Maybe, I thought, although the teenagers who had robbed me resembled little more than normal, run-of-the-mill hoodlums.

With the next leg of my journey set and the office air conditioning revitalizing my spirits, I continued to chat with Alisha and Cleveland, steering the conversation toward specific guidebook-related topics such as the birth of Wonderland Tours, the must-see Guyana attractions, and the overall health of the country's tourism industry. I mentioned that I had just returned from Mahdia, and described the method I had used to get to Kaieteur Falls. They found it hard to believe.

"You're lucky you came back in one piece!" said Cleveland, laughing.

Alisha was shaking her head. "You're probably the first person I know that's ever done that. How much do you think you spent overall?"

I quickly tallied up the various costs. "Probably around $500 or so."

"Hmm. So you saved $300," said Alisha, explaining that Wonderland Tours offered a two-day overland trip to the falls for $800. "That's pretty good." It was the ultimate compliment for a guidebook-less traveler; not only had I executed a popular trip somewhat flawlessly, I had done it under budget.

I explained, however, that I had rarely felt welcomed. That I had felt more like an intruder, or at the very least, an unexpected visitor, than an actual tourist. "There just didn't seem to be any real desire to help me, no matter how much money I had."

"You're right," said Alisha. "I can't say for sure but I think it's a generational thing. Our generation—those in their late twenties or thirties—understood the opportunities. That if you treat people the right way, they'll come back, they'll tell their friends and most importantly, they'll spend money. But the younger generation doesn't think that way. Until we figure out a way to show them how tourism can actually benefit their lives, they won't be motivated to change."

"And remember," Cleveland said, "eighty-five percent of this country is still rainforest. So developing infrastructure is hard no matter what. That's why so many people leave. There are one million Guyanese living in New York alone."

That number seemed high and when I looked it up later, I found the true figure to be closer to around 150,000. But the fact that New York could *possibly* have more Guyanese than Guyana itself said wonders about the country's inability to nurture growth and promote sustainability. I told them that I was from New York and had at one time lived on the edge of a popular Guyanese community. Alisha was delighted.

"I went to school in Queens, and lived there for many years," she said, as we exchanged the names of major streets and landmarks. "Have you ever been to Sybill's on Liberty Ave.?" I mentioned that I had heard of the place but had never been there; it was probably the most famous Guyanese restaurant in the city. "Well you have to go now. And when you do, ask for Cookie. Uncle Cookie. He was my dad's best friend growing up. Tell him I sent you."

Before I left, Alisha dug through some drawers in the back of the office and brought out a few postcards, a bracelet, and a keychain. "We can't let you leave without a few souvenirs," she said. The postcards were of Kaieteur Falls and the Cock-of-the-Rock; the bracelet and the keychain had the colors of the Guyanese flag. I thanked them for the gifts and the guidance and walked out of the office refreshed, encouraged by the conversation, and ready to continue my journey east.

JOURNAL ENTRY — GEORGETOWN

Day 8—Georgetown, Guyana: Another night at the Sleep-In, another night eating unremarkable chicken curry and watching small children splash their way through the pool. This hotel has become my anchor, the place to which I escape periodically throughout the day when I become overwhelmed by Georgetown's incessant vitality. I sit here because I am too leery to wander the streets at night, too suspicious of anyone who tries to approach me—like a small child hiding in a safe zone during a rambunctious game of tag.

But that is the talk of a coward, a wimp, a travel bore. I'm reminded of my first trip through the guidebook-proof world of India, cowering in my air-conditioned hotel room, eating chips, drinking soda, and watching English-language television. It was too difficult to venture out, I had told myself, too challenging to navigate the cluttered alleyways of Jodhpur, the frantic avenues of Mumbai, so I will sit here on my bed, hidden from view, my guidebook utterly inadequate in a completely foreign land.

My first Indian experience had been a test and I had failed; this guidebook experiment was a way to atone for that failure. If I had learned from my first Indian journey—and I believe I had—then I must not only vow to continue my experiment, but also promise to tear myself away from my hotel, to explore these countries, and, most importantly, to embrace interaction with the people around me.

Many travelers would argue that the quality of a journey is often determined by the value of its encounters. Following this logic, one could then say that the importance of these encounters for a traveler like myself—one who relies on these interactions for recommendations on where to go and for directions on how to get there—are magnified. To hide in my hotel room and dwell upon a single unfortunate experience would stall if not stop both the journey and the experiment.

A few nights ago, I had met the lowest Guyana had to offer—opportunistic petty thieves. But today, I had met the opposite, two benevolent souls who understood the troubles their country faced and vowed to remedy the image it projected to the rest of the world. They had made me laugh and had given me gifts, hoping that my memories of their dear country would be fond ones. They had also provided me with the information needed to travel east, over the border to Suriname, on my path to Cayenne, French Guiana.

Hostility and hospitality—those are the extremes. And to reject the latter due to fear of the former is to travel as if wrapped in a protective bubble, the very thing I'm trying to avoid. Tomorrow I say goodbye to the Sleep-In and its myriad comforts. Suriname, here I come.

INTERLUDE — LEWIS AND CLARK: ENCOUNTERS

History has rightly determined the Lewis and Clark expedition to be among the most remarkable journeys of all time. Children study it; hobbyists reenact it; historians dissect it. But what is it about this journey that so captivates the imagination? What is it about this group of men that encourages us to pour over every word they wrote, to walk in their footsteps, and to recreate scenes as we want them to be remembered?

One could argue it is simply the grandeur of the landscape through which the expedition passed, a fantastic world of wild game, jagged gorges, and roaring rivers. But there's another side, a *human* side, which has perhaps elevated the journey in the annals of history. Because if the land through which the Lewis and Clark expedition traveled had been unpopulated, the narrative suddenly loses much of what makes it remarkable in the first place—the individual tension, the personal drama, the human intrigue. You can't negotiate with mosquitoes; there's no trading with a buffalo. And so part of what makes the Lewis and Clark expedition such a memorable and captivating tale is not that they were two solitary men exploring unknown land but rather that they were, in fact, rarely alone.

Even before the expedition left St. Louis in 1804, Thomas Jefferson, like the proud father of thirty teenage boys, was concerned with how the men would behave during their encounters with the Indians. As historian James P. Ronda writes, "what [the President] feared was that after months of hardship and frustration, some small incident might touch off a sudden burst of violence." Most of the time, Jefferson's fears proved unfounded—encounters between the men and the Indians were often festive, with laughter, dancing, singing, and smoking. At Fort Mandan, for instance, the cold, dark days of the North Dakota winter were alleviated by the frequent gatherings between the expedition and their neighbors. The biggest party was saved for New Year's Day, 1805. "The day was ushered in by the discharge of two cannon," wrote Clark in his journal, and continued with sixteen men joining the Indians for a day of revelry. One expedition member played the fiddle, another a tambourine, while a French trader charmed the crowd by dancing on his hands. Relations were cordial; times were merry. Lewis and Clark even developed, uncharacteristically so, a certain fondness for their companions. Toward the end of the winter, as the men prepared to resume their journey west, the explorers paid a visit to Black Cat, one of the local chiefs and a man who Lewis said, "possesses more integrity, firmness, intelligence, and perspicuity of mind than any Indian I have met with in this quarter." They relaxed, smoked, and exchanged presents, thanking the Chief for his continued geniality.

The most frequent form of hospitality encountered by the expedition, however, was provided not by the Indian chiefs but by their women. When Thomas Jefferson wrote, "In all your intercourse with the natives, treat them in the most friendly and conciliatory manner which their own conduct will permit," it is doubtful that this innocent command was meant as a lewd invitation for the expedition's collection of lonely young men. But regardless of Jefferson's intent, sex between Indian women and the men was rampant. And the relationships, not surprisingly, were often quite complicated. At Fort Mandan, there was a belief that the hunting prowess of the men could be transferred to the Indians through sexual relations with their wives. While Ronda writes it is unknown "how many men in the expedition obligingly took part in the ritual," he also cites one trader as reporting that "many Mandans believed their prompt success in the January hunts was due to white participation in the ceremony." And this ability to transfer power through sex was not relegated solely to the expedition's *white* men. For one tribe, in fact, Clark's slave York became what Ronda describes as "the central attraction of the Lewis and Clark expedition"—to sleep with him was to "get in touch with what seemed awesome spirit forces." One man even invited York back to his home, offered up his wife, and stood as a sentry outside the door, lest anybody try and interrupt the potentially lucrative encounter.

Knowing full well how easy it was for the men to succumb to sexual temptation, the captains did what they could to mitigate the potential consequences of these liaisons. As the expedition spent time with one relatively "chaste" tribe, Lewis wrote, "I have requested the men to give them no cause of jealousy by having connection with their women without their knowledge" while later acknowledging the difficulty he would have in executing such a request: "To prevent this mutual exchange of good offices altogether I know it impossible to effect, particularly on the part of our young men whom some months abstinence have made very polite to those tawny damsels." Several months later, as the expedition hunkered down on the shore of the Pacific Ocean for the 1805-06 winter, the men enjoyed the generous hospitality of a particularly randy group of women. To quell the hemorrhaging of goods needed to engage in this type of revelry, the captains initiated an ad hoc sex budget, dividing "some ribbon between the men of our party to bestow on their favorite lasses, this plan to save the knives and more valuable articles."

But apart from a needed dose of morale, these incidents of sexual release should also be viewed as the necessary antidote to the hostility the men faced throughout their prolonged journey. Two particular incidents stand out. The first occurred in September 1804 at the present site of Pierre, South Dakota during a meeting with the notoriously aggressive Teton Sioux. After stumbling through an initial introduction, the Indians refused to allow the expedition to set off from shore, complaining that the gifts they were being offered were inadequate. In many ways, the Indians' tactics resembled a shakedown, a test to see how far Lewis and Clark would go—in essence, to see how vulnerable these travelers actually were. If the captains wilted and gave in, they would give the Sioux the upper hand. But if they didn't give in at all, tempers would boil over, enemies would be made, and the incident could potentially end in bloodshed. As historian Stephen Ambrose explains, "They were Virginia gentleman who had been challenged. They were ready to fight." Luckily for both parties, one of the Indian chiefs, Black Buffalo, kept his calm during the encounter, diffusing the standoff and ordering a more diplomatic approach to the situation. Over the next few days, the men of the expedition visited the Teton villages, smoking, dining, and dancing. And while tensions would flare up yet again as the expedition prepared to continue upriver (this time over a few carrots of tobacco), the situation never escalated beyond some shouting and posturing.

Unfortunately, this kind of restraint was absent in a skirmish nearly two years later. After successfully navigating the Rocky Mountains for the second time, the captains had split up in order to increase the scope of the exploration as they traveled east. In July 1806, Lewis found himself traveling through precarious Blackfeet territory with only three other men. The seasoned explorers knew the dangers in dividing an already small team; Lewis furthermore understood the ruthlessness of the Indians who inhabited the land he would be crossing. "They are a vicious, lawless and rather an abandoned set of wretches," he wrote in one journal entry. "I have no doubt but they would steal our horses if they have it in their power and finding us weak should they happen to be numerous will most probably attempt to rob us of our arms and baggage." Despite the risk, Lewis traveled on, ultimately confronting a band of territorial Blackfeet. Although the initial meeting was tense, both sides put aside their apprehensions and agreed to spend the night together in the same camp. In the morning, however, chaos ensued, as Lewis and his men awoke to find the Indians attempting to steal their guns and horses. When it was all over, two Indians lay dead, one stabbed and one shot, with the Americans fleeing before the Blackfeet could take revenge.

No time period, however, illustrates the full range of Indian encounters better than the spring of 1806, as the expedition scrambled to gather enough food and horses for the perilous journey east over the still snow-packed Bitterroot Mountains. With the crew anxious to begin the journey home but dependent on the Indians for supplies, tensions were high. On April 20th, Lewis records an occurrence of petty thievery: "This morning I was informed that the natives had pilfered six tomahawks and a knife from the party in the course of the last night." The next day, a similar incident ignites a particularly harsh reaction:

> I detected a fellow in stealing an iron socket of a canoe pole and gave him several severe blows and made the men kick him out of camp. I now informed the Indians that I would shoot the first of them that attempted to steal an article from us, that we were not afraid to fight them, that I had it in my power at that moment to kill them all and set fire to their houses, but it was not my wish to treat them with severity provided they would let my property alone.

A week later, the expedition had moved on from the hostile territory of the Chinooks and into the hospitable care of the Wallawallas. There, they traded for horses, received valuable information, partied, danced, and ate. On April 30th, 1806, Clark describes the Wallawallas as "honest friendly people"; the next day Lewis concurs: "I think we can justly affirm to the honor of these people that they are the most hospitable, honest, and sincere people that we have met with in our voyage."

For the guidebook-less traveler, then, there is no check-list of stops—only a series of arbitrary meetings along an uncharted path that may or may not end at a specific location, site, or destination. Viewed this way, the process in which the journey unfolds has been flipped, with the encounters dictating the destinations rather than the other way around. The men of the Lewis and Clark expedition would certainly remember their first view of the Great Falls or their first night alongside the mighty Rocky Mountains. But the stories they would tell when they returned home would not be of waterfalls and buffalo and rapids; instead, these stories would undoubtedly follow the narrative arc of tales told by men for countless generations—accounts of fierce battles, yarns of passionate sex. And taken holistically, so that no single incident merits more attention than it properly deserves, what happens in those encounters, for better or for worse, is often the barometer upon which the entire trip's value is judged.

I was told that to arrive in Paramaribo by evening, I had to leave Georgetown at four in the morning. So on the day of my departure, I woke at half past three, packed my bag, and sat on a bench in the hotel lobby, listening to the howling street dogs, the twittering crickets, and the wailing sobs of a hysterical woman at the hotel bar. Next to the woman sat her friend, rubbing her back as she cried into the table. Eventually, they both stood up and left, exiting stage right, and leaving the late night performance in the hands of the dogs and the crickets.

The van arrived fifteen minutes later and it was obvious that the ride would be much smoother than the one to Mahdia; the van was noticeably newer, the air-conditioning was humming, the upholstery was spotless, and the ceiling was slightly elevated, eliminating the agonizing claustrophobia that had plagued my previous Guyanese trips. We drove through the Georgetown suburbs, revealing an entirely different city than the one to which I had been confined. This was no longer a city of sketchy ghettos and crowded markets. It was, instead, a town of Hindu temples and Islamic Centers, its broad residential avenues flanked by fenced-in, two-story houses with concrete driveways and Japanese sedans. The only signs of movement were the occasional farm animals that wandered aimlessly through the streets, and as we turned down narrow alleyways, we often had to slow down to avoid the sleepy gait of a crossing donkey or horse. It was a tranquil scene, a far cry from the frenzy of Stabroek Market, and as dawn slowly approached, the towering palm trees that lined the streets were gracefully silhouetted against the brightening cerulean sky.

After a few stops, we screamed off down the highway to the east, the driver unimpeded by the usually congested streets. I had an entire bench seat to myself, and I stretched out comfortably, nodding off during large stretches of straight road. When awake, I stared out the window, watching an uninterrupted procession of villages pass by. Each one of these towns was designated by its own sign ("Welcome to Portuguese Quarter," "Welcome to #1 Road") and I soon determined that the bizarre names often fell into one of two distinct categories: those that were suitable for a Dr. Seuss nursery rhyme (Letter Kenny, Cotton Tree, Golden Fleece, Whim) and those more appropriate for a map of the United Kingdom (Brighton, Belvidere, Williamsburg).

We reached the border after a few hours. In the parking lot, a moneychanger and I used a calculator to transform $55,000 Guyanese dollars into $846 Surinamese dollars since, as Alisha had warned me, Guyana currency was worthless in Suriname. I was clueless concerning the appropriate rate and relied on the bus driver and the other passengers to assure me that my conversion was indeed a fair proposal. After completing the exchange, the man said quietly, "Now, let me ask you something. Did you keep enough Guyanese money to pay for the ferry?" I said I had—the driver had counseled me about that—but wondered if he would have shrewdly charged me an additional fee to change some of the Surinamese money I just received back into Guyanese had I not been so informed.

Like I had done in the airport in New York before my flight to Georgetown, I spent the pre-departure time carefully observing my fellow travelers. They were clearly more affluent, and likely more educated, than many of the people I had met during my time in Guyana. Most spoke perfect English and many seemed to be traveling for holiday, clumsily dragging their large rolling suitcases behind them as they poked around the terminal. They flaunted their wealth proudly, parading around in a litany of brand name clothing and accessories: Lacoste shirts and Gucci sunglasses, Prada purses and Louis Vuitton bags. And they made conversation by doing what rich people of any country do best, complaining about things completely out of their control—"the sun is too hot," "the wait is too long," "there's not enough food available."

There was one jester among the crowd and he proved to be a great source of entertainment for everybody there. He was tall and middle-aged, with greasy long hair and a dark wispy moustache. His hat was constantly askew, and he restlessly switched its position from front to back and from back to front. When he wasn't lounging against a wall, he stomped around the waiting area's benches exclaiming, "I wanna git drunk!" He walked with a lean, as if his right hip carried an extra ten-pound weight, and his high-pitched nasally whine elicited mostly rolled eyes from the amused onlookers. A large black woman (sister? girlfriend? caretaker?) with gap teeth, giant hoop earrings, and streaked blond hair dutifully followed him around, occasionally whispering advice or directions into his ear. She had to physically intervene only once—to stop him from opening the giant bottle of Chardonnay that had been hidden inside his luggage. He listened, leaving the bottle closed, and instead fondled it with a loving caress.

After a few hours, I grew impatient and left the cool shade of the station's interior to peer across the river at our destination— Suriname. I wasn't sure what to expect there. If I had known little about Guyana prior to arrival, I knew even less about Suriname. My instincts told me it would be similar, that all three of these mostly forgotten countries contained enough common history and geography to warrant the broad classification of the "Guianas." But I also knew that borders, whether culturally, economically, or physically, had the ability to be transformative demarcations. The US/Mexico border is a good example. So is the DMZ between North and South Korea. And crossing into Nepal from India is like entering a world in slow motion.

So as I boarded the ferry, I began to wonder what I would encounter when I reached the other side. Where did the visitor go in Suriname? Was there a Kaieteur equivalent? A stunning and marketable touristic highlight? What would the food be like? Would they have a similar system of minibuses? Did everyone speak at least a passable form of English? Would I be able to find comfortable accommodation? I had no idea. But for every ounce of apprehension and trepidation, of which I had many, I possessed a similar amount of anticipation and exhilaration.

I knew nothing about Suriname. And for the purposes of my experiment, that was perfect.

CHAPTER 9

❧ ❧ ❧

Paramaribo

*T*he road from Georgetown to the ferry terminal had been dotted with a procession of unassuming villages, hugging the road and virtually unbroken until the border-delineating river. The road in Suriname, however, was noticeably different, with large, sweeping farms reaching out into the horizon, where a wall of forest, ringing the edges in all directions, signaled the beginning of an entirely new world. The plantation vistas were interrupted only occasionally, sometimes by a colorfully adorned colonial church, other times by a modest farmhouse or barn. I stared out the window into panoramas of banana farms and rice fields and wondered if Suriname was even less populated than Guyana.

Our van rumbled east down a two-lane highway so cramped that passing trucks caused our vehicle to shiver. Halfway through the journey, an Indian man turned around and asked me where I was headed. "On my way to Paramaribo," I told him.

His name was Raghoenedh (or at least that's what I wrote down after he quickly rattled off the spelling) and was dressed in a battered white dress shirt, creased brown pants, and a pair of worn loafers. He mentioned that he operated a tour business in his free time—taxi rides, trips into the jungle, sightseeing walks through the capital. I asked him about the few Surinamese attractions Alisha had mentioned but he hadn't heard of them, so I dug into my backpack and brought out my map, wondering if he had other suggestions.

Raghoenedh studied it cautiously, squinting around its borders. "Yes, Suriname big country," he said eventually. "Six hundred thousand people!"

I took the map back and put it away. "So what about Paramaribo? Any recommendations on where to stay?"

"Oh yes. I can find you a hotel. There are many different parts of Paramaribo—good parts, bad parts. It's because of the diversity—there are many different kinds of people in Suriname." He held up both his hands and began to count off one ethnicity per finger. "Japanese, Chinese, Dutch, Spanish, Brazilian, Indian, black people." He paused. "How long were you in Guyana?"

"About ten days," I said.

He scowled. "Too long in that country," he told me. "Lots of black people there—here in Suriname, much bigger mix. So it's calmer." I had noticed this tension a few times in Guyana, an unmistakable strain between the blacks and the Indians. But this man, speaking honestly in the comforts of an empty van, was the first one to mention it directly.

As we approached the city, Raghoenedh and the bus driver exchanged a few words about possible hotels. Soon, we were pulling the van up on a crumbling sidewalk in front of a three-story building, its tall reflective windows crowning a metallic semi-circle marquee on which was emblazoned, in bronze lettering, its tropical name: The Flamingo Hotel and Casino. Raghoenedh motioned for me to follow him inside and the two of us approached the front desk, where a young woman was shuffling through some scattered papers. Raghoenedh nodded in my direction, silently instructing me to talk.

"Do you happen to have any single rooms available for tonight?"

"We have one room," the woman said, looking up. "It's $49 a night."

I asked if we could take a look. She found the key in the safe deposit box, came out from behind the desk, and told us to follow her up the hotel's faux-marble staircase. We walked down the second floor hallway until we reached Room #9. Swinging open the door, I peered into what would become my home for the next few days.

The room was large, dingy, and windowless. In one corner was a small kitchenette, with a two-burner stove, a tiny microwave, and an elevated table. In the other corner was a cheap wooden armoire, its doors ripped off its hinges, holding nothing but a single hanger. A queen-size mattress and box spring lay directly on the floor. There were two televisions, one high on the wall next to the bathroom door and the other on a folding chair next to the table. A massive air-conditioner was built into one of the walls but was quiet. There wasn't a single decoration and the entire place smelled like mold. It was dreadful, the worst of what many guidebooks would classify as "budget" accommodation, but I had been traveling for twelve hours, was starving, and had little energy to search for something more comfortable.

"I'll take it," I said, and as we went downstairs to fill out the necessary paperwork, Raghoenedh said goodbye, disappearing through the doors in the lobby marked "Casino."

After dropping my bag in the room, I left the hotel, hoping to explore the surrounding area. The Flamingo was located on what seemed like a semi-developed commercial avenue, but it was late and most of the shops were closed. Much of the limited evening activity was concentrated inside the wide dirt meridian, with idle loiterers sitting among feral dogs and scattered garbage. A few food shacks remained open, music videos flickering from their televisions, and I approached one of them, hoping for my first taste of Surinamese cuisine.

"Have anything for dinner?" I asked the man behind the counter.

"Fish. All we got is fish," he said.

"Okay, I'll have some fish then."

"Anything to drink?"

I scanned the fridge. "A Heineken," I said, remembering the Dutch names I had read on the Suriname section of the map.

The beer was good, cold and refreshing. The meal was not, a bland spongy filet on white rice with a side of chewy vegetables—yet it cost nearly ten American dollars. Still hungry, I left the shack and wandered through the side streets until I stumbled upon a Chinese-run bakeshop. Pointing to the pastry-filled cabinets, I ordered two slices of cake—one carrot and one chocolate—and ate them with my hands as I stood on the sidewalk.

Finally content, I turned to the small Paramaribo inset on my map. Knowing that all of Suriname would be closed the next day, a Sunday, I began to make my way down toward the tour company I had heard about in Guyana. I walked east along the river, and the shoddiness of the area surrounding the Flamingo Hotel and Casino soon transformed into the splendor of a historic and well-maintained European colonial city. Multi-colored spotlights lit up grand government buildings and smooth lounge music streamed from a cluster of open-air cafes. There were tourists everywhere, more than I had seen during my entire time in Guyana. I had been grateful for Raghoenedh's advice and appreciated his candor regarding the city, but the liveliness of this area confirmed I had once again been led astray, and that my hotel, while affordable, was located on the periphery of touristic Paramaribo. I imagined what the city map looked like in the guidebook: the riverside area would be highlighted, recommended as a neighborhood of interest and dotted with restaurant and bar icons, while my area, home of the Flamingo Hotel and Casino, would remain invisible, languishing off the edges of the map.

I found the tour agency and was relieved to see the lights on and the door still open. The worker behind the desk, a young man named Gio, sat patiently as I described my current situation: the recent robbery, the lack of funds, and my desire to head south into the jungle to see the rest of Suriname. He mentioned that there were a few trips leaving the next day, but the tour company required the customer to pay in full before departure. I pleaded my case, begging Gio to call his boss and to see if I could provide a down payment (my wife had been able to wire me a few hundred dollars in Georgetown) and pay the rest when I returned. The owner would have none of it though—he had been cheated before by customers and would have to adhere, even in my admittedly unusual case, to the company's firm policies. Relenting, I asked Gio when the next tours were departing. But my timing, he explained, was unfortunate—the next day was not only Sunday, but a national holiday, meaning that the entire country would be closed for the next two days. The earliest I could transfer additional funds from the United States and book the trip, then, was Tuesday, delaying my departure into the interior until Wednesday.

The unexpected halt meant I would be spending several days both in Paramaribo, and, unless I found more agreeable yet similarly affordable accommodation, at the Flamingo Hotel and Casino. I thought of Paul Theroux musing that, to the traveler, a public holiday is "hell: no one working, shops and schools closed, natives eating ice cream, public transport jammed, and the stranger's sense of being excluded from the merriment—from everything." Hell was a little much, especially to someone who had recently dealt with the bureaucratic ineptitude of Guyanese law enforcement, but the delay was discouraging, and I couldn't help but wonder how I would fare in this strange city, with limited cash, sequestered away from the palatial glitz of the riverfront area.

I thanked Gio for his time, promised to return in a few days, and, being in no rush to return to the squalor of my hotel, followed a pack of British tourists into one of the dimly lit, posh bars clustered together on the riverside. There was both a hip, lounge-type feel to the place—with pillowed couches, low lying tables, and illuminated Grey Goose bottles—as well as a more traditional bar vibe—with wooden stools, picnic tables, and sports memorabilia littering the cluttered walls. The waitresses were beautiful and spoke perfect English. A sign on the wall said: "Where Real People Make Great Friends."

I sipped my beer from a stool at the bar, regretting my fish dinner as I watched the group of men I had followed there devour enormous plates of steak, French-fries, and spaghetti. They drank pints, cursed loudly, and argued about soccer, seemingly at home in this setting. I guessed the bar was owned and managed by an Irishman or Australian, and that it rarely catered to anybody other than pasty tourists or government workers. I immediately conjured the hackneyed description of a homesick guidebook writer: "Join Paramaribo's expats at Zanzibar to watch daily international sporting events. The bartender pours a tremendous pint of Guinness." Still, the bar was comfortable, familiar, and when I finished my drink, I thought of having another before I remembered that it was getting dark and my hotel was at least a half hour walk away. And so I paid my bill, and began the trek back to the Flamingo.

The demarcation between touristy riverside Paramaribo and the rest of the city was abrupt and as I retraced my route from earlier in the evening, the chatty tourists in lively cafes were soon replaced by whispering vagrants in shadowy corners. I put my head down and walked quickly, ignoring the catcalls and whistles of the nighttime loiterers. Gio had assured me that Paramaribo was much safer than Georgetown, but I was still spooked, and I passed up obvious shortcuts to stay on the wider and more crowded two-lane streets. I eventually emerged in front of the artificial glare of the Flamingo Hotel and Casino, but it was only 10 o'clock and having no desire to spend the rest of the night locked in Room #9, I decided to check out the casino.

It was one long room, a smoke-choked corridor of flashing slot machines and felt tables. The patrons were a mix of Asian and black men, all ages. They fingered stacks of chips nervously and stared obsessively at the blinking numbers, tumbling dice, and shuffling cards. The atmosphere was loud, but with little conversation; the noise came from the spins of the roulette wheels and the clamor of the slots. Toward the back, a stage had been set up for a four-piece band, with drums, guitars, and microphones. But there were no musicians, only the promise of future entertainment.

I walked over to the bar and ordered a drink. It came in a tiny plastic cup, the kind you might give to a young child. When I tried to pay, a small Chinese man grabbed me by the arm, leading me away and hissing cryptically in my ear, "It's free. Everything here is free," sweeping his arm across the room. *What is everything?* I wondered.

I slunk back against a wall sipping my beer, watching the Surinamese lose their money. After a few minutes, I decided I had had enough, and went upstairs to my room.

JOURNAL ENTRY — PARAMARIBO

Day 9—Paramaribo, Suriname: Only one of the televisions in this room works—that's the reason, I suppose, why there are two of them. I had turned it on earlier, hoping to find a soccer game, but there were only a few stations and most of the programs were in Dutch. I couldn't understand anything anyone was saying.

It has been an interesting night. But I wonder if it has been a memorable one. Will I remember this night five years from now? Ten? Will I remember this room—its two televisions, its empty armoire?

Will I remember Zanzibar? The lounge existed as a sliver of implicit tranquility in an otherwise foreign landscape. I can picture hordes of European tourists crowding the place, ordering pints and vodkas and hamburgers and chatting animatedly about sports and politics and jungles and snakes, as their vacations slowly ticked away. There were to be no revelations in that environment, no unforgettable vistas or memorable meals or life altering events. Only the unmistakable cadence and comfort of the universal pub experience: the hum of sports highlights, the clatter of bar glasses, the drone of useless conversation. It had taken a while but I had finally crossed over into what I believed to be the standard guidebook path. Instead of feeling irritated, I had felt relieved and took pride in the fact that nobody had led me there. It was as if I had been thirsty, and had stumbled upon a shimmering oasis of guidebook familiarity.

But if Zanzibar had been the pinnacle of the guidebook-recommended, expat-haven, tourist bar, the Flamingo Casino was the opposite—a hidden bastion of vice, immorality, and addiction built to harvest and subsequently annihilate the dreams of Paramaribo's lower class. Sure, it was off-the-beaten-path, but in the wrong direction—the type of place the braggart traveler would attempt to romanticize, transforming the simple experience into an intrepid adventure among an unknown subsection of Paramaribo society. That tale, of course, would have to be embellished: the lights would be dimmer, the men would be dressed in suits, and there would be mysterious side rooms from which would emerge exotic, scantily clad women.

But there was, of course, nothing of the sort in the Fla-
mingo, only the hypnotic rhythm of sad, cyclical, everyday
life. So which of the two bar experiences will ultimately
prove to be the most rewarding? It's impossible to tell. Only
after sufficient reflection do many of travel's truly poignant
and fulfilling experiences become discernible. So unlike the
immediate gratification I had felt during my trip to Kai-
eteur, any epiphanies concerning my first night in Paramar-
ibo would have to wait. Instead, my only choice is to simply
absorb the experience of the Flamingo, however banal and
depressing it seems to be.

Both the tour guide and a worker at my hotel had alerted me
the previous night that Sunday was a holiday in Suriname,
but it wasn't until I went downstairs that morning that I realized it was one of the more important days of the year—the
anniversary of the Abolishment of Slavery. "What's it going to
be like?" I asked the woman working the front desk.

"It's going to be wonderful," she said, her eyes glowing.

I left my hotel and walked toward the water. Turning onto
the main riverfront avenue, I noticed that despite the early
hour, several proprietors had already erected their stalls,
advertising their goods with homemade signs. Like most
street festivals I had experienced in New York, many of the
booths offered menus of similar items—rice dishes with
barbecued meat, shaved ice, beer. I bought a pair of chicken
skewers and a congealed mass of coconut shavings that looked
like a potato pancake.

The crowd was still light but those who did gather, mostly
women, were clad in colorful outfits—long, flower-patterned
dresses with elaborate fabric woven around their hair. Together,
we marched down the Waterkaant, past what my map called
the "Paramaribo Historical District." To the right was the

river; to the left was a row of colonial houses, multi-terraced and ornate. Just beyond the historic district was the collection of government buildings I had seen the previous night. I walked past the largest of these buildings, a stately wooden mansion adorned with a row of tall symmetrical archways, and discovered it was the Presidential Palace. But the building seemed empty and in disrepair, its opulence diminished by the scaffolding that surrounded its bottom floor.

I turned off the main avenue into a park called the Palmentuin, where towering rows of identical palm trees formed a welcome shield against the growing heat of the sun. Lining the park's winding paths were additional booths, some of which housed various carnival-type games. I stopped for a few minutes to watch one particularly intriguing contest—a game called "Hang On To Win," where teenaged boys demonstrated their strength by competing to see who could hang vertically from a metal pole the longest. This type of bravado exemplified the theme of the day—that of Surinamese pride. Freedom Day seemed to be both a familial affair, with baby buggies and strollers clogging up the park's paths, as well as a cultural one, with traditional music, as opposed to the reggae and club music I had become accustomed to, projecting loudly from many of the booths. The people even dressed the part, with chattering partygoers of all age groups flaunting "I Love SU" t-shirts.

As the air grew stickier and the sun reached its high point, the rows of cooked meat that occupied nearly every booth, so enticing earlier in the day, became decidedly less appetizing. Keen for a short hiatus, I found one of the open-air bars I had passed the previous night, sat down, and ordered a beer.

I was soon joined by Steve, an Irish mining consultant who worked for a Canadian company ninety miles away, but who was in Paramaribo for a quick holiday. He was a big man, with a slight paunch, and when he talked, his face grew serious and his piercing blue eyes opened wide as if he was constantly astonished. We chatted a bit about soccer and the United States; after a while I asked him what his company was looking for in Suriname.

"Gold," he said. "There's gold everywhere in this country. Anywhere you walk." As he said this, he waved his hand over the ground right next to our bar stools, as if he literally meant *anywhere.*

"So where exactly is this mine? South of here? East?"

He took a sip of his beer. "Fuck if I know," he replied, explaining that the owner of the mine had given him a driver. Together, they had come to Paramaribo for the weekend and would return the next morning.

"So you came just for the holiday?"

"I guess so. Freedom Day they call it, right?"

"Yeah. You know anything about it?"

He shook his head. "I don't know. I guess it's kind of like Labor Day in the United States."

That wasn't true, of course, but I didn't say anything. Labor Day, to most Americans, meant little more than the end of summer vacation. To compare the end of Hamptons' season to the anniversary of the abolition of slavery seemed, at the very least, incongruous.

"This your first time in Suriname?" I asked.

"Nah, I've been here before—six or seven times I think."

"What's the route? You come through Amsterdam?"

"Yep," he said. "It's the only way to arrive from Europe." His eyes grew wide, and he rose up a little out of his chair. "And it's always fucking packed! Locals, Dutch, people and a million fucking languages! Everyone here speaks like four different languages. You notice that?"

I said I had.

"You want to know why?"

"Why?"

"Because everyone's shagging everyone! It's crazy! That's why you have all these mixed race people running around." As Steve said this, his voice got louder and he rocked back and forth in his chair, laughing.

He paused for a minute before continuing in a lower voice. "You know, when I came here for the first time, I thought it was a Third World country. But they've got Porsches, Mercedes, everything. I'm staying right across the street, right there." He pointed to the Toraica; someone had told me earlier that it was the most expensive hotel in Suriname. "I go in and they ask for $195 a night. I said 'Fuck off, I'll go next door, down the road.' That's exactly what I said, 'Fuck off.' The guy says, 'Hold on. I'll talk to my manager.' He comes back five minutes later and tells me the price is $115." He paused, hoping for a reaction, before finishing his thought. "No third-world country has a hotel that costs $195."

I nodded, digesting his vigor.

"So what brings you to Suriname?" he finally asked.

I explained that I was there on holiday, and told me about my trip to Mahdia and Kaieteur Falls. When I mentioned the robbery, he grew livid, delivering a barrage of curses the likes of which only an Irishman can dispense. "Cunts man! Fucking cunts!" The muscles on his face tensed up as he reached for his beer. "Cunts, cunts, cunts," he kept mumbling as he swiveled in his chair. His cheeks had turned red and I saw that he was visibly disgusted.

"Really, it could have happened anywhere."

But he ignored my plea. "Did you fight back? Did you hit them or anything?"

"Not really," I said. "I didn't think it was worth it. And I was outnumbered at least five to one."

"I would've just . . . bam, bam, bam," and as he said it, he jerked his head forward, pretending to head-butt the pack of thieves standing in front of him. "That would've scared those cunts anyway. Made them fuck off." He shook his head again and we both looked out onto the road. Steve's anger was making me uneasy; I didn't want to talk about the robbery anymore.

A bus passed with a large billboard tacked to its side, offering a way out of our current conversation. "That's the company I work for," he said, pointing to the advertisement. "They're based up in Toronto—came down here looking for gold. They're making an absolute killing."

I told Steve about my conversation with the ranger up at the top of Kaieteur Falls, about how he mentioned that there were so many diamonds in the park that some workers would find them just walking along the paths. He shook his head, "Nah, that's not how it works. It's not that easy."

As he explained the intricacies of the international mining industry, I noticed that the irrational swearing from only a few minutes before had been replaced by a sophisticated knowledge of geological details. He stressed that finding the source of the minerals is often the hardest part. "If you ever get the chance, find a geologist and buy him a few beers. They always have the best stories."

"So who's getting rich off this stuff?"

"Well, certainly not me and you huh? Just those Canadian cunts!" He clinked his bottle against mine and took a swig.

Outside, the music was picking up, and the streets were becoming more crowded. Three young girls had sat down directly behind us, and during the last part of our conversation, I had noticed Steve periodically glancing their way. They hadn't ordered anything from the bar and, despite it being only early afternoon, I wondered if they too were miners but of a different sort, interested in potential clients, rather than gold or diamonds.

"That girl's certainly got a nice ass, doesn't she?" Steve said. Uninterested in the path down which that conversation led, I paid my bill and went back to my hotel for a midday respite, promising Steve I'd come back to watch the big soccer match later that evening.

When I returned several hours later, Steve was slumped in his chair, his head propped up by his right hand and a large warm bottle of beer in front of him. It was obvious that he hadn't left during the entire time I had been away. The bar was now bustling, filled with hundreds of Europeans enthusiastically awaiting the start of the match. When it finally began, the crowd's noise grew in anticipation, while Steve continued to stare blankly through the television. His vocabulary had significantly deteriorated and most of the questions I now posed to him (Who are you rooting for? Who do you think will win?) were countered with an empty and indifferent scowl. At one point during the first half, a helicopter roared over the bar. When I asked Steve who he thought the occupants were, he glared at me wildly and spit out, "Some cunt!"

In the end, Steve turned out to be the worst kind of traveling companion—an insufferable, stubborn lout whose idea of sightseeing was the bar across the street from the hotel. He had no desire to see Suriname. His goals, cheap beer and loose women, were some of the most easily attained assets in any country. Steve would not, as Theroux had said, be excluded from the merriment of the national holiday. Instead, he would create his own gaiety, a Western cocoon of monetarily achieved enjoyment. The locals might laugh behind his back as he slurred his words and slumped over in his chair, but tempted by the almighty dollar, they would ultimately acquiesce to his demands—another beer, another woman.

Say what you will about a guidebook addict's dependence; at least he or she cares enough to bring one along—to venture beyond the hotel, the bar, and the brothel. Steve's reliance on Suriname's vices was a different kind of addiction, one established centuries ago by conquering armies who ravaged rather than enjoyed foreign lands, pillaging their goods and raping their women. In this sense, the guidebook has civilized "travel," directing the wanderer toward new, often esoteric, and often innocent, attractions.

Having nowhere in particular to go, I could have sat in that bar all night, next to Steve, watching him sloppily down liters of beer while obnoxiously gawking at uninterested women. But I decided instead to wander into the crowded streets of Suriname's most important holiday and listen to the music of the city's bands, before returning to my voluntary detainment at the Flamingo Hotel and Casino.

The morning after Freedom Day was quiet. All the city's shops were shuttered and the downtown streets surrounding the Presidential Palace, which had been filled the day before with snow cone trucks, barbeque stands, and carnival games, were empty. The only signs of movement were the solitary sweepers methodically cleaning up the celebration.

I left the Flamingo early in the morning and had the streets to myself, strolling down nearly deserted alleyways. Without the crowds and pageantry, the area looked much more like the historical district it was, and the two-story houses, with their peeling paint, slanted balconies, and colorful facades, reminded me of the more neglected side streets inside New Orleans' French Quarter. I knew that each building, especially those down by the riverfront, had a story, probably a fairly interesting one, but my map was useless for sightseeing and the area was apparently not "historic" enough to warrant tourist-friendly placards. My morning tour of the city, then, quickly became an aimless wander and I decided instead to try to find new lodging.

I had asked Steve the previous night if he knew where all the tourists we saw at the bar were staying. But he had flatly rejected the notion that they were with him at the Toraica, the swankiest hotel in town. "Those cunts can't afford that!" he had snorted. So where? Without a guide to point me in the right direction, I wasn't even sure where to begin, and feared that Paramaribo's most popular options—the trendy guesthouses that attracted seasoned travelers, loyal reviewers, and repeat visitors—would remain hidden down unassuming side streets and behind inconspicuous facades.

I decided to walk east past the Toraica, and past Zanzibar, into a neighborhood I had not yet explored. Rounding a corner, I spied a young blond woman carrying a plastic bag filled with groceries. Wearing shorts and flip-flops, she had the confident gait of a seasoned backpacker, and I began to follow her, hoping she was headed back to her hotel or guesthouse. I trailed her for a few blocks, unable to catch up and get her attention, until she eventually turned into a shaded pathway underneath a sign that read "Eco Resort Inn."

The entrance to the hotel was gated off, its circular driveway dotted with stunted palms and bright flowers. A large porch with rocking chairs and wicker side tables welcomed visitors into the main building where the lobby, cool and breezy, held a small, well-stocked bar and a sitting area with a giant flat screen television. Through the back of the building was another large patio, with round wooden tables and a long buffet table. Most noticeable of all, however, was the tranquility; there were no sounds besides the faint rustle of the wind and the soft calls of roosting birds. A guidebook narrative slowly formed in my mind: "The Eco Resort Inn: A soothing oasis tucked into a tranquil corner of busy Paramaribo . . ."

I approached the front desk and inquired about available rooms. Not wanting to admit to myself that I had been getting ripped off, I irrationally hoped that the Eco Resort's prices were at least double what I was paying at the Flamingo. But the nightly rate was only twenty American dollars more and included both a free continental breakfast and daily access to the Toraica's pool, sauna, and workout facilities. I confirmed availability for the following night and vowed to move early the next morning, giving myself at least one full day in relative Paramaribo luxury.

I left the hotel, retracing my steps to more familiar territory. As I approached the office of the tour company with whom I had been speaking, I noticed that I was being followed, more curiously than aggressively, by a tall ragged man dressed in a muddy t-shirt, rumpled corduroys, and a baseball cap. He asked if I could spare a moment; I, of course, stuck in Paramaribo, could spare several.

The man's name was Mike, a currently out-of-work airplane pilot. He told me that he spent most of his time in this neighborhood, washing cars for Paramaribo's elite. But business was slow: "All this rain, nobody needs their car washed anymore. I'm just looking for a little money to get something to eat—you can even buy the food for me, I don't care."

I explained that I had my own short-term money issues to deal with and told him that I had little to spare. He was disappointed; most likely he thought I was lying. So I changed the subject.

"Why aren't you flying anymore?" I asked.

"There are no jobs," he said, adding that his demeanor never properly conformed to the Surinamese pilot community. "All drug runners and ass lickers if you ask me. I'm just a regular guy, you know? I talk with regular people. I'm no different than anyone else." He had worked all around North America—in Texas, New Jersey, and the Caribbean. His last job had been in Curacao, as a charter pilot for a rich Dutch businessman. "He had a refinery up there, and he would buy barrels of slush for $6—you know, the leftover stuff from oil—refine it, and sell it back for $74. He made a killing." But this man's need for a charter pilot ran out and Mike found himself back in Suriname without a job. "What about you, what brings you to Suriname?"

"Just a vacation," I replied.

He frowned. "Aren't there better places to go on vacation than Suriname?"

"I suppose so," I said. "But there seems to be a decent number of tourists in Paramaribo."

"I guess."

"What kind of people do you usually see here?"

"Oh all types. Dutch, Americans, Germans."

"Americans? Really?" I hadn't met a single American since I landed in Georgetown.

"Oh yeah. Especially for work. It's like a gold rush down here—they're finding the stuff everywhere. And they make aluminum of course. They go into the interior to find it. You know bauxite right? They take it, bring it to the factories, and turn it into aluminum. Then they sell it all over the world." Despite his shabby appearance, Mike spoke confidently and intelligently. When he couldn't remember a certain word—like bauxite, for example—he would curl his pointer finger and bring it up just below his lower lip, staring at the sidewalk until it came to him. It made him seem almost wise.

He mentioned the company Steve worked for and explained how Suriname was getting screwed in the deal. "You see, the previous president made an agreement where the Canadians got 95 percent of the profits. It was all done on bribery—that's how everything gets done around here. All corruption and greed." As he talked about the incompetence of the national government, his eyes scanned the sidewalk and street behind me.

"Have you heard about the current President?" he asked. I shook my head. "Oh you will—he was in power back in the early eighties. When a bunch of people threatened to overthrow his regime, he and his men took them away and executed them—fifteen people in all."

I later found that this incident had a name, the December Murders, and that it was probably the most infamous event of Suriname's recent history. Mike was particularly disgusted that this man, so obviously corrupt, had charmed his way back into the Suriname government. He shook his head dejectedly and said, "Everyone who voted for this President is either one, uneducated, or two, stupid."

I mentioned that I was eager to see the rest of the country, but had resorted to using a tour company because independent travel seemed utterly impossible.

"That's probably true," he said, "but I don't think it's too hard to get a guide. And this company here"—he motioned to the one I was heading to—"is certainly a good one."

I told Mike I was happy to hear that and dug through my pockets to collect whatever change I had available.

"Barely a dollar," he said softly. "Well, if there's anything else you need, you know where to find me. I'll be here. And hopefully it'll stop raining."

I wished him luck.

JOURNAL ENTRY — PARAMARIBO

*Day 11—**Paramaribo, Suriname:** The national holiday has brought this entire country to a halt. Shops are closed; people are resting. I often strike up conversations with folks simply because I have no idea what else to do. Nevertheless, I seem to be slowly learning quite a bit about the country, as if each person I speak with has been assigned his or her own section—greed, incompetence, corruption—in the introductory portion of a Suriname guidebook.*

This is new territory for me—both literally and figuratively. I've never been much of a conversationalist, on the road or off. And my guidebook dependence has only fueled this behavior: why confer with a random local when I have

an entire library of maps and recommendations at my dis-
posal? I've always thought that those who procure advice
from strangers while traveling are the same people who go to
a restaurant and ask the waiter what dish they should order.
Such behavior confuses me. Even if you conveniently ignore
the server's obvious incentive to recommend the most expen-
sive item (which, of course, was my own strategy when I
waited tables), how on earth is the waiter supposed to know
what kind of food you like? "Get the halibut," she may say.
But I hate halibut, you think to yourself.

I have frequently been scolded for this introverted trav-
eling approach. "Oh, but you're missing out on the best
parts of travel," advises the travel world's avant-garde. Duly
noted. But while you're talking to Stan the local carpen-
ter, I'll be off using my guidebook to see a world-renowned
piece of art or to eat at a universally lauded four-star restau-
rant. And so while I did indeed vow to embrace encounters
moving forward and while my Paramaribo conversations
have undoubtedly been rather informative, I'm less con-
vinced that my interaction with Mike the car washer was
a more valuable traveling experience than seeing whatever
five-star attractions lay within Paramaribo's guidebook-
recommended interior. And if that's an unpopular observa-
tion, then so be it.

Paramaribo finally went back to work the next day and the
area surrounding my hotel, so desolate the previous forty-
eight hours, burst alive with the habitual hustle of weekday
life. The street's dusty meridian, formerly a wasteland for stray
dogs and loose garbage, was now filled with parked vehicles,
and the shops lining the boulevard teemed with the energy
of regular business. When I left my hotel for the first time
that morning, I immediately realized that the neighborhood

in which I was staying was not the dodgy ghetto I had created in my mind, but instead an ordinary commercial sector that had used the government-appointed holiday to take a well deserved break.

Despite the unexpected transformation of its setting, I was still excited to put the Flamingo behind me, so I grabbed my bag, left the hotel, and checked in to the cleaner and quieter resort I had stumbled upon the previous day. My new room had only one (working) television and no microwave, but the bed was off the floor, fresh towels hung in the bathroom, and there was no need to manually tighten each individual light bulb. I lay down on the bed, flipping through thirty channels of English-language television, and continued the hotel's imaginary guidebook description in my mind: A midrange accommodation, "clean and relaxing," with a tiny thumbs up next to its name—Author's Pick!

Eager to take advantage of my last day in Paramaribo, I left my room and went for a walk. Unfortunately, the museum I had wanted to visit, the one housed inside Fort Zeelandia, was closed for the second time in a few days, so I gave up on sightseeing and instead decided to get lunch at the outdoor food stands sandwiched between Paramaribo's crumbling historical district and the river. As I weighed the available options, I spotted Gio, the tour guide I had been talking with, killing time before work. He invited me to join him.

"So, what's the deal with this place?" I asked.

"Well, each booth is run by its own ethnicity." He pointed to a particularly shabby looking stand. "That one, for example, is run by the Chinese. I wouldn't eat anything from them. They leave their food out way too long." He pointed to another. "That one's not bad. Japanese. They serve rice, noodles, that type of stuff. It's pretty clean too. But this one," he said, swiveling to a corner booth, "serves the stuff that black people eat. You know, chicken, rice, greens. Very good." His recommendation bore out; the chicken was delicious. And as I ate, Gio and I chatted about my trip.

"So, what have you been doing the past few days?" he asked, leaning back in his chair. I told him about my stay at the Flamingo, my experience during Freedom Day, and my auspicious discovery of the Eco Resort Inn.

"Oh yeah, I know it," he said. "It's a good hotel. And it's in a much more tourist-friendly neighborhood."

I admitted that I felt much more comfortable in Suriname than I had in Georgetown. "To be honest," I said, "walking around Paramaribo just feels different, as if people actually have things to do."

He agreed. "The Guyanese have a different mindset than the Surinamese, both socially and economically. The Guyanese President once famously said, 'Why do you need a Mercedes for a bicycle economy?' What he meant was that there was no reason for his people to buy bigger and better things—the country just isn't built to sustain that type of lifestyle. But here in Suriname, as soon as people get any money, that's what they do—they buy a brand new car. I'm sure people think that way in New York too, right?"

I said that while that was generally true, the reality was a little more complicated. I explained that the New York he had seen in movies and television shows—the city of big dreams and big money—clashed with the reality I encountered on a daily basis. "My neighborhood is actually kind of like Suriname—a giant mix of cultures and ethnicities. The block I live on is filled with people from Asia—Indians, Pakistanis, Bangladeshis. But go two blocks to the east, and you begin to run into people from Latin America—Peruvians and Ecuadorians and Mexicans. Everyone just mingles together because they have no choice. It's kind of like this food court, actually." I explained that the fusion had created a unique tourist environment in which the visitor could experience different cultures, but that tensions and territorialities often created a difficult living situation. I figured it was the same way in Suriname.

"What's the breakdown of ethnicities here?" I asked.

"I don't know," he said, "but I do know that the Chinese are moving in fast. They're attracted to the growing economy—mostly the timber. And it's impossible to compete with them. Their work ethic is just so much higher than the Surinamese. They come in and they rent out businesses from local shopkeepers, offering them the usual monthly revenue because they know that they'll be able to increase it going forward. It's a good deal for the local guy because he's making the same amount of money without having to work. But after a couple months, he realizes the business he had started years before is now gone, it's no longer what it used to be, and it's being completely run by the Chinese." He brought his hands together and then released them, palms up—poof!—before smiling and lowering his voice. "You know, I heard a rumor. I have no idea where it came from, it's just a rumor. But somebody told me that the government was planning on importing two million Chinese workers into the country."

I laughed. "Wouldn't that quintuple the population?"

"Yeah. But whether it's true or not, it at least means people want to come here."

"And that's not such a bad problem to have," I said.

"Not at all." He grinned. "Look at you guys and the Mexicans!"

It was getting late and Gio had to leave for work. "I'll be taking you guys down to the boat tomorrow," he said, referring to the tour I had signed up for. "It looks like it'll be you and seven other people."

"You're not coming with us?" I asked.

"No, wish I could. But they need me here, just in case somebody needs a one-day tour or something."

"Too bad," I said, adding that maybe in a few years, when tourism grows and business improves, the company will let him accompany the visitors throughout the entire tour.

"Maybe," he said chuckling as he hopped aboard his motorcycle. "But I'm more concerned about what I'm gonna do when two million Chinese get here."

INTERLUDE — LEWIS AND CLARK:
RELIANCE

The decision to designate this endeavor *the* guidebook experiment rather than *my* guidebook experiment was not a frivolous one. It instead emerged from a recognition that my journey would be as much about the people I encountered as it would be about my own experiences. And my time in Paramaribo, as I patiently waited out the unexpected delay of a national holiday, was perhaps the clearest illustration of this assumption brought to life—without Steve and Mike, it's likely I would have left Paramaribo knowing little about the country's economy or government; without Gio and his tour company, it's likely I would never have left at all (an exaggeration, of course, but you get the point).

Popular culture, meanwhile, has bestowed upon the historical journey at the center of this narrative the designation "the *Lewis and Clark* expedition." And yet there is perhaps no phrase less appropriate in describing the intricacies of the voyage than that very title. Because while the expedition was indeed led by Meriwether Lewis and William Clark, undoubtedly two of the finest explorers in American history, at no point were the captains ever left to fend entirely for themselves, alone in the wilderness, back-to-back, fighting grizzly bears and hunting buffalo. The phrase, therefore, is a bit of a misnomer, an inaccuracy; Lewis and Clark, two of the most famous travelers of all time, were in fact as dependent and reliant upon those around them—be it for knowledge, food, lodging, or directions—as I was on my own journey.

Most important to the success of the expedition was the selection of a capable crew, young men who could adequately compensate for the gaps in a journey through unknown territory by building shelter, gathering food, and transporting supplies. As Lewis told Clark before they set off from St. Louis, the expedition "must depend on a judicious selection of our men; their qualifications should be such as perfectly fit them for the service, otherwise they will rather clog than further the objects in view." Fortunately, their pool of potential crewmembers was deep. "What young unmarried frontiersman—whether gentleman's sons or the sons of whiskey-making corn farmers—could resist such an opportunity?" asks historian Stephen Ambrose. "It was the ultimate adventure."

The captains chose wisely, enlisting a diverse crew with varied talents. Some men were relied upon to keep the expedition fed, by hunting game and cooking meals. And when food ran low, the expedition relied on individuals like Private John Shields, who, as mentioned previously, used his talents as a blacksmith to trade for corn. Other men were asked to simply raise the expedition's morale. Private Pierre Cruzatte, for instance, is remembered fondly for his fiddle playing, a festive antidote to the hard slog of the expedition's daily routine. But no expedition member was as appreciated, adored, or revered as much as the veteran frontiersman George Drouillard. Of the man's hunting, Clark wrote, "I scarcely know how we should subsist, I believe but badly if it was not for the exertions of this excellent hunter," while Lewis applauded the outdoorsman's role as intimidator: "The Indians witnessed Drewyer's [they loved the man dearly but routinely misspelled his name] shooting some of those elk, which has given them a very exalted opinion of us as marksmen and the superior excellence of our rifles compared with their guns; this may

probably be of service to us, as it will deter them from any acts
of hostility if they have ever meditated any such."

The son of an Indian woman, Drouillard was also utilized
as an interpreter. On August 14th, 1805 Lewis acknowledged
this contribution when he wrote: "The means I had of communicating with these people was by way of Drewyer who
understood perfectly the common language of gesticula-
tion or signs which seems to be universally understood by
all the nations we have yet seen." Still, while sign language
is effective for certain travel needs—food (bunched fingers
to mouth), drink (tip of a cup), hotel (hands under head)—it
lacks the nuance necessary for more sophisticated conversations, the kind of vocabulary a traveler might pick up in the
"Language" section of a guidebook (Where is the hospital? =
¿Dónde está el hospital?).

To counter this deficiency, Lewis and Clark enlisted the
human equivalent—men and women who could communicate with the Indians in their native tongues. One of these
men was Toussaint Charbonneau, a French Canadian who
lived with the Hidatsa Indians and who joined the group
during the winter at Fort Mandan. Charbonneau, according to author W. Dale Nelson, was "a poor and timid sailor
and hiker, not good qualities for a man on a transcontinental
trek, but a good enough interpreter, and frequently a valuable
source of the kind of information about the Indian tribes that
Jefferson wanted his explorers to gather." Along with Charbonneau came his wife Sacagawea, an Indian woman who
had been purchased from the Hidatsas a few years earlier.
And with several languages on board, Lewis and Clark were
then able to create a complicated, albeit effective game of tele-
phone. Ambrose describes one of these chains, a tiered system
used to communicate with the Shoshone Indians: "Dispens-
ing with Drouillard and the sign language, [Lewis] decided
to use a translation chain that ran from Sacagawea, speaking

Shoshone to the Indians and translating it into Hidatsa, to Charbonneau, who translated her Hidatsa into French, to Private Francis Labiche, who translated from French to English."

Communicating with the Indians was crucial—the expedition's members depended on the tribes as much as they depended on each other. And at no time was Lewis and Clark's dependence on Indian resourcefulness, skill, and knowledge more evident than during the expedition's two crossings of the Bitterroot Mountains. These mountains were unlike any the Americans had ever seen, a complex labyrinth of towering peaks and deep valleys. And with limited options, the expedition was forced to depend on a man whom the Shoshones called "Old Toby" to lead them through the uninhabited terrain. As a tour guide, Old Toby struggled—he got lost, making a difficult crossing even more so—but in the end steered the expedition safely to more manageable ground. In a later letter to an unknown recipient, Lewis recalls the trust the men had put in Old Toby as they launched their assault on the Rocky Mountains: "We attempted with success those unknown formidable snow clad mountains on the bare word of a savage, while 99/100th of his countrymen assured us that a passage was impracticable."

But the mountains, of course, would need to be crossed again. Eager to get moving after a long winter of harsh weather, Indian tension, and a monotonous diet, the substantial patience that had guided the men to the shores of the Pacific Ocean had evaporated. In a May 17th, 1806 journal entry, Clark writes of "that icy barrier which separates me from my friends and country, from all which makes life estimable." Despite warnings from the Indians to wait out the spring thaw, the expedition set out on its own and was quickly stalled by fallen trees and massive snow drifts. On June 17th, 1806, Clark writes, "Under these circumstances we conceived it madness in this stage of the expedition to proceed without a guide." And so the expedition gave in, retreating back the way they had come, and enlisting three Nez Perce guides to take them all the way to Traveler's Rest. According to Ambrose, the skill displayed by the Indian guides during this two-week trek was nothing short of remarkable: "Their sense of distance and timing, not to mention their sense of direction and ability to follow a trail buried under ten feet of snow, was a superb feat of woodsmanship."

The elimination of the guidebook does not entail traveling independence but rather a transfer of the elements on which a traveler depends. Lewis and Clark were unshackled from the sometimes immovable route of previous explorers yet were entirely reliant on their crew and the tribes they encountered for a successful journey. Without the help of others, in fact, there would have *been* no Lewis and Clark expedition, no great traverse of the continent, no opening of the American West. And so perhaps Paul Theroux was writing about the guidebook-less traveler when he said, "Most travel, and certainly the rewarding kind, involves depending on the kindness of strangers, putting yourself into the hands of people you don't know and trusting them with your life. This risky suspension of disbelief is often an experience freighted with anxiety. But what's the alternative? Usually there is none."

CHAPTER IO

ß ß ß

Isadou

Writing about a small Brazilian village in which his Amazon expedition had been momentarily stalled, travel writer Peter Fleming once wrote that, "enforced familiarity bred something more bitter than contempt." But the opposite had happened to me in Paramaribo; with ample time to properly explore it, I had grown fonder of Suriname's capital. I had found places to eat lunch, discovered pleasing spots from which to view the water, and had met some interesting people. It had been an uneventful but pleasant few days in a city I hadn't known existed a month ago. But I was ready to continue the experiment, eager to keep moving through the Guianas. And so, having booked a three-day trip to a Surinamese jungle resort called Isadou with an influx of wired funds from my wife, I packed my bag and sat in a chair on my hotel's porch waiting for the tour company to pick me up. Shortly after nine, the bus rumbled into the parking lot.

Many of the brochures and advertisements I had seen for the company had been written in English and I had assumed that its tours would be primarily English-language excursions. But my assumptions were wrong—not only were most of the other passengers already on the bus related (there was one family of seven and one married couple) but they were also all Dutch, and when Gio announced that he would be speaking English, I knew that it was my presence alone that had necessitated the linguistic shift. No worries, the other passengers assured me, they were all sufficiently bilingual.

Three hours after leaving Paramaribo, we reached the launching point for trips into the jungle—a bustling dock named Atjoni located, according to my map, at the tip of the southernmost road branching out from the capital. The dock was a transportation hub for both locals and tourists and the small beach that led down the road to the river was lined with brightly painted canoes, half of which served as shuttles for the villages located deep inside the jungle and half of which were used by Suriname's various tour companies. It was easy to tell the difference—the tourist canoes were comically stacked with orange life vests, cases of Coca-Cola, and oversized backpacks.

Gio introduced us to our river guide, a weathered, energetic man named Boris, who spoke little English. We remained on the beach for about a half hour, observing the constant stream of passengers arriving and departing, while Boris and Gio gathered supplies for the trip from the dock's popular covered market. As we prepared to push off for Isadou, I bid Gio, and his mastery of the English language, farewell, entrusting my enjoyment and understanding of the rest of the journey to the Dutch-speaking Boris.

The river was more populated and active than the one I had traveled down in Guyana. As we chugged upstream, we passed scenes of everyday riverside life—young boys bouncing off rocks into the water, weary mothers fussily washing laundry on the dirt shores, and a solitary grandmother bathing in a secluded inlet, her head barely visible above the river's surface. We proceeded at a touristic pace, gingerly navigating our boat through the water, while locals careened past, at ease with the dangerous obstacles in the river.

Soon, the traffic dissipated, each boat branching off onto its own respective course, and after forty-five minutes we reached our destination—Isadou. It was a small island, easily traversed from one end to the other in a couple of minutes. Its center had been cleared of trees, forming what was essentially a ring of protective vegetation around a wide grassy lawn. Surrounding the field was a collection of buildings—a spacious open-air kitchen, a makeshift DJ booth with a full drum set and speakers, a row of identical huts for the visitors, and a few larger residences for the island's workers. There was no activity and little noise besides the occasional squawk of a passing bird.

I settled into the visitor hut closest to the edge of the river, and after being told that the afternoon was ours to relax, dragged a chair from my deck to an elevated clearing overlooking a series of rapids. I sat there for a few hours, reading my book and staring into the verdant emptiness of the forest. Across the narrow section of river was another island, undeveloped and thick with a vertical layer of bush. The scenery was spectacularly still until the late afternoon, when a family of spider monkeys emerged from the interior, swinging their way high across its canopy.

I darted back to the huts, eager to inform my fellow tourgoers about the wildlife encounter. They readily followed me back to the river's edge, just in time to watch the last of the monkeys disappear into the vast forest. Afterwards, the group lingered, comparing notes about their first few hours on the island. Most were pleased with the tranquility, seclusion, and overall condition of the island's facilities. Others, such as one despondent, camera-equipped woman, had decided to wage a hopeless struggle against nature.

"There's a frog in my toilet," she said, as she brought up a picture of a frog in her toilet. "It looks like I haven't flushed," she said glumly.

And with that, so began our stay at Isadou, Suriname's premier jungle paradise.

෨ ෨ ෨

The itinerary of the multi-day tour was built around a handful of short, active excursions. One trip took us to an island
that had previously been used to harvest fruit and vegetables.
As Boris led us through the island's narrow trails, he explained
(in Dutch and therefore translated to me by the closest family
member) the odd facts of its history and the strange particulars of its ecosystem. Another trip, this one at night and on the
water, took us in search of nocturnal caymans, small alligator-
like creatures endemic to Central and South America. Most
of the excursions, though, were designed to expose the tourgoers to Suriname's collection of isolated jungle communities.
Boris would take us into the heart of these villages, parading
our group down dirt paths and pointing out the significance
of each building. "This one is a church built by the Americans," he would say, or "This one is used for funerals." The
cultural exposure, however, was two-fold; as we marched
through schools and into homes, disrupting the pace of typical
rural life, the villagers would gather on the edges of our route,
children mocking, men posturing and flaunting, and women
shying away with a reserved curiosity.

Before one of these trips, Boris, a man who had spent his
entire life in the jungle, looked to the sky and delivered an
ominous warning: "I think we have rain in the afternoon."
A few hours later, as we walked along a dirt road between
villages, the sky became gray and the dark, swollen clouds
that had surreptitiously congregated directly above us burst,
unleashing a downpour that bellowed through the partial
protection of the forest's canopy and forced us to take cover
inside one of the town's huts.

When the rain finally stopped, we thanked the owners of the
house for their hospitality, left the village, and walked down to
the river to wait for our boat. Once back in my hut, I hung up

my clothes and returned to the chair I had set up at the edge
of the water. As the sun lowered, and the sky shattered into
the magnificent shades of a tropical dusk, I stared across at the
island on which I had seen the spider monkeys frolicking, hoping for additional clues as to what lay inside its hidden interior.
But this time, nothing happened—no trees rattled, no sounds
echoed, no animals stirred. After some time, I heard the call
for dinner and I abandoned my post for our nightly meal of
chicken and vegetables.

JOURNAL ENTRY — ISADOU

*Day 14—Isadou Resort, Suriname: I'm the only member
of the tour traveling alone and so have been assigned my
own hut on the island. There's an attached bathroom with a
functioning shower (a plus) and a covered front porch from
which I can sit and watch the afternoon thunderstorms (a
big plus). A single orange light bulb flickers from the beams
above my head, dimly illuminating the hut's ceiling yet not
bright enough to reach my notebook. And so I write this
entry using the light from my headlamp, like a teenager
recording his intimate secrets while the rest of his family
sleeps soundly nearby.*

*We have spent only forty-eight hours in Suriname's inte-
rior but I am anxious to break free and return to Paramaribo. It's not the other tourists, who are quite friendly, nor
the guide, who is perfectly adequate, nor the environment,
which is, in many ways, the epitome of Amazonia. Instead,
I have grown increasingly wary of the manner by which
our group is ferried around like a band of roving voyeurs,
a camera-toting herd of interlopers gawking at the geologi-
cally and culturally unfamiliar.*

*Today's afternoon rainstorm, during which we were
trapped at one of the region's small jungle communities,*

serves as an apt example. For the people of the village, the downpour was an opportunity. Children undressed and washed themselves between the huts; grandmothers collected buckets of rainwater. For our group, however, the rain was akin to captivity; until it abated, we were trapped, unable to reach our boat and unable to return to our island.

Had I stumbled into the experience alone, perhaps I would have construed the delay as a poignant anthropological encounter, a stirring and unexpected glimpse into the lives of an unfamiliar society. But I hadn't been alone; I was instead part of a large tour group. And so the excursion had felt more like an intrusion, a contrived encounter with an uninterested party prolonged only by the rain.

This feeling, a nagging sense of passive imprisonment, has been amplified by the tour's rigid and structured itinerary. In Guyana, I had traveled into the interior independently and, through perseverance and luck, had "discovered" the country's primary attraction. In Suriname, the path had been less clear, and with limited funds and diminished motivation, had chosen to enlist a tour company to escort me into the jungle.

Although I'm not yet at the end of my experiment, I can't help but think that these two distinct experiences sufficiently embody and accurately represent the inherent contradiction of guidebook-less travel. Because although the guidebook-less traveler is blessed with an infinite amount of autonomy—the freedom to decide where to go, when to go, and how to get there—that autonomy is far too often hampered by the very conditions from which it is spawned—the traveler doesn't know where to go, doesn't know when to arrive, and doesn't know how to get there. And, in those cases, absolute autonomy succumbs to absolute dependence.

☙ ☙ ☙

Before my trip into the jungle, I had told my bank to send my new debit card to the Flamingo Hotel and Casino, and when I returned from the excursion, I was mildly surprised (and greatly relieved) to find it waiting for me behind the front desk. Flush with new funds, and wanting to celebrate my last night in Paramaribo, I decided to try a Chinese restaurant I had passed several times on my way to the riverfront.

"Going out?" asked the woman behind the front desk.

"Yeah. Going to dinner," I said. "Do you know anything about the big Chinese restaurant down the road on the way to the river?"

"Oh sure. It's okay," she replied, tepidly.

"Well, any other suggestions?"

"Why don't you try the Ambassador's restaurant? I've never been there but I've heard good things."

And so, taking the advice of my hotel's "concierge," I abandoned my original plan and walked across the street to the Flamingo's twin sister, the Hotel Ambassador and Casino, where the casino's signature restaurant, Ambrosia, was located on the second floor. Outside the restaurant, a sign posted to the wall advised potential patrons that shorts and sneakers, both of which I was wearing, were forbidden. But when I asked a nearby security guard if I was allowed to enter, he quickly rescinded the apparently flexible rules, smiling and extending his arm as if to open an imaginary door. I soon understood why; despite being Saturday night, only one of the twenty or so tables was occupied. The diners were a group of affluent Indian women, chatting, sipping champagne, and playing music through one of their mobile phones. When nobody appeared to greet me, I decided to seat myself, choosing the only table in the place set for two.

The restaurant itself was handsomely decorated with long white curtains, potted palms, and elegant glass chandeliers. One corner had a modest bar, its twelve bottles artfully arranged among long stemmed wine glasses. The other corner had an elevated platform and a microphone stand. I snuck a peak at the bottom of my bread plate: Royal Ceramicor Porcelain, the kind of china a couple might put on its wedding registry. The restaurant was clearly ready for business, eager to serve Paramaribo's elite. But no one was there.

After several minutes, the waitress finally emerged from the kitchen. I ordered French Onion soup, a Chef's salad, and a beer—a combination I felt would sufficiently transition my palate away from chicken and rice. After delivering my drink, the waitress disappeared again, scurrying back into the kitchen. A moment later, I heard the clank and clamor of pots and pans—was she the restaurant's only employee?

I spent the next half hour watching the waitress/cook sprint back and forth between the kitchen and the dining room. She spent an inordinate time catering to the whims of the Indian women—another napkin, more water, different silverware. My meal, when it was finally delivered, reminded me of my first dinner in Suriname, flavorless and insufficient, and left me hungry for another course. But the prices on the menu scared me away; listed in U.S. dollars, the entrees alone cost almost as much as a night at my hotel. I knew it was all a part of the restaurant's contrived luxury, an attempt to elevate itself above the city's other offerings. Even the restaurant's logo was a farce—the name Ambrosia topped by a line of five stars, as if it had received the industry's highest possible honor.

After paying the bill, I sat at my table finishing my drink and wondered what the Chinese restaurant would have been like. The atmosphere would have certainly been different— less opulence, more reality. And the prices would have surely been lower. But, considering the ups and downs of my journey through the Guianas, Ambrosia's bizarre style seemed appropriate for my final meal in Paramaribo, an aesthetically lavish yet fundamentally unsatisfying experience.

The next day, I found a bus headed back toward the Guyana border. I had decided during my trip into the jungle that I would not be traveling all the way to French Guiana. While the setbacks from the robbery had contributed to the decision, the ultimate reason was something much more tangible—the Guianas were really expensive, often prohibitively so. And from what I had heard of French Guiana, especially its capital city of Cayenne, the prices were only going to get worse. While I had not yet been forced to part with some of my dearest possessions (unlike Meriwether Lewis who had been forced to trade his personal uniform coat for a horse), I could still see my bank account dwindling fast, and so decided to reverse course, to head back to Georgetown where I could catch a flight back to the United States. The guidebook experiment was coming to an end.

I chose to spend my final night halfway between Paramaribo and Georgetown—in Nieuw Nickerie, one of the few landmarks in western Suriname listed on my map. The approach to the city took us past rice fields and cow pastures so remote that as we rumbled down the two-lane highway, I wondered how inviting the city could possibly be. But my fears proved to be unfounded; Nieuw Nickerie was a pleasantly quiet town whose most distinctive feature stood out immediately—a broad, main thoroughfare lined with towering palms and bisected by a lily pad-saturated creek. I assumed the street served as the city's iconic sight, the primary image for the town's postcards. I also assumed those images omitted the attraction's principal scar—desperate men, pants rolled up to their knees, wading through the murky water looking for frogs and fish.

In Paramaribo, I had taken the advice of Gio and had used the Internet to book a room at Nieuw Nickerie's Residence Inn. But when the bus dropped me off in front of the hotel and I attempted to check-in, I was told that my reservation had been lost and that the hotel was full. When I asked for another hotel suggestion, I was dismayed to be directed to another hybrid establishment, the Regency Hotel and Casino. But the Regency was tolerable: a comfortable option with helpful staff and I soon had an air-conditioned room (for a price significantly less than the Residence Inn), a taxi to the ferry the next morning, and a cold beer at the hotel's patio bar.

My peace was soon interrupted by a rambling Guyanese businessman seated at an adjoining table. He was a tiny man with the face of a mouse and his stylish suit drooped pathetically off his frail body. The row of bottles arranged on his table indicated that he had been drinking for a while and I found it difficult to understand most of what he said. What I did catch: he was from the border between Guyana and Brazil, used to work in Paramaribo, now worked in Nieuw Nickerie, and frequented the Regency because of its amenities.

"Massage," he said, grinning, pointing to a small room off to the side of the bar.

An hour later, the upstairs balcony opened for dinner and I left the bar, grateful to have escaped what had become an utterly inane and increasingly incoherent conversation. But my companion, despite repeatedly saying he had somewhere else to be, followed me upstairs. As I ate my meal, he continued to drink, and stared vacuously at the television attached to the wall. Occasionally, he would try to get my attention, but because of the noise I had no idea what he was trying to say. The one sentence I did make out was puzzling: "Friend, you don't go to America tomorrow, you go to Venezuela!"

When I was ready to leave, I got up and walked over to his table to shake his hand. He held it tightly, and looked me in the eye: "Next time," he stammered, "you come back here."

"Sure," I said. The next time I come back to this city, a place I hadn't known existed a few days ago, in a country I

knew nothing about three weeks ago, I would return to the
Regency Hotel, and I would share a beer with this poor man.
I knew where to find him.

JOURNAL ENTRY — NIEUW NICKERIE

*Day 16—Nieuw Nickerie, Suriname: My guidebook
experiment is nearing its completion, ending earlier than I
would have hoped. Tomorrow I take the ferry to Guyana
and a bus back to Georgetown. From there, it's a quick
flight to New York and my apartment in Queens.*

*Revisiting my notes from the past few days, it's clear
that my trip is sputtering to a rather lackluster conclusion.
My last two days—dinner at the Ambrosia, drinks at the
Regency—were the unfortunate consequence of poor planning and uninspired effort. Seasoned travelers forever plead
with fledgling explorers to "make something happen"—get
out of your comfort zone, take a bus somewhere, talk to a
local. In that respect I admittedly did the bare minimum,
perhaps directly due to my lack of guidebook material but
more likely due to the frustration caused by my lack of guidebook material. In Paramaribo, I was leery of wandering the
city to search for a more enticing restaurant (I had, after all,
wandered into the wrong neighborhood in Georgetown and
had been violently robbed). And so I trusted the advice of my
hotel attendant, eating dinner at the Ambrosia and spending
eight bucks on a lackluster salad. In Nieuw Nickerie, at a
town I recognize to be friendly but touristically insignifi-
cant, I have no interest in sightseeing and was content to find
a comfortable place to stay for the night and a cold drink.
And so, off the advice of another hotel attendant, I settled for
my current abode, the Regency, where I did indeed find a
local to talk to (a "how-to travel" checkmark!). But he was
incoherent and lonely, the most pathetic sort of muse.*

In the end, though, I must continuously remind myself that this trip is an experiment rather than a holiday. And so rather than lamenting my insipid travel-based decisions, I must instead accept those experiences for what they are: valuable data. In short, do those experiences tell us anything about guidebook-less travel?

Perhaps. One of the most noticeable effects of the proliferation of guidebook material—the increased availability of laudatory top ten lists and glossy destination highlight photos—is the transformation of every excursion into a quantifiable event, the conversion of every decision into a measurable occasion. The guidebook is fundamentally designed to enhance the efficiency of a journey, to amplify the good while mitigating the irrelevant. There are no top ten ordinary, run-of-the-mill experiences, only travel apexes, things you must do when you're in France, Thailand, or New Zealand. And while it's true that I've been a guidebook adherent my whole life—and have reaped the efficient rewards of extensive guidebook-aided travel—my experiences during the past fifteen years have also allowed me to realize that for every Taj Mahal, there's an accompanying five-hour wait in the scorching heat of an Indian railway station. For every Machu Picchu, there's an accompanying torturous and unnecessarily lengthy South American border crossing. And without a guidebook to separate the "grain from the chaff," as the guidebook historian Nicholas T. Parsons has said, the "chaff"—in this case the Ambrosia and the Regency—displays a remarkable ability to rise to the top. And with that, the guidebook-less traveler is reminded, often quite crudely and unexpectedly, that sometimes this is what travel is: a shitty meal at an empty restaurant.

INTERLUDE — LEWIS AND
CLARK: FINALE

The end of my trip, marked by "lavish" meals and unfulfilled promises, oddly mirrored the trip I had been attempting to mimic. On September 23rd, 1806, after twenty-eight months and 8,000 miles, the Lewis and Clark expedition arrived back in St. Louis. Although the continuous all-water route had been a chimera, the expedition was by no means a failure—the men had made it to the Pacific Ocean and back, they had gathered an enormous amount of information about the far reaches of the continent, and they had remained remarkably healthy throughout. As Lewis wrote to Thomas Jefferson upon their return: "The whole of the party who accompanied me from the Mandans have returned in good health, which is not, I assure you, to me one of the least pleasing considerations of the voyage."

The crew was eager to celebrate their accomplishments. From the first dinner held in the expedition's honor—a joyous affair two days after arrival—emerged a busy calendar of ritzy banquets and festive gatherings. Lewis set off for Washington, where he was to debrief the man who had made the expedition possible, Thomas Jefferson. It was slow-going, according to Stephen Ambrose, "at least in part because at every town and village the residents insisted on some sort of dinner and ball to honor him." Clark, on the other hand, made his way to Virginia where he would begin a relationship with the woman who would eventually become his wife. But tending to personal matters did little to quell the tide of what biographer Landon Y. Jones called the "fulsome praise of the citizens." During one ceremony, for example, Clark was forced to "endure" the following toast: "You have navigated bold and unknown rivers, traversed mountains, which had never before been impressed with the footsteps of civilized man, and surmounted every obstacle, which climate, nature or ferocious savages could throw in your way."

But outside of the revelry, there were numerous matters to which the captains' attention now turned and no objective was deemed as important as the release of the explorers' journals. This task fell on Meriwether Lewis, and once in Philadelphia, the explorer enlisted scholars who could help with the journals' publication. He found a man who could draw accurate pictures of the flora and fauna and another who could convert the celestial observations into latitude and longitude. By July 1807, writes Ambrose, "Lewis had signed up botanists, ornithologists, naturalists, artists, mathematicians, zoologists, and others to help make his work as good as it could possibly be. He had done everything he could to hurry along the publication process—except one thing. He had not hired an editor."

This is where the story of Lewis and Clark begins to diverge. Clark was put in charge of Indian affairs for the Louisiana Territory. He married a young woman and settled comfortably into his new life. As scholar Clay Jenkinson suggests, "Clark returned from the wilderness in 1806 not diminished by the great adventure but strengthened. . . . It would be hard to imagine a more successful and satisfying post-expedition life than Clark's."

Lewis, meanwhile, was appointed governor of the Louisiana Territory. But unlike Clark, he was unable to find a consistent footing. According to Jenkinson:

> By 1809, Meriwether Lewis had a world of troubles. He was drinking heavily. He was using opium, if only in the form of laudanum, the pain killer of the privileged classes of his day. His personal finances were in terrible disarray. His official accounts as Governor of northern Louisiana were in chaos, and Mr. Madison's War Department [James Madison

had replaced Thomas Jefferson as President] was challeng-
ing his official expenditures.

Through it all, Lewis failed to complete what had been his
"singular objective" upon leaving Washington D.C. in 1807—
the publication of the expedition journals. Jefferson repeatedly
pressed the explorer for an update—in one letter, the former
President wrote, "I am very often applied to know when your
work will begin to appear; and I have so long promised copies to my literary correspondents in France, that I am almost
bankrupt in their eyes. I shall be very happy to receive from
yourself information of your expectations on this subject.
Everybody is impatient for it." But Lewis remained silent.

All of Lewis's problems came to a head in August 1809
when a draft he had submitted to the U.S. government was
suddenly denied, making him personally responsible for the
unforeseen expense, and causing his debtors to abruptly call in
the many loans that the explorer had accumulated. Knowing
he would be unable to pay, Lewis proposed a trip to Washington D.C. to sort the matter out; Clark agreed to meet up
with him via a different route. But Lewis never made it. In the
early morning hours of October 11th, 1809, in an inn seventy
miles southwest of Nashville, Tennessee, Lewis took his own
life. And just like that, one of the most celebrated explorers in
American history was gone.

In the final chapter of *The Character of Meriwether Lewis:
Explorer in the Wilderness,* Jenkinson muses on the reasons for
Lewis's abrupt and unfortunate suicide. Some of the theories discussed by the author include Lewis's lack of support
structures (including his inability to find a wife and the death
of his beloved dog Seaman), his supposed physical and mental illness during the later years of his life, and the friction
between Lewis and certain members of the U.S. government. At the end of the chapter, when Jenkinson is forced to

submit his own hypothesis, he appropriately hedges his bets, arguing that a variety of factors contributed to the explorer's ultimate demise. But while the precise motive for Lewis's suicide remains conjecture for the foreseeable future, the theory most relevant to our current guidebook-related discussion is found in the appetizer version of Jenkinson's work, a smaller book entitled *The Character of Meriwether Lewis: "Completely Metamorphosed" in the American West.* In it, the author introduces a concept called inexpressibility topos, explained as "the idea that some experience, some event is beyond the ability of the writer, perhaps any writer, to describe." Nobody knows why Lewis struggled to publish his journals, but perhaps the silence can be partly explained by the explorer's inability to articulate the experience. "It wasn't that he could not write. It was rather that he could not write prose equal to his own expectations." Maybe, says Jenkinson, "[t]he West was mightier than the pen—at least his pen."

I am not suggesting that Meriwether Lewis killed himself simply because he was unable to adequately express his thoughts—I will leave the suicide postulations to the Lewis and Clark experts. One thing is inarguable—Meriwether Lewis had a host of problems beyond writer's block. But what if "inexpressibility topos" played a role in Meriwether Lewis's depression? What if Lewis, by all accounts a very literate individual, and recently home from one of the greatest adventures ever undertaken, simply couldn't find the appropriate words necessary to construct his narrative? That Lewis, an otherwise erudite and learned scholar, could find no phrase suitable for the monstrous whoosh of the Great Falls, no terminology apt for the remarkable terrain of the Rocky Mountains? What if the experience was, for him, simply indescribable?

· The situation mirrors the travails of a previously mentioned explorer, Marco Polo—a man who, according to at least one writer, strained to convince his readers of the wonders he encountered by utilizing snippets of colorful embellishments. If nothing else, the comparison invites an interesting point—one that suggests some experiences are so transformative for the individual, so distinct from one's day-to-day life, that when asked to describe those experiences to the rest of the world, the author is left dumbfounded on how to do so.

So if the experiences of these men are basically indescribable, what does that say about the guidebook structure? While neither work was initially conceived as a "guidebook" per se, because they described (or intended to describe) previously unfamiliar lands, they inherently contained a large amount of guidebook-related information. But what is the value of this information if the author admittedly struggles to articulate its true meaning? Would Lewis and Polo have found it easier to explain where to go, what they were seeing, and why people should follow them if they could have supplemented their words with GPS coordinates, high definition video, and categorized ratings? Maybe.

Or maybe some kind of travel—the broad, sweeping, ambitious kind—is so intimate, so personal, so transformative, that technology, no matter how advanced or interactive, cannot adequately portray the traveling experience. Some authors, like Polo, approach this inadequacy by embellishing. Others, like Lewis, choose to remain silent, even to their death. In one case the experience has been distorted, in the other it has been hidden. And if this is true, that the information we receive from the world's great travelers, famous or otherwise, is either altered or incomplete, what does that say about our increased use of guidebook-related material—reviews and ratings and blogs and Top Ten lists—to dictate where we go, to describe what we will see and, most importantly, to persuade us why we should go there in the first place?

CHAPTER II

ॐ ॐ ॐ

The Results

My goal when I returned from South America was to digest as much guidebook-related information on the Guianas as I possibly could. It was the final stage of the experiment, an analysis of the journey compared to the multifaceted experience promised by the guidebook spectrum. And as I methodically collected the material (websites, books, essays, blogs, reviews), my enthusiasm was tempered by a shiver of anxiety, like the moment in school right after the teacher returns an important test. I couldn't help but feel I had missed way too much.

Although information on the region was more limited than for other popular South American countries (on one travel blog site, for example, there were 131 entries on Guyana, 92 on Suriname, and 7,660 on Brazil), the sheer breadth of the guidebook spectrum meant that even the most esoteric destinations were covered. In terms of professional guidance, much of the information on the region was contained inside the larger body of South America material. Guyana, Suriname, and French Guiana, for example, made up around fifty pages out of the enormous eleven hundred-page *Lonely Planet—South America on a Shoestring*. I did, however, find one traditional guidebook written specifically for the three countries—Footprint Focus's slim, eighty-page *Guyana, Guyane, and Suriname*, proud recipient of a lone, disappointing two-star review on Amazon.com.

But the amateur guidebook sector, not surprisingly, was able to effectively fill in the substantive gaps. Besides the expected glut of hotel and restaurant reviews, especially for the capital cities of Georgetown and Paramaribo, I found a considerable number of blog posts, photos, videos, and forum contributions. Message board posters pleaded with me to explore certain cities; bloggers urged me to try certain food. Combined with the professional guidance, it was easy to cobble together a holistic picture of this oft-forgotten region of South America.

I quickly surmised, though, that there was no agreed upon path through these countries—no linear, structured itinerary such as the one followed by Tony and Maureen Wheeler forty years ago across Asia. Lonely Planet, for example, covered the countries east to west, explaining that a trip executed in this fashion would allow for slow immersion: "French Guiana, which is technically France, is the most tidy and organized of the three countries; the potholes increase as you travel west through kaleidoscopic Suriname, and by the time you reach Guyana you'll have lost track of the last time you had a hot shower." The Footprint Focus guidebook, on the other hand, covered the countries west to east, making little effort to combine the destinations into a larger more ambitious journey. The book did, however, include a full-page map of the three countries, a short description of the larger region's topography, culture, and history, and a list of seven geographically scattered "Don't Miss" destinations (I had seen only two). Still, despite the ambiguity, it was clear that most travelers to the Guianas were forced to travel the way I had—close to the coast, with occasional forays south into the difficult-to-navigate jungle interior. It was in the more detailed particulars (lodging, food, sightseeing) where my trip had diverged significantly from the recommendations within the guidebook universe.

To begin, my choice of hotels had been dubious. In George-town, off the advice of the airport taxi driver, I had stayed at the Sleep-In International, a centrally located, mid-budget option with a pool and a buffet breakfast. Although I was continually dismayed by the staff's indifference (one reviewer agreed, writing, "I'd say that the staff were not too welcoming in general, and that I often got the feeling that I was a nui-sance, taking their time and attention away from their chat-ting with friends/colleagues or their cellphones"—Exactly!), the hotel had been adequate, and its amenities had elevated it to third out of fourteen on a popular travel review website. It also garnered a mention in one guidebook as the "slightly better" option of the two Georgetown "Sleep-In" options. But despite the praise, I noticed that the hotel was located either right on or outside the edges of many Georgetown tourist maps, perhaps an indication that its surrounding area, an area in which I had been mugged, was less than ideal. The best reviewed, mid-range hotel in Georgetown, in fact, was the Herdmaston Lodge, located in a "pleasant district" several blocks north and closer to the US Embassy. The Herdmas-ton, according to various reviewers, was a "treasure" that was "perfect in every way," a place at which all visitors were pro-vided "service with a smile."

Still, I had been generally happy at the Sleep-In; the same could not be said for my first hotel in Paramaribo. As expected, the Flamingo Hotel and Casino was completely absent from the guidebook spectrum—nobody had reviewed it online and it hadn't been included among the twenty-six hotels mentioned in the Paramaribo section of the Footprint guidebook. The Eco Resort Inn, on the other hand, received mentions in both professional guides, and was described as "good atmosphere and value." Still, what I had initially per-ceived as the finest of Paramaribo luxury was determined by the amateurs to be nothing more than a mundane mid-range option. Apathetic reviews abounded, describing "tired" rooms and extreme air-conditioning "cold enough to preserve the dead." Interestingly, these accounts were accompanied not by a picture of the Eco Resort Inn itself but of a picture of its much fancier, and much more expensive, sister hotel's pool. The mistake may explain the apparent disparity in ratings; travelers expecting five-star service at the Eco Resort Inn were surely going to be disappointed.

But lodging, of course, should be a small sliver in the traveling experience—I was more interested to learn about how my trip had fared outside the confines of my hotels. I started my review with Georgetown, a city that had both captivated and wearied me with its incessant energy. Lonely Planet's introduction to the city succinctly describes this dichotomy: "Georgetown's easy-to-navigate streets, dilapidated architecture and unkempt parks still offer a laid-back feel amidst real-life chaos, and seeking out the city's riches—historic monuments, a thriving intellectual scene and fabulous restaurants—behind its hard-boiled exterior is part of the adventure." Besides the expected references to the city's Town Hall and St. George's Cathedral ("said to be the world's tallest wooden building"), both of which I had seen, and the National Museum, which I had not, there was little mention of traditional sightseeing options in Georgetown. The most interesting tidbit I found, in fact, was offered by a Wikipedia author who claimed that American nineties movie star Pauly Shore owned a mansion on "the outskirts of town in a former mangrove." The entry said that the mansion, named after Shore's movie "Class Act," is home to "invite only" parties "with B-list semi-celebrities like Matt Dillon, Carrot Top and Seth Green." It was the only evidence I could find of this enigmatic hotspot.

It seemed I had fared much better in Paramaribo where, although I had somehow missed one popular website's #1 "Thing to Do" (see Saint Peter and Paul Cathedral—peculiarly also classified as "the largest wooden building in the Americas"), I had still managed to see five of the top ten sights—Fort Zeelandia (#2), the Palmentuin (#3), the Waterkant (#5), the Presidential Palace (#8), and Independence Square (#9). Many of the guidebook extensions shared my enthusiasm for the preserved waterfront district and nearly all noted the city's remarkable convergence of culture, described as "Amsterdam meets the Wild West" by one of the more lyrical authors. And while the maps I saw reaffirmed my suspicion that most tourists avoided the area surrounding the Flamingo, I was surprised to discover that the grungy hotel was located directly across the street from one of Paramaribo's most popular nightclubs, "where you can dance the night away with techno downstairs and salsa upstairs." I had somehow missed its presence entirely.

While my sightseeing performance had been mostly on par with the guidebook standard, my culinary decisions had not. Besides a handful of notable exceptions—my first trip to the Georgetown food cart, the chicken and rice at the Paramaribo waterfront—my meals had failed to live up to what the guidebooks called "often superb" choices from a selection of "wild-hot cuisine." The capital cities, in particular, were praised for their gastronomic delights and reading reviews such as the one for Shanta's in Georgetown ("It's unbelievably inexpensive for how delicious it is. Try everything.") made me yearn for another go-around. Not among these highly recommended options, however, was Ambrosia, my faux five-star dining experience in Paramaribo that was, not surprisingly, unable to garner a mention anywhere I looked.

Kaieteur Falls, on the other hand, was mentioned everywhere: as the #1 "Don't Miss" destination in Footprint, as the #1 ranked attraction on the review websites, and as the most discussed/photographed image among dozens of Guyanese travel blogs. "WOW—wow, wow, and more wow," says one reviewer. "Incredible, wonderful, fascinating and just great," says another. A YouTube search found nearly three thousand videos of the falls, a Google image search over sixty-one thousand photographs. But while imagery for the falls was ubiquitous and praise was unanimous, directions on how to get there were not. Some reviewers were adamant about the need for an aircraft: "YOU MUST FLY IN, not sure how anyone could hike there." Others acknowledged different routes: "There are two ways to visit the Falls, an extended hiking expedition over several days, or a flight from Georgetown. I chose the lazy, but not unexciting, option." One professional guidebook noted the possibility of the overland route yet seemed to exaggerate its length, claiming that a round trip journey to the falls would take eight full days from Georgetown. And little consideration was paid to Mahdia, the town I had passed through on my way to Kaieteur. The most comprehensive review I could find of it was on Wikipedia, where its "relevant infrastructure" was listed as a hospital, three schools, a commercial sector, four hotels, two guest houses, four brothels, a police station, a post office, two artisan wells, a Regional Administrative Office and, of course, an airstrip.

The secluded island I had visited off the Suriname River, Isadou, received a similarly scant level of attention. There was no mention of it in either professional guidebook and an online search found only a handful of short videos, a few links to tour companies, and a sparse website written entirely in Dutch. The resort seemed to be indistinguishable from the country's growing number of island retreats offering foreign visitors the chance to venture deep inside Suriname's vast jungle—all the while in the comforts of your own private hut.

So what had I missed? In Guyana, I wish I had known about the Rupununi Savannah, "an extensive area of dry grassland in the far southwest" of the country, home to a "wide variety of birds" and a "few large cattle ranches." Although only accessible by plane, and not recommended as a viable travel destination during the wet summer season, the region, described as a topographical oddity, sounds fascinating. One guidebook only piqued my interest with the comment, "You'd be hard-pressed to find a safer place in South America." I also wish I had found the time, and had had the money, to make it over to Iwokrama. The tour guide at the Kaieteur Falls guesthouse had mentioned the eco-resort as a popular tourist hotspot, but I had been turned off both by its inaccessibility from Mahdia (I would have had to drive back to George-town before flying to Iwokrama) and the general cost of most eco-lodges in the region. Those who had stayed at the resort, however, had mostly good things to say of the experience: "a unique and special place," "one of my best experiences ever," and "reminds you of what's important in life."

In Suriname, I had heard of the Galibi Nature Reserve, where thousands of giant leatherback sea turtles go to breed every year, but had chosen not to go. That had been a mistake for the more touristy side of me, not only because the area was ecologically unique but also because my visit would have coincided with peak turtle viewing season. I was also a bit dis-appointed to find out that solo trips into the jungle, a traveling method I would have preferred, were indeed possible, albeit a bit unorthodox. Lonely Planet lays out the opportunity in a short sidebar:

If you and a buddy are up for a real Surinamese adventure, grab your hammock, sunscreen and insect repellant and head up the Suriname River by boat, stopping at small Amerin-dian and Maroon villages along the way. . . . A new organi-zation, Stichting Lodgeholders Boven Suriname maintains an online map of villages and lodges that can receive travel-ers and is an invaluable resource if you want to cut a track into this frontier.

And there was, of course, French Guiana (also called Guy-ane). Described as a "tantalizing mélange of visible history, fabulous cuisine and the sultry French language with the vastness and ethnic diversity of Amazonia," the country was generally referred to as one of the most expensive in South America. One guidebook noted that "accommodation in Guyane is more expensive than Paris." And I struggled to find specific information on what to do while in the country—the primary attractions seemed to include the capital city Cayenne and the French space center, Kourou, dubbed "white city" by the country's citizens because of the large influx of French families. Perhaps most telling was the country's "Do" section on its Wikitravel page, ominously blank, as well as a sentence I found in the *Footprint Focus* which seemed more at place in a Pausanias manuscript than a twenty-first century guide-book: "About 28km southeast of Cayenne is the small town of Roura, which has an interesting church."

I had waded through all of this information eagerly, once again amazed at the abundance of material available for seem-ingly every inch of our planet. Most of it had quickly blended together—the hotel review I had read inside the print guide was no more or less memorable than the random reviews I had seen online. In that sense, the guidebook became some-what amorphous, an unstructured mix of arbitrary assistance. But from this nebulous mass emerged two blog postings that had managed to separate themselves from the pack, to remain top of mind long after my initial search.

The first entry had been written by an American real estate broker. His journey had begun as mine had—with a desire to travel, with no particular destination in mind, and with a curiosity about a region he knew little about. "I love to research travel," the blogger admitted and so research he did,

uncovering a handful of intriguing facts concerning Guyana—
only 4,000 tourists visit every year, 65 percent of the country is
virgin jungle, it has excellent rum. These facts encouraged him
to order a guidebook; the guidebook helped him book a trip.
"The next week was a collection of fantastic adventures and
new friendships," he writes, detailing a journey remarkably
different from my own. Little goes wrong during this blogger's travels and a pervasive enthusiasm permeates much of the
narrative: "I will remember these good, generous people. I will
remember a million stars in the sky."

Reading the blog and its sweeping generalities ("these
good, generous people") made me wonder how I would ultimately remember the Guianas. Travel narratives often make
the writer's journey seem more linear than it really is, a distor-
tion of literary necessity. I rarely remember my trips as fluid
affairs; they are instead recalled as a series of fragmented,
mostly brief experiences and encounters. In this way, it would
seem guidebooks are appropriately structured, spending most
of their time not on broad overviews but on specific, individual experiences. "Stand at the top of the world's highest
single drop waterfall!" a guidebook for Guyana might say,
the proclamation accompanied by a stunning panoramic view
of Kaieteur Falls. Coming across such an entry, the expectant
traveler enthusiastically proclaims, "I can't wait to be there!"
thus demonstrating the most marketable aspect of today's
guidebook extensions—the replicability.

It was because of this aspect that I was able to so thoroughly appraise the merits of my own trip. But the analysis
could easily go the other way—to see if my most memorable
experiences were frequently cited by the multitude of guidebook extensions. And of course, many of them were not. I will
always remember, for example, the pool party in Mahdia and
my first business meeting with Trevor inside his pickup truck.
The street on which I was robbed will forever be ingrained in

my mind, as will the shadowy confines of the police station and the apathy of the policeman who begrudgingly listened to every word of my sorry tale. It will also be impossible to forget my time inside the questionable Flamingo Hotel and Casino, as well as my afternoon of drinks with the irascible and profane Irish engineer. These experiences are the ones that would remain with me long after the larger images of the trip had faded away. Perhaps it was because they were unexpected and unanticipated; more likely, it was the intimate and personal nature of the encounters—the knowledge that these experiences combined to form *my* trip, and nobody else's. They were, dare I say, irreplicable, making them completely and utterly guidebook-proof.

This is not to say that guidebook-heavy travel is devoid of these experiences. It is not. A journey conceived primarily through the advice of online reviews and Top 10 lists, however, makes their occurrence less likely, as the traveler—head buried in information, mind focused on efficiency—trudges from checkpoint to checkpoint. Ironically, this effect has not gone unnoticed by the professionals. In Lonely Planet's *New York City* guidebook, underneath a discussion of the city's different boroughs, is a small sidebar entitled "DIY NYC." In it, the author claims that while Lonely Planet is "dedicated to providing comprehensive and in-depth coverage" for every one of its destinations, sometimes, "the greatest adventure is to fly by the seat of your pants":

> *Stroll Central Park or Prospect Park without any agenda. Jump onto a passing bus and ride it until you feel like getting off, then explore the neighborhood you've landed in. Get lost among the illogical, diagonal streets of the far West Village. Read the bulletin board at a local café and find an announcement for a performance going on that night—and then go to it. Hail a cab and ask the driver to take you to*

his favorite lunch spot, where you'll no doubt delight in an
obscure and affordable ethnic feast.

Imagine that—a guidebook imploring its readers not to use it. And yet in a world so inundated with information, so saturated with facts and figures and diagrams and maps, it is hardly surprising that we need a guidebook to tell us not to use a guidebook.

In early August 1806, as the eastbound expedition made its way back toward St. Louis, Lewis and Clark encountered two men traveling upstream, Joseph Dickson and Forrest Hancock, young explorers intent on striking it rich out west. It was the expedition's first indication that the route to the Pacific was now open for business, accessible to a new wave of adventurers, prospectors, and curiosity-seekers. Happy to assist those following in their footsteps (that was, after all, part of the reason for the expedition in the first place), the explorers answered many questions posed by the young traders. As Stephen Ambrose writes, "[Lewis and Clark] gave Dickson and Hancock information on what lay ahead of them, provided them with some sketch maps, and told them where they could find beaver in abundance." The two men also asked the captains if they could sign over one of their most important assets—Private John Colter, an able-bodied veteran who had proved invaluable to the expedition over the previous two years. Lewis and Clark agreed to let their man go (as Clark writes in his journal, "we were disposed to be of service to any one of our party who had performed their duty as well as Colter had done") and so as the expedition approached the finish line, Colter proudly reversed course, heading back into a world of buffalos, grizzly bears, and beavers. George Drouillard, another well-regarded member of the Lewis and Clark expedition, would follow soon after, intent on resuming a life of trade and exploration.

Robert M. Utley, a historian who has studied the lives of the so-called "mountain men," maintains that Colter and Drouillard "made significant contributions to history," traversing and documenting "great tracts of country unseen by either Lewis or Clark." Their knowledge, subsequently, would be passed on to other explorers, who would forge *their* own path, building and adding to previous discoveries. The result of this process continues today, with a perpetual series of incremental contributions slowly unveiling the complexities and mysteries of an entire continent. If Lewis and Clark penned the first true "guidebook" to the land that would eventually represent the United States, then those who followed are the authors of editions two through ad infinitum, contributors tasked with perfecting and supplementing an already established base of geographical and cultural knowledge. My online review of a New York City pizza place, then, is simply an addition to a culinary chapter that begins with Lewis's description of buffalo meat. And because of the increase of traveling motivations and the ease at which material can now be created (my pizza review most likely exists among dozens of other similar evaluations), adding something entirely new to the guidebook spectrum, the goal of many modern day explorers, is an increasingly difficult task. The traveler utopia—"the road less traveled"—has therefore become a gimmick; in order to stand apart from the masses, one is forced to walk across Africa, ski down Mt. Everest, raft down the Congo, or, admittedly, travel to South America without a guidebook.

So with that observation, let's return, finally, to the question around which this entire experiment was conceived: how has the guidebook evolution changed the way we see the world? Not surprisingly, my own experiment suggests that travel is both potentially enhanced *and* potentially hindered by the enormous amount of guidebook-related information currently available. To truly appreciate the beneficial effects of travel, therefore, guidebook use must be tempered, its information used judiciously. While complete reliance is utterly unnecessary, total rejection is similarly foolish. It's hard to imagine that Lewis and Clark's journey would have been any less impressive or exciting had they known how many blue beads to bring, how long the Great Falls portage would take, or what the going price for a Shoshone horse was. In my case, I wish I had known how much hotels were going to cost, how to plan for a Suriname holiday, and what neighborhoods in Georgetown to avoid after dark.

The problem, then, is not that this type of information exists; the ease of knowledge dissemination is one of the great advances of our time. The issue is the exposure to, reliance on, and the credence given to *all* kinds of guidebook-related information, be it objective (bus times, currency conversions) or subjective (Top 10 Lists, hotel reviews). This information subsequently creates benchmarks by which we compare our own trips, a normalized library of traveling experiences. While the information undoubtedly has the power to inspire and to motivate, used blindly, the guidebook spectrum can also muddle the mind, distort experience, and depress revelation. As Paul Theroux has written, "If the Internet were everything it is cracked up to be, we would all stay home and be brilliantly witty and insightful. Yet with so much contradictory information available, there is more reason to travel than ever before: to look closer, to dig deeper, to sort the authentic from the fake; to verify, to smell, to touch, to taste, to hear, and sometimes—importantly—to suffer the effects of this curiosity."

If Meriwether Lewis and William Clark had been able to access this kind of information before their own journey— pictures and videos of the country's plains, blog postings of the Missouri river, reviews of the various Indian tribes—how would they have responded to their various encounters and experiences? It is likely we would have been deprived of this wonderful hyperbole from Lewis as he attempts to describe the lower Missouri region to his mother:

> *This immense river, so far as we have yet ascended, waters one of the fairest portions of the globe, nor do I believe that there is in the universe a similar extent of country equally fertile, well watered, and intersected by such a number of navigable streams.*

One also has to imagine that this account of the White Cliffs would have been (unfortunately) muted:

> *As we passed on it seemed as if those scenes of visionary enchantment would never have an end; for here it is too that nature presents to the view of the traveler vast ranges of walls of tolerable workmanship, so perfect indeed are those walls that I should have thought that nature had attempted here to rival the human art of masonry had I not recollected that she had first began her work.*

And you'd have to assume that Lewis's initial reaction to the Great Falls of the Missouri, the "grandest sight [he] ever beheld," would have been easier to compose, and therefore less memorable, if he had been able to borrow from the descriptions of other travelers:

> *From the reflection of the sun on the spray or mist which arises from these falls is a beautiful rainbow produced which adds not a little to the beauty of this majestically grand scenery. After writing this imperfect description I again viewed the falls and was so much disgusted with the imperfect idea which it conveyed of the scene that I determined to draw my*

pen across it and begin again, but then reflected that I could
not perhaps succeed better than penning the first impressions
of the mind.

All of which brings us to a travel blog written six
months before my own journey detailing an overland trip
from Georgetown through Mahdia and onward to Kaieteur Falls—i.e., the exact route I had followed. Not only
were the author's observations extraordinarily similar to
my own—of the van's music, she wrote "Equipped with
state of the art speakers and a sub-woofer that seemed to
be molded into the doors, or maybe the seats, it ensured for
a continuous ride of blaring Guyanese hip hop music, with
plenty of air-horns"—but her photographs could very well
have been copies of ones I had taken—the cramped interior
of the tattered van, the nose of a blue canoe framed against
the shimmering surface of choppy river water, a tiny yellow frog cowering inside the lip of a large green leaf. She
had even stayed at the RH Hotel and Restaurant (giving it
a surprisingly good review) and gotten a ride from the infamous Gottfried (unfortunately not mentioned by name but
easily discernible in one of the site's photographs). I couldn't
believe it—this was my journey, conveniently laid out in a
series of daily entries and accompanied by inspiring, high
definition imagery.

What I had thought to be the most adventurous, anti-
guidebook portion of my experiment instead turned out to
be a simple reenactment of a trip made months before I had
arrived and fastidiously documented for the whole world to
see. I had known the overland journey to Kaieteur was far
more common than I had originally thought (the man at the
falls guesthouse had told me as much), but I had mistakenly
believed that my specific route—through the crazy mining
town of Mahdia, down the cratered path to Pamela's Landing

and up the river to the rapid-delineated checkpoints of Amatuk, Waratuk, and Tukei—was the rarest of itineraries. I was
wrong.

It was a clear indication of just how far the guidebook
evolution had come, further proof that the amateur sector
has taken the reigns from the professionals and effectively
filled in the proverbial guidebook "map." But more than
anything, I was glad I hadn't seen the blog before my own
journey; it contained very little that would have enhanced
my understanding of the region before I had arrived and
much that would have diluted the experience. So while my
refusal to utilize guidebook information before my trip had
resulted in some sketchy hotels, mediocre food, financial
blunders, and, arguably, a black eye, it had also allowed me
to discover what the region had to offer without the burden of comparison. My first impressions of the cities and the
people and the attractions, therefore, were my first actual
impressions—a rare and valuable occurrence in today's
information-saturated world.

To many pessimistic travelers, then, blog postings like the
one above only confirm their most cynical beliefs—that there
are no new experiences, that the world has been documented
to an incredibly nuanced degree, and that the era of "true"
travel has succumbed to the immediacy of our current culture.
But to me, the blog was merely a reminder that while col-
lectively the world has been trodden, explored, and dissected,
individually it remains wide open—a blank canvas of wonder. And while our content-producing society has produced
an array of tools to assist us in that exploration, those tools
should be used conservatively, allowing enough room for that
wonder to develop independently.

To those of you dismayed by the current state of travel or
overwhelmed by the modern glut of guidebook literature, I urge
you to put down the mobile device, shut off the computer, and

conduct your own guidebook experiment. Go to a restaurant without reading the reviews. Travel to a city you've never heard of. Find a road on a map and drive it beginning to end. Because while what you find will almost certainly be known to mankind, what you discover will forever be your own.

References

GUIDEBOOK HISTORY/BACKLASH

I am greatly indebted to Nicholas T. Parsons as his *Worth the Detour: A History of the Guidebook* served as the impetus to and starting point for much of my guidebook research. It is unquestionably the most thorough and comprehensive account of the genre available today. From there, my research extended into both academic and popular literature; what follows is a select list of the works on which I relied the most.

Background for the section on Pausanias came mostly from Christian Habicht's *Pausanias' Guide to Ancient Greece,* the collection *Following Pausanias: The Quest for Greek Antiquity* edited by Maria Georgopoulou, Celine Guilmet, Yanis A. Pikoulas, Konstantinos Staikos, and George Tolias, as well as various translations of the manuscript including James George Frazer's seminal version. Information and commentary concerning Aymeric Picaud's *The Pilgrim's Guide* was found in the scholarly work and translations of Alison Stones and Annie Shaver-Crandell as well as from *The Confraternity of Saint James* website. Notes on ars apodemica, the Grand Tour, and Richard Lassels's *The Voyage of Italy* were collected primarily from Justin Stagl's *A History of Curiosity: The Theory of Travel 1550-1800* and from *The Norton Book of Travel* edited by Paul Fussell. For the section on the guidebook empires created by John Murray and Karl Baedeker, Lynne Withey's *Grand Tours and Cook's Tours: A History of Leisure Travel, 1750 to 1915,* W.B.C. Lister's *A Bibliography of Murray's Handbooks for Travellers,* and a *Yale Review* articled entitled "Baedeker's Universe" written by Edward Mendelson were all valuable resources. Information concerning the Hippie Trail and the beginnings of Lonely Planet, meanwhile, was pulled from Rory MacLean's *Magic Bus,* Tony Wheeler's *Unlikely Destinations,* and an article written by Tad Friend for *The New Yorker* entitled "The Parachute Artist."

For the background on Marco Polo, I relied heavily on Laurence Bergreen's *Marco Polo: From Venice to Xanadu.* Clay Shirky's *Cognitive Surplus: Creativity and Generosity in a Connected Age* and Jeff Howe's *Crowdsourcing: Why the Power of the Crowd is Driving the Future of Business* helped me contextualize the contributions of amateur guidebook contributors. And Alain de Botton's *The Art of Travel*, Paul Theroux's *The Tao of Travel*, and Pico Iyer's *Video Night in Kathmandu: And Other Reports from the Not-So-Far-East* were all vital in sorting through (and thinking about) what I called "guidebook backlash."

Finally, the same information revolution that has fundamentally altered the guidebook industry has also facilitated the search for and acquisition of coveted historical texts. Some thanks, then, must be extended to Google Books, a portal through which I found dozens of resources to peruse (for free) including most representatives on my Guidebook Hall of Fame *(Description of Greece, The Pilgrim's Guide, The Voyage of Italy, A Handbook for Travellers on The Rhine)* as well as Mark Twain's *Following the Equator, The Travels of Marco Polo,* and *The Travels of Sir John Mandeville.* Additional resources were found at the central branch of the New York Public Library, the University of North Carolina at Chapel Hill's Davis and Park libraries and Elon University's Belk Library. And of course, a bit of gratitude must be shown to the millions of faceless reviewers who continue to update the "map" of our world piece by piece by piece; in many ways, they were the inspiration for this book.

THE LEWIS AND CLARK EXPEDITION

This manuscript should in no way be misconstrued as a proper history of the Lewis and Clark expedition; on the contrary, I relied heavily on and borrowed substantially from those authors who have effectively (and entertainingly) already told the tale from a variety of angles. Stephen Ambrose's popular *Undaunted Courage: Meriwether Lewis, Thomas Jefferson, and the Opening of the American West* served as an accessible entry point. Equally important was Bernard DeVoto's *The Journals of Lewis and Clark*, a condensed and annotated version of the explorers' field notes. Other works on which I relied heavily include: John Logan Allen's *Passage Through the Garden: Lewis and Clark and the Image of the American Northwest*, Paul Russell Cutright's *Lewis and Clark: Pioneering Naturalists*, Bernard DeVoto's *The Course of Empire*, Donald Jackson's *Letters of the Lewis and Clark Expedition, with Related Documents (Volumes 1 and 2)*, Clay S. Jenkinson's *The Character of Meriwether Lewis: Explorer in the Wilderness* and *The Character of Meriwether Lewis: "Completely Metamorphosed" in the American West*, Landon Y. Jones's *William Clark and the Shaping of the West*, W. Dale Nelson's *Interpreters with Lewis and Clark: The Story of Sacagawea and Toussaint Charbonneau*, James P. Ronda's *Lewis and Clark among the Indians*, and Robert M. Utley's *After Lewis and Clark: Mountain Men and the Paths to the Pacific*. There are, of course, dozens of books about the Lewis and Clark expedition and I admittedly consulted but merely a few. For those who wish to read more, I suggest starting with Ambrose and the journals and proceeding from there.

ACKNOWLEDGMENTS

I owe a world of thanks to my mother, Patricia Flanagan, who spent countless hours reading, editing, and re-reading the book from its early stages right up to completion. My appreciation also goes out to Monica Hill, for an early referral that changed the manuscript's trajectory, and Penny Abernathy, for always remembering this project was in the works and encouraging its development. Additional thanks go to Larry Habegger, James O'Reilly, and Sean O'Reilly for giving me the chance to work on this project. And to my wife Emily and son Matthew, thank you for your support, patience, and understanding—I love you both more than you will ever know.

ABOUT THE AUTHOR

David Bockino is an Assistant Professor in the School of Communications at Elon University. He was born and raised in New York and currently lives in Durham, North Carolina with his wife and son.